Date Due

D1367534

Europe's
Ambiguous Unity

Europe's Ambiguous Unity

Conflict and Consensus in the Post–Maastricht Era

edited by
Alan W. Cafruny
Carl Lankowski

LYNNE
RIENNER
PUBLISHERS

BOULDER
LONDON

Published in the United States of America in 1997 by
Lynne Rienner Publishers, Inc.
1800 30th Street, Boulder, Colorado 80301

and in the United Kingdom by
Lynne Rienner Publishers, Inc.
3 Henrietta Street, Covent Garden, London WC2E 8LU

Library of Congress Cataloging-in-Publication Data
Europe's ambiguous unity : conflict and consensus in the
  post–Maastricht era / edited by Alan W. Cafruny and Carl Lankowski.
    p. cm.
  Includes bibliographical references and index.
  ISBN 1-55587-224-7 (hardcover : alk. paper)
    1. European Union. 2. European federation. 3. European Union
countries—Constitutional law. 4. Europe—Economic integration.
I. Cafruny, Alan W., 1951–   . II. Lankowski, Carl F., 1949–
KJE947.E885 1996
341.24'22—dc20   96-32056
                                                                CIP

British Cataloguing in Publication Data
A Cataloguing in Publication record for this book
is available from the British Library.

Printed and bound in the United States of America

   The paper used in this publication meets the requirements
  of the American National Standard for Permanence of
  Paper for Printed Library Materials Z39.48-1984.

5 4 3 2 1

Contents

Preface

This book was originally conceived as a study of the relationship between social movements and the design and trajectory of European integration. The contributors were impressed with the apparent lack of connection between the concerns of social movements and regional integration. A central premise was that what had come to be known as "Euro-skepticism" was by no means exclusively a product of nationalist reflexes to pooled sovereignty and the consequent (relative) decline of national autonomy brought about by regional economic integration. For this reason we focused on new sources of opposition, based on transformations in the social structure and articulated in many cases by social movement activists, organizations, and parties.

The project of European integration had been conceived in large part as a piece of repair work for the economic and political pathologies of the Great Depression of the 1930s. Not surprisingly, its design was oriented to social conflicts of that day and did not anticipate recent developments. Therefore, we expected to find novel forms of opposition and conflict emerging to challenge the original design. We also expected that Europe's institutional tableaux—both in Brussels and in the member states—would channel these conflicts so that they often presented themselves indirectly and in odd combinations when examined separately. For this reason, we believed that only an EC/EU-European perspective would permit an accurate analysis of the kaleidoscope of movement politics across the face of the Community.

As European integration gained momentum in the wake of the Intergovernmental Conference leading to the Maastricht Treaty on European Union, it became increasingly obvious that the challenges and opportunities available to movement actors were being redefined by the evolving institutional and political contexts of action. The unification of the two German states dramatically transformed Europe's political landscape. Before the end of the millennium, Europe's citizens would be compelled to confront the additional challenges of monetary unification and a wider European configuration encompassing not only the Nordic countries but also Austria and, at the very least, the Visegrad Four.

Accordingly, the project itself had to be redefined. The hydraulics of political change and the dynamics of integration worked on the groups and movements we had been observing, rearranging their relationships to Europe's emerging architecture in new patterns of protest and assimilation. The conference at Maastricht simultaneously enlarged and brought greater definition to the scope of the discussion about Europe's future. Europe's political construction was suddenly on the agenda. This led us to commission additional papers on the relationship between the primary representative institutions of the EU and its member states, on the EU's evolving multi-level structure of participation and governance, on the status of the EU's communicative space, on the Nordic countries, and on French politics.

The editors are grateful above all to our contributors for "keeping the faith" over several rounds of rewriting occasioned by historical developments. We also wish to thank the Council for European Studies, Roy Ginsberg and Skidmore College, and St. Lawrence University for supporting the conference at which the initial papers were presented. Special thanks go to Lynne Rienner for encouraging us to proceed with the project, and to Gia Hamilton, who managed the manuscript with great care and skill.

—*AWC*
—*CL*

Europe's Ambiguous Unity
Alan W. Cafruny & Carl Lankowski

This book analyzes the changing configuration of social forces activated by
Western European regional integration. We start from several premises: that
Europe already possesses a constitution, however incomplete and flawed; that
the Treaty on European Union signed in Maastricht established a new set of
problems for Europe even as it partially resolved existing ones; and that
Europe faces intense pressure from within and without to develop novel
forms of participation and legitimation.

Europe's constitution has gradually emerged from the series of treaties
and court decisions beginning with the Schuman Plan of 1950 and culminating in the Maastricht Treaty. The Schuman Plan arose from the conviction
that peace was better than war in Europe and that peace could be nurtured by
building novel forms of regional cooperation. The debate over the European
Defense Community (EDC) in 1954 and the negotiation of the Treaty of
Rome in 1957, establishing the European Economic Community (EEC) and
European Atomic Energy Community (Euratom), made it clear that regional
integration would proceed primarily through economic cooperation—a lesson that retained its validity until political union was written into the Treaty
on European Union.

The Treaty of Rome served for all intents and purposes as a constitution.
To be sure, all actions undertaken had to be justified with reference to Treaty
provisions, and any illusions that states would not play a central role in constructing the Community were finally dispelled by the Luxembourg
Compromise of 1966. Nevertheless, the Treaty did provide a framework
within which broad discretion could be exercised. Policies in areas not stipu-
lated by the Treaty were launched, often well in advance of major treaty revi-
sions.

Europe's original constitution has received two major overhauls since
1958. The first of these, the Single European Act (SEA) of 1987, was devoted primarily to the creation of a European marketplace and secondarily to
institutional development in the interest of greater legitimacy. The second
major overhaul was the process leading to the Treaty on European Union
(Maastricht Treaty) of 1991 (ratified in 1993), which established the
European Union (EU). The treaty-making process leading to Maastricht and
beyond to the 1996 intergovernmental conference (IGC) has already spawned
judicial cases from *Costa v. Enel* (1962) to the German Constitutional Court
ruling (1993). The unfolding of this judicial process shows that a constitutional process is well under way.[1]

Unfortunately, in light of the liberal democratic principles to which all EU members subscribe, leaders have viewed Community politics as a sphere of elite negotiations and bargains precisely because there has been no consensus on the nature of the European project. The result has been a series of brokered deals emphasizing, above all, the continuity of the market creation project and postponing or avoiding altogether discussions of the political basis of Europe's unity. The weakness of Maastricht pillars II and III (Common Foreign and Security Policy and Justice and Home Affairs) only highlights this political gap. The lack of consensus about Europe's unity has several causes. One is the reluctance of European statesmen to call a thing by its proper name. Their denial that a constitutional process is unfolding allows them to carry on while excluding the public. As a result, dissatisfaction with the process and the results is predictably articulated in the national political idiom.

Meanwhile, there has been a growing awareness that even in the absence of democratic participation and legitimation EU politics has infiltrated domestic politics. It has become necessary to develop strategies to influence policies in the European arena. With the conclusion of the Maastricht Treaty it became clear that the constitutional process could not advance without popular assent. The reforms introduced by the SEA and Maastricht, although quite modest when measured against the constitutional norms of democratic governance, nevertheless opened up new channels of democratic participation or strengthened existing ones.

Europe-15 confronts a set of problems arising out of tensions imminent in this complex constitutional design. Since 1989 the community has also had to justify itself in a pan-European setting. Both sets of problems underline the fact that the central thrust of integration politics in the 1990s and beyond concerns the construction of a European polity. The leading issues on the agenda include decisionmaking rules, representation, and the distribution of powers.

On one level, this agenda is driven by a process of global economic liberalization that makes regional cooperation increasingly desirable. This book addresses the relationship between this process of liberalization and the other driving force behind Europe's constitutional agenda: the changing configuration of social and political movements operating at the national, subnational, and, to a much more limited extent, transnational level.

The dynamics of integration have produced a complex but systematic pattern of disruptive effects that mobilize groups to constantly redefine and defend their interests. Advances in regional integration thus set in motion opposite forces of disintegration, and the Union's lack of democratic legitimation and institutionalized processes of political participation becomes increasingly problematic. Because Europe lacks a demos and a symbolic agora that can serve as a communicative space in which conflicts can be directly regulated or resolved, these conflicts usually manifest themselves in traditional, national formats. Until Denmark's resounding *nej* to Maastricht on June 2, 1992, Europe's leaders could insulate the people from what is properly their own constitutional process. After the Danish referendum, their voices could no longer be ignored, a lesson that was reconfirmed in the narrow endorsement of the Maastricht Treaty by the French people later that year.

What are the social and political effects of Europe's current constitutional design? What kinds of strategies have been developed to exercise influence within the evolving institutional structure of European regional integration? When have these strategies been explicitly oppositional and how have the content and form of oppositional strategies evolved as Europe's constitution has developed? What designs are preferred and can they represent the interests of the European people and influence the nature of Europe's ongoing constitutional debate? These questions animate the analyses in the following chapters.

MAASTRICHT: A WORK IN PROGRESS

The Treaty on European Union represented an ambitious attempt to establish the broad framework of a European polity. By establishing the rules and timetable for monetary union, it was supposed to build on the market-enhancing momentum of the SEA. By creating corresponding political institutions giving more power to the European Parliament and the regions, it would promote greater democratic legitimacy at a time when Europe's citizens had begun to recognize that the Community was playing a much more significant role in national life.

Yet while Maastricht did advance the process of market liberalization, attempts to establish a corresponding social and political community largely failed, despite the Treaty's sometimes ambitious rhetoric. The treaty provisions on Economic and Monetary Union (EMU) greatly limit the nature and scope of state intervention in the economy. The treaty establishes explicit targets, rules, norms, and obligations for member states even if these targets may not be met by 1999. By contrast, the provisions on political union are decidedly intergovernmentalist and include numerous loopholes and "opt-out" procedures.[2] A Common Foreign and Security Policy (CFSP) has not emerged. The "social dimension" is based more on voluntary bargaining than on authoritative rule making by political institutions. Social policy is left largely to the hands of the member states, and the Union's capacity to promote redistribution and cohesion is very weak.

Thus, even as it served to undercut the de facto sovereignty of nation-states in the economic sphere, the Maastricht Treaty did not establish a corresponding European political community and even provoked a nationalist backlash. The EU comprises fifteen polities and one transnational economy.

Wolfgang Streeck has characterized it as "an international order controlled by intergovernmental relations between sovereign nation-states, that serves as a domestic order for a transnational economy."[3]

It is possible to explain the relative success of the market-enhancing measures of the SEA—and by implication the willingness of states to surrender de facto monetary authority to a nascent European Central Bank—in terms of the traditional desire of states to preserve sovereignty. Member states find it much more difficult to surrender budgetary authority, the key source of national sovereignty and social cohesion. Within this context, "re-regulation" at the European level primarily on the basis of standards harmonization and free movement constitutes for the Commission the path of least resistance to integration.[4] This emergent form of regionalization, which has been termed *negative integration*, continues to assign the responsibility for social policy to national governments even as it undermines their ability to control or allocate national resources. Steps toward monetary union can also be explained according to a logic of intergovernmentalism: All member states— and especially France—hope to regain at least some measure of monetary control from the Bundesbank and the United States even as they accept the inexorable logic of transnational capital mobility. Yet, negative integration has massive redistributive consequences for classes, regions, and nations. Thus even as it establishes a particular form of economic integration it lays the basis for future instability.

The concept of *Fordism* is also useful in understanding the ways in which underlying regional and global economic, political, and social trends have shaped Europe's constitutional process. Fordism refers to a specific stage or mode of production characterized by fixed product lines, low levels of product innovation, and mass marketing.[5] This productive process was consistent with centralized wage bargaining practices, mass trade unions, welfare as a universal entitlement, and class-based political parties. These practices were institutionalized within the framework of a postwar settlement, which included the more systematic use of Keynesian macroeconomic policies designed to promote full employment and explicit or implicit corporatist arrangements in which wages were linked to productivity. The market was embedded not only within national social compromises but also within a specific international framework: Europe's economic growth was greatly accelerated by foreign direct investments of U.S.-based companies in the 1950s and 1960s, Marshall Plan aid and defense spending, and U.S. willingness to tolerate restrictions on trade and capital within the context of a European payments bloc.[6] Keynesian macroeconomic management worked as long as financial capital was subordinated to national economic plans. National systems of corporatism and extensive state intervention in industry, labor markets, and social systems were viewed across the political spectrum as legitimate and complementary to economic development.

While asserting the analytic utility of the concept of Fordism, we do not suggest that regional integration can be explained adequately only with reference to alleged imperatives of capital accumulation. To be sure, institutions and ideas have their own autonomy and influence outcomes; but the fact that any explanatory framework for the EU must necessarily emphasize historical contingency and unintended consequences warns against reductionism. Nevertheless, at a broad level of generality the original project of the EEC, although strongly shaped by the idealism of the founding members, fit the Fordist regulatory pattern. The EEC served to buttress nation-states— and particularly the national welfare state—through the collective management of market forces. Significantly, the only sector to be organized along transnational lines was agriculture, and even here the Common Agricultural Policy (CAP) functioned less as a vehicle for integration than as a means to circumscribe the potentially disruptive effects of the free market in agriculture. The new customs union did establish a more open regional marketplace, but extensive national financial controls, corporatist bargains, and industrial policies remained. The state thus maintained its capacity to intervene in the national economy and, in this sense, sovereignty was indeed rescued.[7]

As the postwar settlement began to unravel in the 1970s, governments embarked initially on a restorative effort based on more extensive programs of national planning. By shifting to flexible exchange rates, governments hoped to insulate national economies from each other and thereby liberate themselves from balance of payments constraints. What was now called the European Community (EC) seldom figured prominently in strategies for industrial restructuring, and when it did so it was largely as a means to support national economic champions and coordinate ambitious national industrial policies. Under the leadership of European commissioner for industry Etienne Davignon, for example, the EC took on a decidedly dirigiste tone, and many observers of the EC in the late 1970s and early 1980s anticipated the construction of a "Fortress Europe."

The accession of conservative governments to power in Germany and Britain, the failure of British and French experiments in economic nationalism, the international capital markets, and the increasing acceptance of neoliberal cures for Europe's economic disease (Eurosclerosis) all contributed to market liberalization in the mid-1980s. This process was given further impetus by the collapse of the Soviet Union, whose economic travails convinced many that state planning did not allocate resources efficiently or justly. The numerical decline of the traditional working class and the corresponding growth of the service sector, and the declining power of trade unions, increased confidence in market rationality. All of these factors supported the tendency to view economic problems in terms of consumption rather than production.

Yet efforts to impose market rationality have been partial and contested and have failed to produce the desired results. Considered as a defensive response to the crisis of Fordism, the neoliberal model has not resolved structural unemployment and Europe's relative decline vis-à-vis East Asia and the United States. Indeed, the high-water mark of neoliberalism was reached in the late 1980s and now appears to have receded. The Cecchini Report of 1988, which provided the theoretical underpinnings of the single market, boldly predicted that the single market would boost Europe's growth while reducing unemployment.[8] By contrast, the Delors White Paper on Competition, Employment, and Growth issued at the beginning of 1994 is a far more sober and cautious document.[9] It recognizes that the two central problems of the European economy—mass, structural unemployment and relatively low productivity—cannot be resolved simply by market forces.

Thus the project of market liberalization embodied in the SEA and the Maastricht Treaty has not resolved the crisis of legitimation associated with Europe's structural economic problems. Rather, it has served to deepen citizen discontent and transfer it to the European level. The SEA and the Maastricht Treaty have effectively taken power away from nation-states without recreating comparable political structures at the level of the Union. An uneasy alliance has formed between a supranational authority able to expand its powers largely on the basis of market rationality and states that preserve their sovereignty only by "liberating" themselves from economic obligations that they are no longer able or willing to undertake.

SOCIAL FORCES AND THE CONSTITUTIONAL AGENDA

Integration on the basis of market liberalization thus set in motion corresponding processes of disintegration. At the broadest level, the transformation of the Community into an instrument of market rationality altered its character and created a pressing need for constitutional elaboration and reform. During the 1960s and 1970s Community policies seldom generated public interest because they did not, with the exception of agriculture, have great redistributive consequences. By contrast, the SEA and Maastricht Treaty have had a much greater impact on European citizens.

At the same time, attitudes toward the EU changed, dramatically in some cases, as parties and movements discovered new opportunities and constraints in Brussels or Strasbourg, as the scope of national economic management narrowed in the face of global economic interdependence, and as the distribution of costs and benefits of membership for nation-states, regions, and classes was altered.

Structured Ambiguity: Europe's Inauthentic Polity

The original treaty structure and successive amendments to it powerfully imply a European polity. Freedom of movement guaranteed under the SEA is virtually inconceivable without corresponding rights of place. The single market program thus created an intermediate political status somewhere between citizen and foreigner. This same process also provoked demands for compensation by the labor movement and the postindustrial movements, above all the environmental movement. Indeed, integration's market vocation disappeared from the title of the European constructs in the Treaty on European Union, whose first pillar is a European Community. Moreover, a Union citizenship was conferred upon all nationals of EU member states. At the same time, EC areas of responsibility grew to encompass a social dimension as well as environmental and "cohesion" policies. The position of the European Parliament was also upgraded, an ombudsman was created, and a new body—the Committee of the Regions—was established to anchor the principle of subsidiarity at the subnational level.

In pressing forward with institutional development, Europe's leaders acted according to models of democratic legitimation that linked individuals politically to the Brussels institutions via novel mechanisms of representation. Large tracts of ostensibly national legislation have become Europeanized. Most fundamentally, these innovations promise nothing less than a social contract that can create a relationship of authority between Europeans and the EU. Europe's ambiguous unity derives from a variety of causes, but two stand out: the incompleteness and weakness of European institutions and lack of consensus among political leaders about Europe's constitutional vocation. Together, they generate skepticism and even cynicism about the capacity of the EU to deliver the goods and the sincerity of efforts to make it do so.

Despite significant advances in the position of the European Parliament since 1979, the year of the first direct elections to that body, EU institutions still are unable to command media attention that rivals what national polities get. This will not change unless and until the Parliament acquires the power to initiate legislation and raise revenues. Absent that, members of the European Parliament (MEPs) tend to form broad alliances across parties to advance the Parliament's institutional interests. This array of heterogeneous interests only adds to the resulting weakness of transnational political party federations, and, in turn, undermines clear partisan lines that could serve as the basis for conducting meaningful European political campaigns. Party systems remain nationally focused, even if they are increasingly compelled to cope with global and regional economic processes articulated at the European level.

Form matters. A European polity already exists, but it is severely distorted by the systematic excision of the European dimension from public discourse. An ever greater slice of public life possesses a significant European, if not global, dimension. Pollution, product standards, immigration, and of course macroeconomic policies must be handled jointly by member states and between these states as a group and third countries. More and more legislation originates in Brussels, but this condition is largely hidden from view by use of the directive, the EU's dominant legal instrument. The political significance of this form can scarcely be overestimated. Simply put, directives express a joint European decision in a national idiom. In addition to the flexibility of application this permits, it serves the inestimably important function of presenting European law as if it were locally made. Governments can take credit or place blame as they see fit. Generally speaking, this situation has concealed the day-to-day effects of the EU from Europeans.

At its core, the skepticism that breeds ambivalence derives from both unfulfilled promises of a social contract that will adhere to parliamentary forms and declarations of a "citizen's Europe." Institutions also matter. The continued centrality of the Council of Ministers in the EU institutional matrix in and of itself betrays the constitutional pretensions of a European social contract. Incentives to promote community behavior are constantly overwhelmed by the impulse to pass the costs of market creation to other member states. Market liberals have always found it difficult to admit that markets must be purchased with the currency of compensation and aid in any social arrangement that calls itself a community. This solidarity is manifest in fiscal transfers and public goods provided by the center; the jump in EU budgetary outlays associated with southern enlargement as well as the politics of the cohesion fund illustrates this process. If mutual recrimination between member states has been on the rise since Maastricht, it is surely associated with the fiscal squeeze in the member states occasioned by recession and economic restructuring. Efforts to remain in the club by adhering to the convergence criteria for monetary union only increase governments' tendency to scramble for tax bases. Under these circumstances, is it any wonder that the EU is viewed as an austerity cartel aimed at Europeans' living standards?

If national self-interest so characterizes the behavior of the member states, what prevents the unraveling of the integration process? With the end of the Cold War, there is less incentive to come together. However, German unification prompted a return of the "Schuman syndrome," according to which cooperating with Germany in the hope of influencing its policies costs less than going it alone. Moreover, European governments have decided they need the EU to advance the internal market project, so much so that they deploy the rhetoric of solidarity to win support for it. Europeans' ambiguity feeds on the all-too-transparent hypocrisy of governments that talk about citizenship and community against the background of beggar-thy-neighbor policies. The inclusion of Nordic countries and Austria in the EU can only deepen this ambiguity because their membership was sold in part on the basis of their contributions to democratizing Brussels institutions, to enhancing the social and environmental profile of the Union, and to increasing prosperity.

In sum, Europeans' ambiguous relationship to the EU is an artifact of its ambivalent post-Maastricht design features, division among governments over its constitutional vocation, and conjunctural developments such as the business cycle and enlargement. This situation confronts not a static society but one whose developmental dynamics produce typical spatial and demographic constellations of support and opposition. It is to these patterns that we now turn.

Rationalization, Regionalization, and Tertiarization

Far from solving the old political problems that Europe inherited from the 1980s and the new ones it encountered after the fall of the Berlin Wall, the Maastricht Treaty only weakly acknowledged them and, in some cases, made them worse. Treaty articles addressing a wide variety of institutional and substantial policy concerns created an expanded framework for more intensive forms of cooperation, but the result was far from satisfactory. As the social bases of politics evolved, traditional forms of political organization declined relatively in importance and new forms developed. New issues emerged even as traditional ones remained unresolved. Responses have ranged from persistent attempts to introduce new themes to stability-oriented crisis management to resentful defense of deteriorating positions. In sum, Maastricht is equally a crisis of European integration and a crisis of national integration within the member states.

What processes are at work generating the patterns we identify? Consider the functioning of integration and legitimation mechanisms commonly present at the national level in European welfare states. In the current period of transition, piecemeal perspectives offer inadequate points of departure for effective reform. Analysis must encompass not only the ensemble of social, economic, and political structures that must be adjusted to each other but also multiple levels of governance.

Viewed from this perspective, Europe's *décollage* makes sense in terms of the combined operation of three processes resulting from the weakening of Fordism and the subsequent trend of market liberalization: *rationalization, regionalization,* and *tertiarization.* Each of these processes is associated with different conceptions of European integration and correspondingly differentiated constitutional design preferences. Moreover, each is manifested in every European state in varying degrees. The resulting heterogeneity gives rise to a complexity that precludes any facile solutions and has injected an unusual degree of political contingency into the debate over Europe's constitutional future.

Rationalization, the first of these processes, arises out of the traditional contest over the distribution of social goods (primarily employment and income) by participants on either side of the labor market. Rationalization refers to the functional logic of cost cutting both at the point of production and in the fiscal environment, and its major pathological manifestation is social marginalization—the breakdown of systems of social solidarity. With the collapse of communism and globalization of production and finance, the dominant response to rationalization involves adaptive strategies based on remaining within the Fordist regulatory regime, even as new production forms challenge it.

Given the link between the construction of the European welfare state and the project of regional integration,[10] one might expect that political backing for strategies to defend Fordist arrangements would come mainly from the original supporters of the European Community. Indeed, the "rationalizers" do tend to be central actors in Europe's corporatist tradition: employers associations; trade unions; and parties of the center-right and center-left, especially in the original six member states. Because the postwar system was built for and by them and European integration emanated from this system, most supporters of the federalist vision of European integration are located within this constellation. European federalism in this sense refers to a strategy aimed at recapturing lost sovereignty at a higher level of organization. Its utopia is the European federal state. Christian Democracy provided much of the original impetus and legitimation for the SEA and Maastricht treaties. But the specific political achievements of the treaties, such as the Social Charter and attempts to curb the power of the Council of Ministers, have been overshadowed by the process of liberalization.

Britain's response to the Maastricht Treaty helps to clarify the political dynamics of this rationalizing project. The Maastricht Treaty, with its greater emphasis on federalism and regulation at the European level, greatly deepened the traditional fault lines in the Conservative Party over Europe. The anti-European wing of the party is fighting a rearguard action to sustain the form and reality of national sovereignty even as the pro-European wing and, since 1988, the Labour Party seek to reestablish corporatism on a European level. The nationalist reaction achieves its greatest resonance in unitary states such as Britain and France, but its economic program has been undermined by the internationalization of finance and production.

Especially with the enlargement of the common market from six to twelve members (including Ireland, the U.K., Denmark, Spain, Portugal, and Greece), a second process with its own constitutional logic began to unfold. *Regionalization* refers to the spatial differentiation attendant upon rationalization when territorially defined units compete for resources as the size of the resource pool shrinks. It is the territorial manifestation of the struggle over the distribution of social goods. The specific response to this process depends on the location of a given region. As Stuart Holland pointed out some time ago, territorial fragmentation can be either an enormous benefit or a crippling loss, depending on available externalities.[11] Response to the process of regionalization may or may not involve regionalism, that is, the cultivation of a territorially based identity to defend positions already achieved or to attract resources from other parts of the system. Taking advantage of constitutional provisions or cultural identities, solidarity is redefined in opposition to Jacobin traditions.

Because of these factors, the behavior of regions can change quickly as they develop their own attitudes toward European constitutional developments. This reactive behavior results in a level of self-referentiality that, while serving as an important condition for regional precociousness, breeds intolerance and diminishes social solidarity. In this context, one can point to recent developments in Flanders and Lombardy and, more generally, the surge of ethnic nationalism in wealthy regions seeking to escape their obligations to poorer ones.

With reference to regionalization, it is abundantly clear that the deepening of European integration has provoked intense reactions from EU regions whatever their precise cultural or political status. Part of the motivation for their impressive mobilization comes from the desire to lay claim to the EU budget and European Investment Bank (EIB) loans. The telos for the prosperous regions, in contrast to that of the federalists, is a system of multilevel governance that maximizes the autonomy and resources available to regional authorities. In contrast to the antifederalists, the regions are firmly committed to a version of subsidiarity that devolves powers to the subnational level. The situation for weaker regions is, however, more ambiguous, since they often rely on "their" central governments to capture resources on their behalf from Brussels. Therefore, political unity among regions—either in the Committee of the Regions created by the Maastricht Treaty or in the constitutional debate over Maastricht II—is unlikely.

The third process associated with the decline of Fordism is that of *tertiarization*, which refers to the partial displacement of conflict from issues of production and distribution to issues of quality of life, questions of personal identity, and forms of participation in all social spheres. The partial decoupling of production from consumption results from rule-based reductions in working time, the emergence of a dominant postindustrial milieu, and increasing general education opportunities for a broader stratum of the population, all of which have taken place within the context of a regime of more or less comprehensive social insurance.[12]

The postindustrial politics associated with the tertiarization process flourishes in the most economically successful European welfare states. Although it is localized geographically, its pretensions are universalist and, for the most part, republican and liberal. It is associated with the proliferation of citizens' initiatives and "new" social movements that bloomed in the 1970s and comprised a kind of *fronde* against the political establishment.

That rebellion directed itself against all institutions of the postwar settlement in Western Europe, including those associated with the project of regional integration. The North Atlantic Treaty Organization (and the Warsaw Pact) expressed the Cold War logic of extermination; the EC the relentless commodification of every social sphere. International cooperation, however, held great appeal for postindustrialists, who dreamed of an escape from the harsh discipline of economic logic and the confining logic of nationalist particularism. Here was fresh energy to be tapped for regional integration, if only it could be shown that republican values and democratic participation could advance in that context.

Special circumstances had to be present for postmaterialists to condense out of the social solution into a political force of their own. These conditions first occurred in Germany, where the Green Party managed to stabilize itself as the country's third political force in the mid-1990s. Consequently, as representatives of the most coherent alternative vision of Europe at the parliamentary level, the evolution of the German Greens' analysis of and strategy toward Europe has particular relevance for the discussion of the EU's constitutional future.

THE INTERGOVERNMENTAL CONFERENCE: TOWARD A STABLE SOLUTION?

If Europe's recent attempts to overhaul its constitution resolved some problems, they created a host of new ones. By alluding to European citizenship, the Maastricht Treaty evoked the prospect of a European constitutional order but did not define the rights of citizens in that order. By undermining individual governments' vetoes, it limited national democratic influence over the Union but provided few effective and routine means to participate in the decisionmaking process at the European level. By moving ahead with EMU, Maastricht raised the specters of cores and peripheries, insiders and outsiders, social dumping, stagnation, and high unemployment. By calling for a common foreign and security policy, the framers created confusion about the scope of EU membership as well as the EU's mission in the world.

It follows from the foregoing that the basic question for the 1996 IGC is, can an acceptable and practical alternative to the European state system be found? By this measure, the IGC will certainly fail. The reasons range from the principled defense of the state as guarantor of the values of the French Revolution to the opposite, a distinct absence of transnational solidarity.

The Maastricht review agenda has emerged through three channels. The original mandate, articulated in Article B of the Treaty on European Union and decisions of the European Council, an interinstitutional initiative by the European Parliament, the Council, and the Commission, called for a review of the Maastricht Treaty and specified four areas of special scrutiny: the scope of the co-decision legislative procedure; security and defense; the policy areas of energy, tourism, and civil protection; and the hierarchy of the legal acts of the Community. The European Council added to these items the number of commissioners, the weighting of member-state votes in the Council, and institutional changes required by enlargement. Finally, the interinstitutional agreement added consideration of budgetary procedures and the exercise of executive power by the Commission as a result of co-decision procedures.

In June 1994 on Corfu the European Council took the first steps toward organizing the IGC. A "reflection group" was mandated to meet in June 1995 to prepare the agenda. Members of the group included representatives of each of the member-state foreign ministries, the Commission, and two representatives of the European Parliament. Prior to convening the reflection group, initial assessments were prepared by the Commission, the Parliament, and the Council.

The mandate given and the procedures adopted suggest, not surprisingly, that the IGC will provide incremental solutions to the perceived central problems of the European constitutional order. IGC preparations have left much intact: EMU will not be revisited, nor will there be a retreat from Maastricht pillars II (Common Foreign and Security Policy) and III (Justice and Home Affairs). Indeed, among the participants in the reflection group consensus reigns that the purpose of the amending exercise is to improve the functioning of established institutions. This consensus extends to the perceived need to clarify Brussels' powers, simplify the EU's Byzantine decisionmaking procedures, and render the treaties more comprehensible to citizens of the Union.

In light of EU institutional characteristics, it is not surprising that the documents of the Commission and the Parliament converge and that for the Council even basic aims of the integration project are in dispute. The Commission and Parliament both advocate unification of all procedures under a unified treaty, including pillars II and III. The Commission argues for greater adherence to the Maastricht Treaty's allowance for decision by qualified majority vote under pillars II and III. Regarding legislation, the Commission would like to reduce the current twenty-plus procedures to three, whereas the Parliament insists on equality with the Council in all "normal" legislation (a single procedure for everything other than treaty amendment) with equally comprehensive qualified majority votes in the Council. Another point of convergence between Parliament and the Commission concerns the EU's military vocation. Both advocate formalizing a link to a revived Western European Union (WEU). The path to this link was paved by the 1994 and 1996 NATO summits, whose communiqués confirmed NATO's willingness to make forces available for that purpose.

In sum, barring some major unforeseen political disruption, the IGC will produce a streamlined version of the Maastricht Treaty, preserving the current separation of powers among the Council, Parliament, and Commission and increasing the EU's capacity to act externally. Having already broadened the scope of its policymaking competence, Maastricht had made a gesture, however hesitant, to tertiary or postindustrial politics. In establishing the Committee of the Regions it acknowledged the process of regionalization. The establishment of a social policy for the EU indicates the continuing influence of ideas of social solidarity both in the Commission and in member states.

These elements notwithstanding, it is clear that Europe's constitutional debate remains rooted in the traditional federalist-nationalist system of coordinates and is still greatly influenced by neoliberalism. Many hard boards will have to be bored before this coordinate system can change. It will require the powerful presence of a new political subject capable of projecting an alternative vision of Europe's polity in its own interest. The debate over design criteria has been taken up in many member states though its character still looks more like a diplomatic negotiation than a constitutional event. Less coherently, the federalist model is being challenged by the regions, which are eager to preserve or expand their influence and scope for self-determination. At one level, these challenges are products of the clash between the normative foundations of Western European politics, some of which are still evolving. It is important to note that the dynamics of opposition and reform emerge not only in constitutional moments but also in the policymaking process itself.

In diplomatic settings it is vital to narrow the agenda for negotiations in order to increase the chances that agreement be reached on something. If, as many have argued, EU politics is a species of European domestic politics, then the movement should be in the opposite direction, toward a much more open process of constitution building that can articulate a social contract able to secure allegiance and hold decisionmakers accountable. Until a new synthesis is attained, future intergovernmental conferences will be unconvincing and Europe's disorganization will persist.

PLAN OF THE BOOK

This volume is divided into two parts. The first considers the basic economic, political, and social contours of the Union; the second focuses on particular

countries and social movements. All of the chapters in the first section emphasize the incomplete, contested quality of the EU's constitutional design.
Liesbet Hooghe and Gary Marks, Thomas Hueglin, and Michael Shackleton
focus on the separation of powers among the Commission, the Council, and the
European Parliament. Hooghe and Marks, in Chapter 1, contend that the sites
of authority—and hence of political conflict—are, as a result of the SEA and
the Maastricht Treaty, simultaneously supranational and intergovernmental.
They describe a complex system of multilevel power sharing in which constitutional change has compelled subnational groups to establish direct connections to Brussels even as states struggle to maintain their status as brokers.

Hueglin (Chapter 2) finds similarities in the political interlocking federalism of the EU and the Federal Republic of Germany; yet the differences are
crucial for understanding the nascent European constitutional order. The
German system of political interlocking contains a strong social dimension
that is almost entirely absent in the European federal order. The application
of the principle of subsidiarity, moreover, serves to frustrate the development
of a social dimension.

In Chapter 3, Shackleton argues that the Maastricht Treaty provoked an
internal crisis of legitimacy for the Union by raising unfulfilled expectations
concerning popular participation and that the future development of the
Union will greatly intensify the problem of the democratic deficit. He pro-
poses a number of institutional reforms that might increase democratic participation and foster a clearer sense of the European public interest.

Shalini Venturelli (Chapter 4) also addresses the concept of a European
public interest, with particular reference to the possibilities of establishing a
European public space. She shows that the Union's policies toward information have great implications for the possibility of democratic participation
and expression, and delineates three rival conceptions of public service arising from European political and social thought. She also describes the growing conflict between the demands of private contractual law, itself influenced
by U.S. firms and Anglo-American traditions of property rights, and the more
inclusive forms of public constitutional law.

The emergence of a nascent constitutional order on the basis of a neoliberal agenda has obvious implications for the European Left. Alan Cafruny, in
Chapter 5, argues that although the SEA and the Maastricht Treaty do
advance the constitutional agenda, thereby deepening the crisis of the
European Left, the possibility of a more Social Democratic Europe cannot be
discounted. It is doubtful that Europe can establish a stable monetary zone
without simultaneously building for itself at least some aspects of the national welfare state at the level of the EU.

Part 2 examines the constitutional order from the perspective of some
member states and, more particularly, those parties and movements that
have developed reformist or oppositional strategies toward the Union. The

chapters by Pia Christina Wood, Carl Lankowski, and Michael Keating show how the domestication of EU politics has different impacts on the three most powerful member states. Wood (Chapter 6) describes the evolving reaction of the French Right to a strategy that tied the fortunes of the French economy to that of the Bundesbank. Persistent levels of high unemployment in France have established the conditions for the growth of nationalism. However, despite its strong statist orientation, the French Right has not articulated a convincing alternative to the integrationist strategy that developed in response to the failure of Keynesian strategies from 1981 to 1983.

Carl Lankowski (Chapter 7) describes Germany's transition from a "penetrated state" to a powerful state that now transmits conflicts and policy debates to the rest of Europe. A three-cornered conflict now rages among Germans over the deregulatory implications of economic globalization, Europe's social welfare legacy, and the postindustrial politics of new social movements. Germany is acting as a locus classicus for shaping Europe's emergent development path. Lankowski documents the increasingly important role played by the German Green Party—presently Germany's third parliamentary political force—in Europe's constitutional debate.

As Michael Keating shows in Chapter 8, changes in the agenda of the EC have strongly influenced attitudes toward Europe within the United Kingdom. As long as the EC was viewed primarily as a prop to the welfare state, it could elicit strong support from the Conservative Party and the Labour Right, while the Labour Left and the Scottish nationalist movement opposed it. However, as the EC's neoliberal character emerged in the 1980s and the Maastricht Treaty began to erode rather than buttress Westminster, both the Labour movement and the Scottish national movement have viewed further integration with the continent as a means of liberation from a declining United Kingdom. John Coakley, Michael Holmes, and Nicholas Rees (Chapter 9) point to a similar phenomenon operating in the Republic of Ireland, which retains a strong core of nationalist and anti-EU sentiments; as in Scotland, attitudes toward Brussels have often been shaped by anti-British attitudes.

In the final chapter, Christine Ingebritsen explores the potential impact of the Nordic states on the EU. Because of their strong social democratic and solidaristic traditions, these states have regarded the EC/EU with considerable ambivalence. On the one hand, their entry into the Union might be expected to strengthen the forces of social democracy against neoliberalism. On the other hand, the tradition of Nordic aloofness might instead lead to a strategy of exit or partial disengagement.

NOTES

1. Martin Shapiro, "The European Court of Justice," in Alberta Sbragia, ed., *Europolitics: Institutions and Policymaking in the New European Community*

(Washington, D.C.: Brookings Institution, 1992); Anne-Marie Burley and Walter Mattli, "Europe Before the Court: A Political Theory of Legal Integration," *International Organization* 47 (winter 1993); Martin Shapiro and Alec Stone, "The New Constitutional Politics of Europe," and J.H.H. Weiler, "A Quiet Revolution: The European Court of Justice and Its Interlocutors," in Martin Shapiro and Alec Stone, eds., *The New Constitutional Politics of Europe Comparative Political Studies* (Special Issue), 26 (January 1994).

2. William Nicoll, "Maastricht Revisited: A Critical Analysis of the Treaty on European Union," in Alan Cafruny and Glenda Rosenthal, eds., *The State of the European Community: Theory and Research in the Post-Maastricht Era* (Boulder, Colo.: Lynne Rienner Publishers, 1993); see also Wolfgang Streeck, "Neo-Voluntarism: A New European Social Policy Regime?" *European Law Journal* 1 (March 1995).

3. Streeck, "Neo-Voluntarism," p. 31.

4. Giandomenico Majone, "The European Community Between Social Policy and Social Regulation," *Journal of Common Market Studies* 31 (1993).

5. Alain Lipietz, *Towards a New Economic Order: Post-Fordism, Ecology and Democracy* (Cambridge: Polity Press, 1989); Michael Rustin, "The Politics of Post-Fordism," *New Left Review* 175 (1989).

6. John G. Ruggie, "International Regimes, Transactions, and Change: Embedded Liberalism in the Postwar Economic Order," *International Organization* 36 (spring 1982); Charles C. Maier, "The Two Postwar Eras and the Conditions for Stability in Twentieth-Century Western Europe," *American Historical Review* 86 (April 1981).

7. Alan Milward, *The European Rescue of the Nation-State* (Berkeley: University of California Press, 1992).

8. Paolo Cecchini, *The European Challenge, 1992: The Benefits of a Single Market* (Aldershot, U.K: Gower, 1988).

9. Commission of the European Communities, *Growth, Competitiveness, Employment: The Challenges and Ways Forward into the 21st Century White Paper* COM(93) 700 Final (Brussels, December 5, 1993).

10. See, especially, Milward, "European Rescue."

11. Stuart Holland, *The Regional Problem in Europe* (New York: St. Martin's Press, 1976).

12. Herbert Kitshelt, *The Transformation of European Social Democracy* (New York: Cambridge University Press, 1994); Frances Fox Piven, ed., *Labor Parties in Postindustrial Societies* (New York: Oxford University Press, 1991).

1

THE EUROPEAN UNION IN THE 1990s: CONTRADICTIONS OF ECONOMIC AND POLITICAL INTEGRATION

1

Contending Models of Governance in the European Union

Liesbet Hooghe & Gary Marks

Developments in the European Union (EU) over the past decade have revived debate about the consequences of European integration for the autonomy and authority of the state in Europe. The scope and depth of policymaking at the EU level have dramatically increased. The Union has almost completed the internal market and has absorbed the institutional reforms of the Single European Act (SEA, 1986), which established qualified majority voting in the Council of Ministers and increased the power of the European Parliament. The Maastricht Treaty (1993) further expanded EU competencies and the scope of qualified majority voting in the Council and gave the European Parliament a veto on certain types of legislation. The Maastricht Treaty is a landmark in European integration, quite apart from its ambitious plan for a common currency and a European Central Bank by the end of this century.

In this chapter we take stock of these developments. What do they mean for the political architecture of Europe? Do these developments consolidate national states or do they weaken them? If they weaken them, what kind of political order is emerging? These are large and complex questions, and we do not suppose that we can settle them once and for all. Our strategy is to describe two basic alternative conceptions — state-centric governance and multilevel governance — as distinctly as possible and then evaluate their validity by examining the European policy process.

The core presumption underlying the state-centric governance model is that European integration does not challenge the autonomy of national states.[1] State centrists contend that EU membership preserves or even strengthens state sovereignty and that European integration is driven by bargains among member-state governments. No government has to integrate more than it wishes because bargains rest on the lowest common denominator of the participating member states. In this model, supranational actors exist to aid member states, to facilitate agreements by providing information that would not otherwise be so readily available. Policy outcomes reflect the interests and relative power of member-state executives, not those of supranational actors.

An alternative view is that European integration is a polity-creating process in which authority and policymaking influence is shared across multiple levels of government—subnational, national, and supranational.[2] Although national governments are formidable participants in EU policymaking, they have relinquished control to collective EU institutions and supranational institutions. As a result, states have lost some of their former authoritative control over individuals in their respective territories. In short, the multilevel governance model claims that the locus of political control has changed. Individual state sovereignty is diluted in the EU by collective decisionmaking among national governments and by the autonomous roles of the European Parliament, the European Commission, and the European Court of Justice (ECJ).

TWO MODELS OF THE EUROPEAN UNION

The models that we outline below are drawn from a body of work on the European Union and are elaborated in somewhat different ways by different writers. We aim here to set out the basic elements that underlie contending views of the EU so that we may evaluate their validity, not to replicate the ideas of any particular writer.

The core ideas of the *state-centric model* are put forward by several writers, most of whom call themselves intergovernmentalists.[3] This model views states (or, more precisely, national governments) as ultimate decisionmakers, devolving limited authority to supranational institutions to achieve specific policy goals. Decisionmaking in the EU is characterized by bargaining among state executives. To the extent that supranational institutions arise, they serve the ultimate goals of state executives. The state-centric model does not maintain that policymaking is determined by state executives in every detail, only that the overall direction of policymaking is consistent with state control. States may be well served by creating a judiciary, for example, that allows them to enforce collective agreements or a bureaucracy that implements those agreements, but such institutions are not autonomous supranational agents. Rather, they have limited powers to achieve state-oriented collective goods.

EU decisions, in the state-centric model, reflect the lowest common denominator among state executive positions. Member-state executives need not swallow policies they find unacceptable because decisionmaking on important issues operates on the basis of unanimity. This allows states to maintain individual as well as collective control over outcomes. While some governments are not able to integrate as much as they would wish, none are forced into deeper collaboration than they really want.

State decisionmaking in this model does not exist in a political vacuum.

In this respect, the state-centric model takes issue with realist conceptions of international relations that focus on relations among unitary state actors. State executives are located in domestic political arenas, and their negotiating positions are influenced by domestic political interests. But—and this is an important assumption—those state arenas are discrete. That is to say, state decisionmakers respond to political pressures *nested* within each state. Thus, the fifteen state executives bargaining in the European arena are complemented by fifteen separate state arenas that provide the sole channel for domestic political interests to the European level.

One can envision several alternatives to this model. The one we present here, which we describe as *multilevel governance*, is drawn from several sources.[4] Once again, our aim is not to reiterate any one scholar's perspective but to elaborate essential elements of a model that makes the case that European integration has weakened the state.

The multilevel governance model does not reject the view that state executives and state arenas are important or that these remain the *most* important pieces of the European puzzle. However, if the state no longer monopolizes policymaking at the European level or the aggregation of domestic interests, a very different polity comes into focus. First, according to the multilevel governance model, decisionmaking is shared by actors at different levels rather than monopolized by state executives. That is to say, supranational institutions—above all, the European Commission, the European Court of Justice, and the European Parliament—have independent influence in policymaking that cannot be derived solely from their role as agents of state executives. State executives may play an important role, but so too do European-level actors.

Second, collective decisionmaking among states involves a significant loss of control for individual state executives. Lowest-common-denominator decisions can be made on only a subset of EU issues, mainly those concerning the scope of integration. Decisions concerning rules to be enforced across the EU (e.g., harmonizing regulation of product standards, labor conditions, etc.) have a zero-sum character, and necessarily involve gains or losses for individual states.

Third, political arenas are interconnected rather than nested. Although national arenas remain important for the formation of state executive preferences, the multilevel model rejects the view that subnational actors are nested exclusively within states. Instead, they act directly in both national and supranational arenas, creating transnational associations in the process. States do not monopolize links between domestic and European actors but are one among a variety of actors contesting decisions that are made at a variety of levels. In this perspective, complex interrelationships in domestic politics do not stop at the national state but extend to the European level. The separation between domestic and international politics, which lies at the heart of the state-centric model, is rejected by the multilevel governance model. States are an integral and powerful part of the EU, but they no longer provide the sole interface between supranational and subnational arenas, and they share, rather than monopolize, control over many activities that take place in their respective territories.

POLICYMAKING IN THE EUROPEAN UNION

The questions we ask have to do with who decides what in European Union policymaking. If the state-centric model is valid, we would find a systematic pattern of state executive dominance. That would entail three conditions. States, by virtue of the decisions their representatives make in the European Council and the Council of Ministers, should be able to impose their preferences collectively upon other European institutions (the Commission, the Parliament, and the Court). In other words, the latter three European institutions should be agents effectively controlled by state-dominated European institutions. Second, states should be able to maintain individual sovereignty vis-à-vis other member states. And third, states should be able to control the mobilization of subnational interests in the European arena. If, however, the multilevel governance model holds true, we should find first that the European Council and Council of Ministers share authority with supranational institutions; second, that individual state executives cannot consistently deliver the outcomes they want from collective decisionmaking; and, finally, that subnational interests mobilize directly in the European arena or use the EU as a public space to pressure state executives into particular actions.

In the following sections, we describe four sequential phases of the policymaking process: policy initiation, decisionmaking, implementation, and adjudication. We focus on informal practices in addition to formal rules to explain how institutions actually shape the behavior of political actors in the European arena.

Policy Initiation

In political systems that involve many actors, complex procedures, and multiple veto points, the power to set the agenda is extremely important. The European Commission alone has the formal power to initiate and draft legislation, which includes the right to amend or withdraw a proposal at any stage in the process, and it is the think tank for new policies (Article 155, EC). From a multilevel governance perspective, the European Commission has significant autonomous influence over the agenda. In the state-centric view, this formal power is largely decorative: In reality the European Commission draws up legislation primarily to meet the demands of state executives.

At first sight, the practice of policy initiation accords with a state-centric interpretation. Analysis of five hundred recent directives and regulations by the French Conseil d'Etat found that only a minority of EU proposals were spontaneous initiatives of the Commission. Demand, not autonomous supranational action, drives regulatory initiatives at the European level, but the demand comes not only from state actors. A significant number of initiatives originate in the European Parliament, the Economic and Social Committee, regional governments, and various private and public interest groups (Majone 1994).[5]

However, such data should be evaluated carefully. For one thing, regulatory initiative at national and European levels is increasingly intermeshed. In its report, the Conseil d'Etat estimated that the European Commission is consulted beforehand on 75 to 80 percent of French national legislation. Former President of the European Commission Jacques Delors's prediction that by the year 2000 about 80 percent of national economic and social legislation would be of Community origin has a solid base in reality.[6] Moreover, it is one thing to be the first to articulate an issue, and quite another to influence how that issue will be taken up, with whom, and under what set of rules. And in each of these respects the influence of the Commission extends beyond its formal role, partly because of its unique political and administrative resources, discussed later, and partly because the Council is stymied by intergovernmental competition.

An institution that may serve as a powerful principal with respect to the Commission is the European Council, the summit of the political leaders of the member states (plus the president of the Commission) held every six months. The European Council has immense prestige and legitimacy and a quasi-legal status as the institution that defines "general political guidelines" (Treaty on European Union, Title 1, Article D). However, its control of the European agenda is limited because it meets rarely and has only a skeleton permanent staff. The European Council provides the Commission with general policy mandates rather than specific policy proposals, and such mandates have proved to be a flexible base on which the Commission can build legislative programs.

More direct constraints on the Commission originate from the Council of Ministers and the European Parliament. Indeed, the power of initiative is increasingly a shared competence, permanently subject to contestation, among the three institutions. The Council (Article 152, EC) and, since the Maastricht Treaty, the European Parliament (Article 138b, EC) can request that the Commission produce proposals, although they cannot draft proposals themselves.[7] Council presidents began to exploit this window in the legal texts from the mid-1980s, when state executives began to attach higher priority to the Council presidency.[8] Some governments bring detailed proposals with them to Brussels when they take over the Council presidency. Another way for the Council of Ministers to circumvent the Commission's formal monopoly on legislative proposal is to make soft law by ratifying common opinions, resolutions, agreements, and recommendations. [9]

The effect of this on the Commission's agenda-setting role is double-edged. On the one hand, the Commission finds it politically difficult to ignore detailed Council initiatives or soft law, even though their legal status is vague.[10] On the other hand, state executives use the European arena to attain a variety of policy goals, and this gives the Commission allies for integrationist initiatives.

The European Parliament gained new influence from Article 138b. In return for its approval of the Santer Commission in January 1995, it extracted from the European Commission president a pledge to renegotiate the code of conduct (dating from 1990) between the two institutions in an effort to gain greater influence on the Commission's right of initiative.

The European Council, the Council of Ministers, and the European Parliament have each succeeded in circumscribing the Commission's formal monopoly of initiative, though one cannot claim that they have reduced the position of the Commission to that of an agent. All four European institutions now share and compete over agenda setting.

The diffusion of control over the EU's agenda does not stop here. Interest groups have mobilized intensively in the European arena, and although their power is difficult to pinpoint, it is clear that the Commission takes their input seriously. The passage of the Single European Act precipitated a rapid growth of European legislation and a corresponding increase in interest group representation in Europe. An outpouring of case study research suggests that the number and variety of groups involved is as great as, and perhaps greater than, that in any national capital. National and regional organizations of every kind have mobilized in Brussels, flanked by a large and growing number of European umbrella organizations and individual companies from across Europe. According to a Commission report, some 3,000 interest groups and lobbies, or about 10,000 people, were based in Brussels in 1992.[11] Most groups target the European Commission and the European Parliament, for these are perceived to be more accessible than the secretive Council of Ministers.[12] In addition, subnational authorities now mobilize intensively in Brussels. Apart from the Committee of the Regions, established by the Maastricht Treaty, individual subnational authorities have set up almost one hundred regional offices in Brussels and a wide variety of interregional associations.[13]

It is often difficult to apportion responsibility for particular initiatives. This is true for the most intensively studied initiative of all—the internal market program—which was pressed forward by business interests, the Commission, and the European Parliament, as well as by state executives.[14] Because the Commission plays a subtle initiating role, its influence is not captured by analysis of which institution formally announces a new policy. For example, the Delors White Paper on Growth, Competitiveness, and Employment was publicly mandated by the European Council in June 1993, but it did so in response to detailed guidelines for economic renewal placed on the table by the Commission president.

The Commission has considerable leverage, but it is conditional, not absolute. It depends on its capacity to nurture and use diverse contacts, its ability to anticipate and mediate demands, its decisional efficiency, and the unique expertise it derives from its role as think tank of the European Union. The Commission is always on the lookout for information and political support. It has developed an extensive informal machinery of advisory committees and working groups for consultation and prenegotiation, some of which are made up of member-state nominees but others of interest group representatives and experts who give the Commission access to independent information and legitimacy. The Commission has virtually a free hand in creating new networks, and in this way it can reach out to new constituencies, including a variety of subnational groups.

For example, in 1988 the Commission created a Consultative Council for Local and Regional Authorities to provide advice on cohesion policy. The Commission hoped to mobilize support from below for a partnership in which the Commission and national and subnational authorities would jointly design, finance, and implement economic development programs. Jacques Delors and the Commission realized that they would need significant external support to overcome the reluctance of several member-state governments to give subnational governments greater influence over economic development policy. One of the Commission's longer term-goals was to institutionalize regional participation, and a step was taken in this direction with the establishment of a Committee of the Regions in 1993. Although the Commission alone was not responsible for this outcome—pressure by the German Länder and the Belgian regions on their respective governments was pivotal—the experience of creating the Advisory Council laid the groundwork.[15]

The extent to which the Commission initiates policy (Article 155) depends also on its alacrity. Consider the European Energy Charter, a formal agreement between Russia and Western European states guaranteeing Russian energy supply after the collapse of the Soviet Union.[16] An EU policy came into being because the Commission preempted an alternative intergovernmental approach preferred by the Dutch, German, and British governments. Acting on a vague mandate from the European Council in June 1990, the Commission negotiated a preliminary agreement with the Russian government in 1991. Member-state executives, presented with a fait accompli, accepted the European Community (EC) as the appropriate forum for the charter and gave the Commission a toehold in international energy policy,[17] a noteworthy incursion into a policy area that had been dominated by national governments.

The Commission's capacity to move quickly comes from its internal cohesion. An example from industrial policy illustrates the limits of the Commission's agenda-setting power when it is internally divided. In spring 1990, Europe's largest electronics firms pressured the Commission for a European strategy in the semiconductors sector as a means of securing EU financial support and market protection. The Commission was paralyzed for months as a result of internal disagreements. When it eventually produced a policy recommendation for a European industrial policy in the beginning of 1991, most firms had shifted their strategy to other arenas. The French firms Bull and Thomson had obtained guarantees from the French government for financial support, while others like Siemens and Olivetti were exploring strategic alliances with U.S. or Japanese firms.[18]

As the think tank of the European Union, the Commission investigates the feasibility of new EU policies, a role that requires the Commission to solicit expertise. In this capacity it produces 200 to 300 reports, papers (white, green, nonpapers), studies, and communications annually.[19] Some are highly technical studies about, for example, the administration of milk surpluses. Others are influential policy programs such as the 1985 White Paper on the Internal Market,[20] the 1990 reform proposals for Common Agricultural Policy that laid the basis for the European position in the General Agreement on Tariffs and Trade (GATT) negotiations, or the 1993 Delors White Paper on Growth, Competitiveness, and Unemployment, which argued for more labor market flexibility.

As a small and thinly staffed organization, the Commission has only a fraction of the resources available to central state executives, but its position as interlocutor with those executives, subnational authorities, and a large variety of interest groups gives it unparalleled access to information. The Commission has formidible in-house expertise in agriculture, where one-fourth of its staff is concentrated, and in external trade and competition, two additional areas where Commission competence is firmly established. In other areas, the Commission relies on member-state submissions, its extensive advisory system of public and private actors, and paid consultants.[21] The European Commission is a critical actor in the policy initiation phase, whether one looks at formal rules or practice. After surveying the evidence one cannot conclude that the Commission serves merely as an agent of state executives. We discern instead a system of multilevel governance involving contention and interdependence among the Commission, Council of Ministers, and European Parliament, each of which commands impressive resources in the intricate game of policy initiation.

Decisionmaking

According to the Treaties, the main legislative body in the EU is not the European Parliament but the Council of Ministers, an assembly of member-state executives. Until the Single European Act, the Council was the sole legislative authority.

In the state-centric model, state executives determine decisionmaking. They adjust policies to their collective preferences, define the limits of European collaboration, share the role of the European Commission and the Court, and, if need be, curtail their activities. If previous decisions have unintended consequences, these can be corrected by the Council.

There is some plausibility to this argument, but it is one-dimensional. First, individual governments have operated under serious constraints since the Single European Act. Second, even collectively, state executives exert conditional, not absolute, control. State executive dominance is eroded in the decisionmaking process by the legislative power of the European Parliament, the role of the European Commission in overcoming transaction costs, and the efforts of interest groups to influence outcomes in the European arena.

The most transparent blow to state sovereignty has come from the successive extension of qualified majority voting under the Single European Act and the Maastricht Treaty. Qualified majority voting is now the rule for most policy areas covered by the original Treaty of Rome, including agriculture, trade, competition policy, transport, and the internal market, though important exceptions include the budget, taxation, capital flows, self-employed persons and professions, visa policy (qualified majority voting after January 1, 1996), free movement of persons, and rights of employed persons.[22] The decisionmaking rules are complex, but the bottom line is clear: In broad areas of EU competence individual state executives may be outvoted.

The practice of qualified majority voting is complicated by the Luxembourg Compromise and by a "veto culture" that is said to have predominated in the Council of Ministers. Under the Luxembourg Compromise state executives can veto decisions subject to majority rule if they claim that their vital national interests are at stake. However, the Luxembourg Compromise features far more strongly in academic debates about the EU than in the practice of European politics. It was invoked less than a dozen times between 1966 and 1981 and even less frequently since that time. The Luxembourg Compromise was accompanied by a veto culture that inhibited majority voting if a state executive expressed serious objections. During the 1970s this led to the virtual paralysis of the European Community as literally hundreds of Commission proposals were blocked. But the effectiveness of the veto culture was its undoing. It eroded during the 1980s as a result of growing intolerance with deadlock on the part of the European Parliament and most national leaders.[23] The turning point came in 1982 when the British government was unable to veto a decision on agricultural prices to extract a larger British budgetary rebate. A qualified majority vote was taken at the meeting of the Council of Ministers despite British objections.

Thereafter, state executives became more reluctant to invoke the compromise or tolerate its use by others. The last successful use of the Luxembourg veto was in June 1985, when the German government blocked a Council decision to reduce agricultural prices for cereals and colza. Since passage of the Single European Act, which made majority voting the norm in a large number of areas, there has been just one attempt to invoke the compromise, which failed. The Greek government vetoed a Council proposal concerning adjusted green exchange rates (used for calculating agricultural prices) in 1988 in order to extract a more favorable exchange rate for the green drachma but found itself isolated in the Council and retracted the veto. In 1992–1993, the French government threatened to veto the agricultural package of the GATT, but eventually settled for a financial compensation package to cover what amounted to a "discreet climbdown."[24] As Neill Nugent has observed, the Luxembourg Compromise "is in the deepest of sleeps and is subject only to very occasional and partial awakenings."[25]

In this context, second order rules about the adoption of alternative voting procedures are extremely important. Amendments to the Council of Ministers Rules of Procedure in July 1987 have made it much easier to initiate a qualified majority vote. Although previously only the Council president could call a vote, it now suffices that one representative—and that could be the Commission—demands a ballot and is supported by a simple majority of the Council.[26]

One of the most remarkable developments in the 1980s was the transformation of the notion of vital national interest. State executives wishing to exercise a Luxembourg veto have become dependent on the acquiescence of *other* state executives; they can no longer independently determine whether their vital national interest is at stake. As the British (1982), German (1985), Greek (1988), and French (1992–1993) cases suggest, the conditions are restrictive.[27] The Luxembourg Compromise operates effectively only for decisions that involve some combination of the following characteristics: the perception of an unambiguous link to vital national interests; the prospect of serious domestic political damage to the government concerned; a national government that can credibly threaten to damage the general working of the European Union. Although the notion of vital national interest originally legitimized unconditional defense of state sovereignty (French President Charles de Gaulle vetoed the budgetary reform of 1965 on the grounds that it was too supranational), it evolved to justify only defense of substantive interests, not defense of national sovereignty itself.

Even if a member-state executive invokes the Luxembourg Compromise, the veto remains a dull weapon. It cannot block alternative courses of action, as the German government experienced in 1985 after it had stopped a Council regulation on lower prices for cereal and colza. The Commission simply used its emergency powers and achieved virtually the same reductions unilaterally.[28] Moreover, a veto rarely settles an issue, unless the vetoing government prefers the status quo. But even in the two cases in which the status quo was more desirable than the proposed change (the German and French cases), neither government could sustain the status quo. The German government was bypassed by the Commission; the French government failed to block the GATT accord and, moreover, received only modest financial compensation in return for its acquiescence.[29]

All in all, since the mid-1980s, the Luxembourg Compromise has been a weak instrument for the defense of state sovereignty. The British, German, Greek, and French governments did not gain much by invoking or threatening to invoke it. Each came to accept that European decisions severely constrained its options. The Luxembourg Compromise is now mainly for domestic consumption. In each of the four cases the ensuing crisis enabled embattled governments to shift responsibility in the face of intense domestic pressure. Although national governments did not realize their substantive aims, they could at least claim they fought hard to achieve them.

State executives built a variety of specific safeguards into the SEA and the Maastricht Treaty, including numerous derogations for particular states, especially on matters of taxation, state aids, monetary policy, and energy policy. These treaties preserve unanimity for the most sensitive or contested policy areas.

These constraints on qualified majority voting soften the blow to national sovereignty. Nevertheless, a sensible discussion of the overall situation turns on the *extent* to which national sovereignty has been compromised rather than on whether this has happened. State sovereignty has been pooled among a group of states in most EU policy areas.[30]

Collective state control exercised through the Council of Ministers has diminished, partly because of the growing role of the European Parliament in decisionmaking. The SEA and the Maastricht Treaty established cooperation and co-decision procedures that have transformed the legislative process from a simple Council-dominated process into an complex balancing act among Council, Parliament, and Commission. The Council cannot make legislative decisions without the support of at least one of the two other institutions unless it is unanimous. Both procedures enhance the agenda-setting power of the European Parliament, [31] and the cooperation procedure in particular gives the Commission significant agenda-setting capacity.[32] Since the Maastricht Treaty, the two procedures apply to the bulk of EU legislation.

The intermeshing of institutions is particularly intricate under the co-decision procedure, under which the Parliament obtains an absolute veto, although it loses some agenda-setting power to the Council of Ministers. If the Parliament or Council rejects the other's positions, a conciliation committee, consisting of representatives from both institutions, with the Commission sitting in as broker, tries to hammer out a compromise. An absolute majority in the Parliament and a qualified majority in the Council must approve the compromise. If there is no agreement, the initiative returns to the Council, which can then make a take-it-or-leave-it offer, which the Parliament can reject by absolute majority. Thus the Parliament has the final word.

Even though the outcome of the co-decision procedure is likely to be closer to the preferences of the Council than those of the Commission or Parliament,[33] it does not simply reflect Council preferences. Under both procedures the Council is locked in a complex relationship of cooperation and contestation with the two other institutions. This is multilevel governance in action, and it is distinctly different from what would be expected in a state-centric system.

However, the erosion of collective state control goes further. It is difficult for state executives to resolve transaction costs in the egalitarian setting of the Council of Ministers, particularly now, given that there are fifteen such actors.[34] The Council usually lacks information, expertise, and the coordination to act quickly and effectively, and this induces it to rely on the European Commission for leadership.[35] The Commission, as a hierarchical organization, can usually present a more coherent position than the Council. Furthermore, Commission officials bring unusual skills to the negotiation table. As administrators, they have often been working on a particular policy issue for years; career mobility tends to be lower than for top echelons of most national administrations.[36] In addition, they have access to information and expertise from a variety of sources in the European Union. They tend to be exceptionally skilled political negotiators accustomed to the diverse political styles of national representatives and the need to seek consensus.[37] Formal decision rules in the Council help the Commission to focus discussion or broker compromise. While member-state representatives preside at Council of Ministers meetings and working groups, the Commission sits in to clarify, redraft, and finalize the proposal—in short, it holds the pen.

Recent theoretical literature has often stressed the intergovernmental character of the European Union, whereas most of the empirical literature has emphasized the influence of the Commission.[38] Cohesion policy offers an example of how the Commission may step beyond its role of umpire to become a negotiator. In establishing the framework for structural funds for 1994–1999 in the summer of 1993, Commission officials negotiated bilaterally with officials from the relevant states. The Belgian presidency acted as umpire. In such cases, the Commission becomes effectively a thirteenth (or, since 1995, a sixteenth) partner around the bargaining table.[39] This can be true even for the most intergovernmental aspect of European Union politics, treaty bargaining, as an example from Maastricht illustrates. When Britain refused the watered-down social provisions in the Maastricht Treaty, Jacques Delors put on the table his original, more radical, social policy program of 1989 and proposed to attach it as a special protocol to the Treaty, leaving Britain out. Faced with the prospect that the whole negotiation might break down, the other eleven state executives hastily signed up to a more substantial document than they had originally anticipated.[40]

In sum, the Council of Ministers is the senior partner in the decision-making stage, but the European Parliament and the Commission are indispensable. The Commission exercises power by subtle influence rather than sanction. Except for agriculture, external trade, and competition policy, where it has substantial executive autonomy, it gains little by confrontation. Its influence depends on its ability to craft consensus among institutions and among member-state executives. However, extensive reliance on qualified majority voting has enabled the Commission to be bolder because it does not have to court all state executives at once.

The European Parliament's power is based more on formal rules. Its track record under the cooperation and co-decision procedures shows that it does not eschew confrontation with the Council. In return for the Parliament's assent to enlargement of the Union and the GATT in 1994, it extracted from the Council a formal seat in the preparatory negotiations for the intergovernmental conference (IGC) of 1996–1997. In the meantime, it intends to make the most of its power, even if it treads on the toes of its long-standing ally, the European Commission. During the Santer Commission hearings in January 1995, the European Parliament demanded that the European Commission accept parliamentary amendments "as a matter of course" and withdraw proposals that it rejects.[41] Commission officials have described these proposals as "outrageous" on the grounds that the Commission "would more or less lose its ability to operate."[42]

Decisionmaking in the EU is shaped by multiple, intermeshing competencies, complementary policy functions, and variable lines of authority — features characteristic of multilevel governance.

Implementation

Multilevel governance is prominent in the implementation stage. Although the Commission has formal executive powers and national governments are in principle responsible for implementation, in practice these competencies are shared. On the one hand, national governments monitor the executive powers of the Commission closely, though they do so in conjunction with subnational governments and societal actors. On the other hand, the Commission has become involved in day-to-day implementation in a number of policy areas, and this brings it into close contact with subnational authorities and interest groups. As in the policy initiation and decisionmaking stages, mutual intrusion is contested.

The Commission has discretion to interpret legislation and issue administrative regulations bearing on specific cases. It issues between six and seven thousand administrative regulations annually.[43] However, only a tiny proportion of the Commission's decisions are unilateral. Since the 1980s with the institutionalization of comitology, a mechanism for state executive oversight of Commission activities, the Council and the individual national governments have become intimately involved. Many regulations have their own committee attached to them. Balancing Commission autonomy and state executive involvement is an open-ended and contentious process in the European Union. Rules of operation vary across policy areas and lead to contention between the Commission, usually supported by the Parliament, and the Council.[44] Some committees are only advisory; others can prevent the Commission from carrying out a certain action by qualified majority vote; and a third category must approve Commission actions by qualified majority. In each case the Commission presides.

At first sight, comitology seems to give state executives control over the Commission's actions, but the relationship between state actors and European institutions is more complex. Comitology is weakest in precisely those areas where the Commission has extensive executive powers. In competition policy, state aid, agriculture, commercial policy, and the internal market, the Commission has significant space for autonomous action.[45] State centrists may argue that state executives prefer to delegate these powers to achieve state-oriented collective goods, such as control over potential distortion of competition or a stronger bargaining position in international trade. But as a result state executives have lost exclusive control in a range of policy areas. To mention just three examples among the many discussed in this chapter: They no longer control competition within their borders; they cannot aid national firms as they deem fit; they cannot autonomously conduct trade negotiations.

German regional policy had to be recast because it ran foul of the European Commission's policy on competition. The Commission's insistence in the 1980s that regional aid to Western Länder be curtailed has provoked several disputes among Länder and between Länder and the federal government. By 1995, the traditional system of *Gemeinschaftsaufgabe* was on the brink of collapse.[46]

Although comitology involves state actors in the European Commission's activities, this intermeshing is not necessarily limited to *central* state actors. Because the issues on the table are often technical in nature, member-state governments tend to send those people who are directly responsible or who are best informed about the issue at home—including subnational officials and representatives of interest groups or other non-governmental bodies. Subnational participation in comitology is prevalent in member states organized along federal or semifederal lines.[47] But, in recent years, subnational actors have been drawn into the European arena from more centralized member states.[48]

To the extent that EU regulations affect policy areas where authority is shared among central and subnational levels of government, effective implementation requires contacts between multiple levels of government. Environmental policy provides an example of this, for in several European countries competencies in this area are shared across different territorial levels. To speed up implementation of environmental law, in 1990 the Commission began to arrange so-called "package" meetings to bring together central, regional, and local government representatives of a member state. Such meetings are voluntary, but in the first year of its operation seven countries made use of them. The Spanish central government, for example, took advantage of the Commission's presence to pressure its autonomous provinces into compliance with EU environmental law, but in doing so it conceded them access to the European arena.

The majority of participants in comitology are not national civil servants but interest group representatives (particularly from farming, union, and employer organizations) as well as technical experts, scientists, and academics.[49] One can plausibly assume that national governments find it more difficult to persuade such individuals to defend the national interest than their own officials. In practice, therefore, comitology, which was originally a mechanism to allow state review of Commission activities, has had the unintended consequence of deepening the participation of subnational authorities and private actors in the European arena.

A second development that has received little attention in the literature is the direct involvement of Commission officials in day-to-day policy implementation. The Commission was never expected to perform ground-level implementation except in unusual cases (such as competition policy, fraud, etc.), yet in some areas this has changed. The most prominent example is cohesion policy, which now absorbs about one-third of the EU budget. The bulk of the money goes to multiannual regional development programs in the less developed regions of the EU. The 1989 reform prescribed the involvement of Commission, national, regional, local, and social actors on a continuing basis in all stages of the cohesion policy process: selection of priorities, choice of programs, allocation of funding, monitoring of operations, and evaluation and adjustment of programs. To this end, each recipient region or country had to set up an elaborate system of monitoring committees, with a general committee at the top and a cascade of subcommittees focused on particular programs. Commission officials can and do participate at each level of this system. Partnership is implemented unevenly across the EU,[50] but almost everywhere it institutionalizes some form of direct contact between the Commission and noncentral government actors including regional and local authorities, local action groups, and local businesses. Such links break open the mold of the state, so that multilevel governance encompasses actors within as well as beyond existing states.

Adjudication

State centrists have argued that a European legal order and effective European Court of Justice are essential to state cooperation.[51] Unilateral defection from EU policy by a state executive is difficult to detect, and thus it is in the interest of all executives to delegate authority to a European Court to monitor compliance. The ECJ also mitigates incomplete contracting problems by applying general interstate bargains to future contingencies. Thus, the ECJ may be conceptualized as an agent of constituent member states. However, a number of scholars have argued convincingly that the ECJ has become more than an instrument of member states.[52] The Court has been active in transforming the legal order in a supranational direction, but it could not have done this without a political ally at the European level: the European Commission. Nor could it have established the supremacy of European law without the collaboration of national courts, and this collaboration has altered the balance of power between national courts and national political authorities.

Through its activist stance, the ECJ has laid the legal foundation for an integrated European polity. By means of an impressive body of case law, the Court has established the Treaty of Rome as a document creating legal obligations directly binding on national governments and individual citizens alike. Moreover, these obligations have legal priority over laws made by the member states. Directly binding legal authority and supremacy are attributes of sovereignty, and their application by the ECJ indicates that the EU is becoming a constitutional regime.

The Court was originally expected to act as an impartial monitor "to ensure that in the interpretation and application of the treaties the law is observed" (Article 164, EEC; Article 136, Euratom; Article 31, ECSC), but from the beginning the Court viewed these interstate treaties as more than narrow agreements. The Court's expansive role grew out of the failure of the treaties to specify the responsibilities of major EU institutions.[53] Instead, the treaties set out "tasks" or "purposes" for European cooperation, such as the customs union (Treaty of Rome), the completion of the internal market (Single European Act), and economic and monetary union (Maastricht Treaty). The Court has constitutionalized European law and expanded European authority in other policy areas by stating that these were necessary to achieve these functional goals.[54]

Although court rulings have been pivotal in shaping European integration, the ECJ depends on other actors to force issues onto the European political agenda and condone its interpretations. Legislators (the European Council, Council of Ministers, Commission, and Parliament) may always reverse the course set by the Court by changing the law or by altering the treaties. In other words, the ECJ is no different from the Council of Ministers, Commission, or Parliament in that is locked into mutual dependence with other actors.

One outcome of this interlocking is the principle of "mutual recognition," which became the core principle of the internal market program in the landmark case of *Cassis de Dijon* (1979), in which the Court stated that a product lawfully produced in one member state must be accepted in another. Detailed analysis of the evidence suggests that the Court made the decision autonomously, notwithstanding the opposition of the French and German governments.[55] The Commission projected the principle of mutual recognition onto a wider agenda, the single market initiative, and it did this as early as July 1980 when it announced to the European Parliament and the Council that the Cassis case was the foundation for a new approach to market harmonization.[56]

National courts have proved willing to apply another doctrine, direct effect, by invoking Article 177 of the Treaty of Rome, which stipulates that national courts may seek "authoritative guidance" from the ECJ in cases involving Community law. In such instances, the ECJ provides a preliminary ruling, specifying the proper application of Community law to the issue at hand. While this preliminary ruling does not formally decide the case, in practice the Court is rendering a judgment on the "constitutionality" of a particular statute or administrative action. The court that made the referral cannot be forced to acknowledge the interpretations by the ECJ, but if it does, other national courts usually accept these decisions as a precedent. Preliminary rulings expand ECJ influence, and judges at the lowest level gain a de facto power of judicial review, which had been reserved to the highest court in the state.[57] Article 177 gives lower national courts strong incentives to circumvent their own national judicial hierarchy. With their support, much of the business of interpreting Community law has been transferred from national high courts to the ECJ and lower courts.

ECJ decisions have become accepted as part of the legal order in the member states, shifting expectations about decisionmaking authority from a purely national system to a more multilevel one. The doctrines of direct effect and supremacy were constructed over the strong objections of several member state executives. Yet the Court's influence lies not in its scope for unilateral action but in the fact that its rulings and inclusive mode of operation create opportunities for other European institutions, particularly the Commission, for private interests, and for national courts to influence the European agenda or enhance their power.

CONCLUSION

Multilevel governance does not confront the sovereignty of states directly. Instead of being explicitly challenged, states in the European Union are being melded gently into a multilevel polity by their leaders and by the actions of numerous subnational and supranational actors. State-centric theorists are right when they argue that states are extremely powerful institutions that are capable of crushing direct threats to their existence. The organizational form of the state emerged because it proved a particularly effective means of systematically wielding violence, and it is difficult to imagine any generalized challenge along these lines. But this is not the only, nor even the most important, issue facing the institution of the state. One does not have to argue that states are on the verge of political extinction to believe that their control of those living in their territories has significantly weakened

It is not necessary to look far beyond the state itself to find reasons that might explain how such an outcome is possible. When we disaggregate the state into the actors that shape its diverse institutions, it is clear that key decision makers, above all those directing the state executive, may have goals that do not coincide with that of projecting state sovereignty into the future. As well as being a goal in itself, the state may sensibly be regarded as a means to a variety of ends that are structured by party competition and interest group politics in a liberal democratic setting. A state executive may wish to shift decisionmaking to the supranational level because the political benefits outweigh the cost of losing control. Or a state executive may have intrinsic grounds to shift control, for example, to shed responsibility for unpopular decisions

Even if state executives want to maintain sovereignty, they are often not able to do so. A state executive can easily be outvoted because most decisions in the Council are now taken under the decision rule of qualified majority, and, moreover, even the national veto, the ultimate instrument of sovereignty, is constrained by the willingness of other state executives to tolerate its use in particular circumstances. But the limits on state sovereignty go deeper. Even collectively, state executives do not determine the European agenda because they are unable to control the supranational institutions they have created at the European level. The growing diversity of issues on the Council of Ministers' agenda, the sheer number of state executive principals and the mistrust that exists among them, and the increased specialization of policymaking have led the Council to rely upon the Commission to set the agenda, forge compromises, and supervise compliance. The Commission and the Council are not on par, but neither can their relationship be understood in principal-agent terms. Policymaking in the EU is characterized by mutual dependence, complementary functions, and overlapping competencies.

The Council also shares decisionmaking with the European Parliament, which has gained significant legislative power under the Single European Act and the Maastricht Treaty. Indeed, the Parliament may be conceived of as a principal in its own right in the European arena. The Council, Commission, and Parliament interact within a legal order which has been transformed into a supranational one through the innovative jurisprudence of the European Court of Justice. The complex interplay among these contending institutions in a polity where political control is diffuse often leads to outcomes that are unintended by any one of them.

The character of the Euro-polity at any particular point in time depends on tension between supranational and intergovernmental pressures. We have argued that, since the 1980s, it has crystallized into a multilevel polity. States no longer serve as the exclusive nexus between domestic politics and international relations. Direct connections are being forged among political actors in diverse political arenas. Traditional and formerly exclusive channels of communication and influence are being sidestepped.

However, multilevel governance is unlikely to reach equilibrium. There is no widely legitimized constitutional framework. There is little consensus on the goals of integration. As a result, the allocation of competencies between national and supranational actors is ambiguous and contested.

It is worth noting that the European polity has made two U-turns in its short history. Overt supranationalist features of the original structure were overshadowed by the imposition of intergovernmental institutions in the 1960s and 1970s.[58] From the 1980s on, a system of multilevel governance arose, in which the activities of supranational and subnational actors diluted national governmental control.

As the EU reaches into the lives of European individuals and groups, so they are induced to extend their reach to the EU. Societal interests—producer groups, new social movements, and subnational authorities, among many others—have been drawn into this multilevel polity. With its dispersed competencies and contending but interlocked institutions, multilevel governance provides multiple points of access for interest group activity. However, as Cafruny and Lankowski argue in the Introduction to this book, and as subsequent chapters demonstrate for particular issues or actors, the resulting multilevel polity favors certain interests and disadvantages others. It privileges interests that thrive in a post-Keynesian economy and the pluralistic setting of a postcorporatist polity, and it empowers actors who have technical expertise suited to an elitist policy process.

These developments have engendered strong negative reactions on the part of declining social groups represented in nationalist political movements. Ironically, much of the discontent with European integration has been directed toward state executives themselves and the pragmatic and elitist style in which they have bargained for institutional change in the EU.

The EU-wide series of debates unleashed by the Maastricht Treaty have forced the issue of sovereignty onto the agenda. Where governing parties themselves shy away from the issue, it is raised in stark terms by opposition parties, particularly those of the extreme right. Several member-state governments are, themselves, deeply riven on the issues of integration and sovereignty. States and state sovereignty have become objects of popular contention—the outcome of which is as yet uncertain.

NOTES

We would like to thank Kermit Blank, who contributed to an earlier draft of this chapter. We would also like to thank Simon Bulmer, Jim Caporaso, Stephen George, John Keeler, Peter Lange, Andrea Lenschow, Christian Lequesne, Mark Pollack, Michael Shackleton, and Helen Wallace for their criticisms, comments, and suggestions. We are indebted to Ivan Llamazares and Leonard Ray for research assistance.

1. Michael Mann, "Nation-states in Europe and Other Continents: Diversifying, Developing, Not Dying," *Daedelus* 13 (1994), pp. 115–140; John Mearsheimer, "Back to the Future: Instability in Europe After the Cold War," *International Security* 15 (1990), pp. 5–49; Alan Milward, *The European Rescue of the Nation-State* (Berkeley: University of California Press, 1992); Andrew Moravcsik, "Negotiating the Single European Act: National Interests and Conventional Statecraft in the European Community," *International Organization* 45 (1991), pp. 651–688; Andrew Moravcsik, "Preferences and Power in the European Community: A Liberal Intergovernmental Approach," *Journal of Common Market Studies* 31 (1993), pp. 473–524; Andrew Moravcsik, "Why the European Community Strengthens the State: Domestic Politics and International Cooperation" (paper presented at the Annual Meeting of the American Political Science Association, New York, September 1–4, 1994); Wolfgang Streeck, "Neo-Voluntarism: A New European Social Policy Regime?" in Gary Marks, Fritz Scharpf, Philippe C. Schmitter, and Wolfgang Streeck, *Governance in the Emerging Euro-Polity* (London: Sage, 1996).

2. Gary Marks, "Structural Policy and 1992," in Alberta Sbragia, ed., *Euro-Politics: Institutions and Policy Making in the "New" European Community* (Washington D.C.: Brookings Institution, 1992); Liesbet Hooghe, ed., *Cohesion Policy and European Integration: Building Multilevel Governance* (Oxford: Oxford University Press, 1996); Gary Marks, Liesbet Hooghe, and Kermit Blank, "European Integration since the 1980s: State-centric Versus Multi-Level Governance," *Journal of Common Market Studies* 34 (forthcoming).

3. Stanley Hoffman, "Obstinate or Obsolete? The Fate of the Nation State and the Case of Western Europe," *Daedalus* 95 (1966), pp. 892–908; Stanley Hoffmann, "Reflections on the Nation-State in Western Europe Today," *Journal of Common Market Studies* 21 (1982), pp. 21–37; Paul Taylor, "The European Community and the State: Assumptions, Theories and Propositions," *Review of International Studies* 17 (1991), pp. 109–125; Andrew Moravcsik, "Negotiating the Single European Act" and "Preferences and Power"; Geoffrey Garrett, "International Cooperation and Institutional Choice: The EC's Internal Market," *International Organization* 46 (1992), pp. 533–560; Milward, *European Rescue*; Streeck, "Neo-Voluntarism"; for an intellectual history, see James A. Caporaso and John T.S. Keeler, "The European

Community and Regional Integration Theory" (paper presented at the Third Biennial International Conference of the European Community Studies Association, May 1993, Washington, D.C.).

4. Marks, "Structural Policy and 1992"; Gary Marks, "Structural Policy After Maastricht," in Alan Cafruny and Glenda Rosenthal, eds., *The State of the European Community* (Boulder, Colo.: Lynne Rienner Publishers, 1993); Alberta Sbragia, "Thinking About the European Future: The Uses of Comparison," in Alberta Sbragia, ed., *Europolitics: Institution and Policymaking in the "New" European Community* (Washington D.C.: The Brookings Institution, 1992); Alberta Sbragia, "The European Community: A Balancing Act," *Publius* 23 (1993), 23–28; Philippe C. Schmitter, "Interests, Powers and Functions: Emergent Properties and Unintended Consequences in the European Polity," Center for Advanced Study in the Behavioral Sciences, unpublished paper (1992); Philippe C. Schmitter, "The Emerging Europolity and Its Impact upon Euro-Capitalism," in Robert Boyer, ed., *Contemporary Capitalism: The Embeddedness of Institutions* (1992); Giandomenico Majone, "The Development of Social Regulation in the European Community as a Regulatory State," unpublished paper, 1994; Giandomenico Majone, "The Development of Social Regulation in the European Community: Policy Externalities, Transaction Costs, Motivational Factors," unpublished paper, 1995; Paul Pierson, "The Path to European Integration: An Historical Institutionalist Perspective," *Comparative Political Studies* 29 (1996), pp. 123–163; Stephan Leibfried and Paul Pierson, eds., *European Social Policy: Between Fragmentation and Integration* (Washington, D.C.: Brookings Institution, 1995); Marks, Hooghe, and Blank, "European Integration since the 1980's"; see Caporaso and Keeler, "The European Community," for an overview.

5. Majone, "The European Community."

6. Ibid.

7. Neill Nugent, *The Government and Politics of the European Community* (London: Macmillan, 1994).

8. Ibid.

9. Ibid.; Francis Snyder, "Soft Law and Institutional Practice in the European Community," in Stephen Martin, ed., *The Construction of Europe: Essays in Honour of Emile Noël* (Kluwer: Dordrecht, 1994).

10. Snyder, "Soft Law."

11. Audrey McLaughlin and Justin Greenwood, "The Management of Interest Representation in the European Union," *Journal of Common Market Studies* 33 (1995), pp. 143–156.

12. Sonia Mazey and Jeremy Richardson, "EC Policy-Making: An Emerging European Policy Style?" in Duncan Liefferink and Philip Lowe, eds., *European Integration and Environmental Policy* (Scarborough, Ontario: Belhaven Press, 1993).

13. Liesbet Hooghe and Gary Marks, "Birth of a Polity: The Struggle over European Integration," in Herbert Kitschelt, Peter Lange, Gary Marks, and John Stephens, eds., *The Politics and Political Economy of Advanced Industrial Societies* (forthcoming); Liesbet Hooghe, "Subnational Mobilisation in the European Union," *West European Politics* 18 (1995), pp. 175–198; Gary Marks, Jane Salk, Leonard Ray, and François Nielsen, "Competencies, Cracks and Conflicts: Regional Mobilization in the European Union," *Comparative Political Studies* (1996), pp. 164–192.

14. David Cameron, "The 1992 Initiative: Causes and Consequences," in Alberta M. Sbragia, ed., *Europolitics: Institutions and Policymaking in the "New" European Community* (Washington D.C.: Brookings Institution, 1992); Moravcsik, "Negotiating the Single European Act"; Maria Green Cowles, "Setting the Agenda for the New Europe: The ERT and 1992," *Journal of Common Market Studies* 33 (1995), pp.

501–526; Majone, "The European Community"; Renaud Dehousse, "Integration Versus Regulation? On the Dynamics of Regulation in the European Community," *Journal of Common Market Studies* 30 (1992), pp. 383–402; Geoffrey Garrett and Barry Weingast, "Ideas, Interests, and Institutions: Construction of the EC's Internal Market," in Judith Goldstein and Robert Keohane, eds., *Ideas and Foreign Policy* (Ithaca, N.Y.: Cornell University Press, 1993).

15. Liesbet Hooghe, "Building a Europe with the Regions. The Changing Role of the European Commission," in Liesbet Hooghe, ed., *Cohesion Policy and European Integration: Building Multi-Level Governance* (Oxford: Oxford University Press, 1996).

16. Janne Haaland Matlary, "Quis Custodiet Custodes? The European Commission's Policy-Making Role and the Problem of Democratic Legitimacy" (paper presented at the Third Biennial International Conference of the European Community Studies Association, May 1993, Washington, D.C.).

17. Ibid.

18. George Ross, "Sidling into Industrial Policy: Inside the European Commission," *French Politics and Society* 11 (1993) pp. 20–44; George Ross, *Jacques Delors and European Intgration* (Oxford: Oxford University Press, 1995).

19. Peter Ludlow, "The European Commission," in Robert O. Keohane and Stanley Hoffmann, eds., *The New European Community: Decision-Making and Institutional Change* (Boulder, Colo.: Westview Press, 1991).

20. Cameron, "The 1992 Initiative"; Wane Sandholtz and John Zysman, "1992: Recasting the European Bargain," *World Politics* 42 (1989), pp. 95–128.

21. Neill Nugent, "The Leadership Role of the European Commission: Explanatory Factors" (paper presented to the research conference of the University Association for Contemporary European Studies at the University of Birmingham, September 18–19, 1995, Birmingham).

22. Renaud Dehousse, "Integration Versus Regulation? On the Dynamics of Regulation in the European Community," *Journal of Common Market Studies* 30 (1992), pp. 383–402; Nugent, *Government and Politics*; Schmitter, "The Emerging Europolity."

23. Anthony Teasdale, "The Life and Death of the Luxembourg Compromise," *Journal of Common Market Studies* 31 (1993), pp. 567–579.

24. Ibid.

25. Nugent, *Government and Politics*, p. 145.

26. Ibid.

27. Nugent, *Government and Politics*; William Wallace, *Regional Integration: The West European Experience* (Washington D.C.: Brookings Institution, 1994); Teasdale, "The Luxembourg Compromise."

28. Teasdale, "The Luxembourg Compromise."

29. Ibid.

30. Wolfgang Wessels, "Staat and (westeuropaische) Integration: Die Fusionsthese," *Politische Vierteljahrasschrift*, Sonderheft 23 (1992), pp. 36–60; Fritz Scharpf, "Community and Autonomy Multilevel Policymaking in the European Union," *Journal of European Public Policy* 1 (1994), pp. 219–242.

31. George Tsebelis, "The Power of the European Parliament as a Conditional Agenda Setter," *American Political Science Review* 88 (1994), 128–142; George Tsebelis, "Will Maastricht Reduce the Democratic Deficit?" *APSA Comparative Politics Newsletter* 6 (1995), pp. 4–6.

32. Tsebelis, "The European Parliament"; Garrett and Weingast, "Ideas, Interests, and Institutions"; Schmitter, "Interests, Powers and Functions,"; Joe H.H.

Weiler, "The Transformation of Europe," *Yale Law Review* 100 (1991), pp. 2403–2483; compare with skeptical early prognoses: Roland Beiber, J. Pantalis, and J. Schoo, "Implicatons of the Single Act for the European Parliament," *Common Market Law Review* 23 (1986), pp. 767–792.

33. Tsebelis, "Maastricht."

34. Garrett and Weingast, "Ideas, Interests, and Institutions"; Fritz Scharpf, "The Joint Decision Trap: Lessons from German Federalism and European Integration," *Public Administration* 66 (1988), pp. 239–278; Giandomenico Majone, "The European Community."

35. Nugent, "Leadership Role."

36. Irene Bellier, "Une culture de la Commission européene? De la recontre des cultures et du multilinguisme des fonctionnaires," in Yves Mény, Pierre Muller, and Jean-Louis Quermonne, eds., *Politiques Publiques en Europe* (Paris: L'Harmattan, 1994).

37. Giandomenico Majone, "Deregulation or Re-regulation? Policy-Making in the European Community Since the Single Act," unpublished paper (1993); Nugent, "Leadership Role"; Bellier, "Une culture de la Commission européenne?"

38. Cowles-Green, "Setting the Agenda"; Volker Bornschier and Nicola Fielder, "The Genesis of the Single European Act: Forces and Protagonists Behind the Relaunch of the European Community in the 1980s: The Single Market," unpublished paper (1995); Sandholtz and Zysman, "Recasting," and Cameron, "The 1992 Initiative," have demonstrated this leadership/broker role for the Internal Market Program: For technology policy (Esprit, Race) see Wayne Sandholtz, "ESPRIT and the Politics of International Collective Action," *Journal of Common Market Studies* 30 (1992), pp. 1–21; John Peterson, "Technology Policy in Europe: Explaining the Framework Programme and Eureka in Theory and Practice," *Journal of Common Market Studies* 29 (1991), pp. 269–290; and Mark A. Pollack, "Creeping Competence: The Expanding Agenda of the European Community," *Journal of Public Policy* 14 (1995), pp. 95–145. For telecommunications see Wayne Sandholtz, "Institutions and Collective Action: The New Telecommunications in Western Europe," *World Politics* 45 (1993), pp. 242–270. For social policy see Laura Cram, "Calling the Tune Without Paying the Piper? Social Policy Regulation: The Role of the Commission in European Community Social Policy," *Policy and Politics* 21 (1993), pp. 135–146. Volker Eichener, *Social Dumping or Innovative Regulation? Processes and Outcomes of European Decision-Making in the Sector of Health and Safety at Work Harmonization*, EUI Working Paper (1992), and Majone, "The European Community." For industrial policy see Ross, *Jacques Delors*. For energy policy, see Matlary, "Quis Custodiet"; For cohesion policy see Ingeborg Tömmel, "System-Entwicklung and Politikgestalung in der Europäischen Gemeinschaft am Beispiel der Regionalpolitik," *Politische Vierteljahresschrift*, Sonderheft 23 (1992), pp. 185–208, Gary Marks, "Decision Making in Cohesion Policy. Describing and Explaining Variation," in Liesbet Hooghe, ed., *Cohesion Policy and European Integration: Building Multi-Level Governance* (Oxford: Oxford University Press, 1996), and Hooghe, "Building a Europe."

39. Hooghe, "Building a Europe."

40. Pierson, "European Integration"; Peter Lange, "The Maastricht Social Protocol: Why Did They Do It?" *Politics and Society* 21 (1993), pp. 5–36.

41. Reiterated by EP president K. Haensch in an interview for *The European*, January 26, 1995.

42. *Financial Times*, January 15, 1995.

43. Nugent, *Government and Politics*; Ludlow, "The European Commission."

44. Kieran St. Clair Bradley, "Comitology and the Law Through a Glass, Darkly," *Common Market Law Review* (1992), pp. 693–721.

45. Lee McGowan and StephenWilks, "The First Supranational Policy in the European Union: Competition Policy," *European Journal of Political Research* (1995), pp. 141–169; Nugent, *Government and Politics*; Nugent, "Leadership Role."

46. Jeffrey Anderson, "Germany and the Structural Funds: Reunification Leads to Bifurcation," in Liesbet Hooghe, ed., *Cohesion Policy and European Integration: Building Multi-Level Governance* (Oxford: Oxford University Press, 1996).

47. On Germany: Klaus Götz, "National Governance and European Integration: Intergovernmental Relations in Germany," *Journal of Common Market Studies* 33 (1994), pp. 91–116; on Belgium: Liesbet Hooghe, "Belgian Federalism and the European Community," in Michael Keating and Barry Jones, eds., *Regions in the European Union* (Oxford: Clarendon Press, 1995), pp. 135–166.

48. For France, see Christian Lequesne, "L'administration central de la France et le système poilitique europeén: mutations et adaptations depuis l'Acte unique," in Yves Mény, Pierre Muller, and Jean-Louis Quermonne, eds., *Politiques Publiques en Europe* (Paris: L'Harmattan, 1994).

49. G. J. Buitendijk and M.P.C.M. van Schendelen, "Brussels Advisory Committees: A Channel for Influence," *European Law Review* 20 (1995), pp. 37–56.

50. Marks, "Decision Making"; Liesbet Hooghe and Michael Keating, "The Politics of EU Regional Policy," *Journal of European Public Policy* 1 (1994), pp. 367–393.

51. Garrett and Weingast, "Ideas, Interests, and Institutions"; Geoffrey Garrett, "The Politics of Legal Integration in the European Union," *International Organization* 49 (1995), pp. 171–181; Moracsik, "Preferences and Power."

52. Anne-Marie Burley-Slaughter and Walter Mattli, "Europe Before the Court: A Political Theory of Legal Integration," *International Organization* 47 (1992), pp. 41–76.

53. Weiler, "Transformation."

54. Ibid.

55. Dehousse, "Integration"; Karen Alter and Sophie Meunier-Aitsahalia, "Judicial Politics in the European Community: European Integration and the Pathbreaking Cassis de Dijon Decision," *Comparative Political Studies* 26 (1994), pp. 535–561; Majone, "The Development of Social Regulation."

56. Alter and Meunier-Aitsahalia, "Judicial Politics."

57. Burley-Slaughter and Mattli, "Legal Integration."

58. Weiler, "Transformation."

2

Europe's Ambiguous Federalism: A Conceptual and Analytical Critique

Thomas O. Hueglin

POLITICAL AMBIGUITY, ECONOMIC RATIONALITY

The inception and original development of the European Community (EC) followed a relatively simple logic of multiple trade-offs among a limited number of participants. The general sociopolitical environment for European integration was dictated by three external factors: a genuine desire for European peace after the devastating experience of World War II, a common perception of vulnerability in the wake of the Cold War, and a growing alarm over the economic hegemony of the United States. Internally, the EC provided a forum of political respectability for postfascist Germany and Italy, offered a significant voice of codetermination to the small Benelux countries, and gave France substantive control over the coal and steel production of its remilitarizing German archenemy. The trade-off between France and Germany in particular can be regarded as the centerpiece of European integration: West Germany regained political respectability and economic strength in exchange for its massive subsidization of French agriculture (in lieu of reparations, which were out of the question after the Weimar experience). At the heart of the arrangement was a common agricultural policy (CAP) in which Germany figured as the crucial net payer.

By the time this chapter was first written, the Community had doubled in size, from the original six to twelve members. By the time it will go into print, the now renamed European Union (EU) will consist of fifteen members, with many more additional membership candidates, mostly from eastern and southeastern Europe, already waiting at the gates. Consecutive rounds of enlargement have changed and will continue to change dramatically the Community's political and economic character. But post-Maastricht Europe is now increasingly questioned by large segments of the European populations. Maastricht was intended both to accommodate changes that had already taken place and to preformulate a viable path into the future. On both counts, a critical examination of the mismatch between the illusionary Maastricht rhetoric about a union that has its destiny under political control and a European reality far removed from such control may help to explain the ambiguity of the Community's character and construction.

What was originally conceptualized as a nascent European federal state soon turned into a loose confederation of partially integrated nation-states with rather vague notions of political union. And what appeared as a relatively homogeneous group of participants in the beginning has by now spread into an extended array of members with widely divergent political, cultural, and socioeconomic bases. The added Mediterranean dimension (Greece, Spain, and Portugal together with the south of Italy and France) in particular had already polarized the Community between a highly developed industrial north and a rural south. One might now speak of a "developing community" instead of an "economic" one. This polarization will doubtlessly become even more pronounced if and when further rounds of enlargment include countries like Turkey or Poland.

The idea of a supranational community with a single decisionmaking center had not even survived the "Europe of the Six." With the retention of de facto national veto power, the EC not only strayed significantly from its original institutional blueprint, but it much more importantly lost sight of a cohesive political architecture altogether. Instead, European integration progressed in a functionalist manner by integrating those sectoral policies that allowed consensus precisely because they were *not* seen as crucial national interests — the CAP being the notable and costly exception, at least in part due to the peculiar historical compromise between Germany and France. Community enlargement became a pragmatic substitute for the development of an adequate institutional framework or a cohesive set of integrated policies, a kind of forward-bound escapism changing the quantity of integration instead of its quality.

It is obvious, of course, why new candidates would line up for membership in what is emerging as the world's strongest and largest trading bloc, a fortress that is well shielded against outside competitors. The most recent junior members, Sweden, Finland, and Austria, while themselves fully developed industrial economies, simply may have had to opt for becoming part of a Union whose overwhelming economic effects they had already been exposed to for a long time. Future members like Turkey or Poland may harbor the additional hope that economic stabilization within the Union will lead to democratic stabilization as well.

However, it is the Union that decides on the path and speed of further enlargement, and its rationale is guided by market expansion now and political consolidation later. In the current neoliberal Union environment such a rationale will increasingly benefit those interests that have been dominant since the Community's inception: the industrialized centers of the north — with German industrial and finance capital at the apex of the agenda-setting power hierarchy. Europe's growing nervousness about a looming crisis in Germany's political economy only underscores its central role in shaping Community fortunes.

The current efforts of intensified market integration are consistent with the resurgence of neoliberal economic restructuring everywhere. The further development of a de facto (or even institutionalized) two-tiered community (*Europe des deux vitesses*) will strengthen those countries and regions that have most obviously succumbed to the pressures of a dominant bloc of multinational corporate interests seeking improved structures of capital valorization. The Union stands today not as a *United States of Europe* but as a *Europe a la Carte* in which money power instead of political cooperation dictates the menu. Like the free trade agreements between the United States, Canada, Mexico, and Chile, Europe's renewed thrust toward the final completion of the internal market must be seen as a poorly prepared and legitimized new round in a zero-sum game in which everybody hopes to gain, while the winners have already been determined backstage (in the boardrooms of those corporations and financial institutions whose multinational transactions already dominate the agendas of national economic policy formation on both continents). As in the American trade deal, multinational capital mobility will be increased at the expense of political control (because the transnationalization of the European capital markets will not be paralleled by an equal increase in supranational decisionmaking power) and at the expense of policy takers and workers (because labor mobility will inevitably lag behind that of capital).

The main argument of this chapter is therefore that the Maastricht Treaty's ambiguous commitment to a new federalism en route to political union is not much more than an institutionalist smoke screen behind which business as usual continues, to the benefit of some but to the detriment of others. I will begin with a critical discussion of federalism, identify some of the winners and losers under the current union arrangement, outline emerging new conflict lines, and conclude with some thoughts about federal renewal.

FEDERALISM WITHOUT A SOCIAL DIMENSION

The original blueprint for European integration at least foresaw the approximation of a political community with a bicameral set of federal institutions: the European Parliament as lower legislative assembly; the Council of Ministers as the upper chamber analogous to, not the American Senate, but to the West German Bundesrat; and the European Commission as a truly supranational executive and collective government with a presidency that rotated among member states. As is well known, the EC's institutions developed quite differently.[1] Executive decisionmaking remained the responsibility of the Council of Ministers, which in turn remained a diplomatic body of *inter*-national negotiation rather then *supra*national policy formation. Contrary to the word and spirit of the Treaty of Rome and especially since the Luxembourg Compromise of 1966, consecutive steps of adopting majority decisions were replaced by a de facto unanimity and the retention of veto power by each member state. The Commission, on the other hand, degenerated into a think tank providing and preparing policy expertise in accordance with national prerogatives and of course administering the myriads of bureaucratic community regulations that indeed accumulated into a major body of supranational law. Both bureaucratic administration and executive policy formation finally remained poorly legitimated in a formal democratic sense because the European Parliament—although meanwhile directly elected—did not assume any significant legislative or budgetary power, thus constituting little more than a talkative forum of suggestive gesturing and opinion formation.

Again, recent efforts at institutional reform have remained largely declaratory or limited in scope. The provisions of the Single European Act (SEA) of 1987 can hardly be seen as a decisive step toward a European federal state. It only endorsed a modest expansion of majority voting, further watered down by opting-out provisions for individual countries. The Maastricht Treaty, concluded in 1991 and finally ratified in 1993, likewise accompanied its declarations of extended Community policy responsibilities with a rather limited commitment to qualified majority voting. Far more significantly, the ambiguous insertion of the subsidiarity principle as a security blanket for the retention of national sovereignty, a price to be paid for even a merely declaratory commitment to European Political Union (EPU), seems to have closed the door to European federal statehood once and for all.

In classical federal states such as the United States or Germany, the allocation of powers between the two levels of government is constitutionally determined, and typically so by strictly enumerating the powers of the federal government, leaving all other or residual powers to the state or Länder governments. Thus, the Tenth Amendment to the U.S. Constitution reserves as states' (or the people's) rights all powers not explicitly delegated to the federal government, and the German Basic Law similarly stipulates that all powers not specifically enumerated as federal are automatically presupposed as Länder powers. This does not eliminate ambiguity and conflict. The constitutional history of the United States has been dominated by the eventual victory of the supremacy clause of Article VI over the Tenth Amendment, hollowing out much of the states' original retention of residual powers. And in Germany, the extensive enumeration of "concurrent" rather than "exclusive" federal powers has similarly proven to be a Trojan Horse of centralist power encroachment.

The subsidiarity principle as contained in the Maastricht Treaty is of an altogether different nature. As Article 3b stipulates, further Community action en route to political and monetary union shall be undertaken only if the same objective cannot be "sufficiently achieved" by the individual member states and can therefore be "better achieved" by the Community. In other words, Community action remains tied to political agreement and to the interpretation and calculus of national self-interest. What matters and decides the overall character of federal union is not whether a particular level of government possesses or does not possess certain powers, but instead whether national governments regard their own regulation of certain matters as sufficient or not. Any extension of Community action therefore remains tied to consent and agreement among the governments of the member states.

There is, of course, nothing wrong with the EU following a different pattern of institutional design. It is not a priori undemocratic that the decisionmaking process should remain based primarily on intergovernmental agreements among government representatives who are, after all, democratically elected to take care of their peoples' business. And indeed, as Fritz W. Scharpf pointed out some time ago,[2] there are essentially two models of federalism, one following the U.S. pattern of institutional power separation, the other more resembling the German pattern of (intergovernmental) power interlocking. From the very beginning, the Community has been institutionally based much more on the latter model. The decisive difference between the U.S. and the German model is the following: Federal powers in the United States are formally independent from state cooperation, and such cooperation is in constitutional terms based on voluntary concessions of the federal government. German federalism requires (majority) consent of the Länder governments in all important acts of legislation and the implementation of such legislation by the Länder administrations. The execution of federal powers is, in other words, de facto dependent on the Länder governments. The European Community constitutes a similar case of institutionalized political interlocking because "important policy tasks have been transferred to the next higher institutional level, whereas policy formation and implementation remained tied to the unanimous agreement of the member-governments." Scharpf concluded by pointing out that the European Community, like German federalism, suffers from a political trap that reduces its problem-solving capacities through a permanent consent requirement. But he insisted that problem solving on the basis of consensual national bargaining, while slow and cumbersome, would not lead to the eventual breakdown of the Community. It would keep going because national political as well as European bureaucratic interests were coalescing in their self-censoring defense of a professional game of influence and obstruction.

At first glance, this kind of institutionalist analysis could not appear more convincing. The EC from its very inception depended more on intergovernmental co-determination, typically on the basis of consent and unanimity, than on some form of central federal government with exclusive or concurrent powers. And intergovernmental bargaining as the "other" model of federalism appears natural and legitimate for a community of nation-states that have all thus far retained predominantly national identities. The old formula of a "Europe of Fatherlands," while defamed by ardent federalists as confederal cop-out from "real" integration, has always been closer to the European reality than the institutionalist dreams of those federalists.

However, at second glance some big questions arise. Can one simply assume that the same system of decisionmaking that has obviously served the needs of the old West German state and society so well will produce similarly satisfactory and legitimate policy outcomes in a future European Union? And, more important, who are the beneficiaries of an institutional design that tends to keep crucial public policy developing at a glacial pace while it promotes national economic interests and multinational market interests at the same time?

The rationale and philosophy of federalism are based on the principle of political equality among unequal partners regardless of size, economic strength, and political clout of the member states in a federation. U.S. pragmatism created the Senate, in which each state is represented by two senators regardless of its size or population. These senators represent regional populations, not state governments. The U.S. model works because the potential for regional conflict has been low (at least after a Civil War had settled the issue of slavery) and because voting behavior in the Senate is not governed by strict partisanship. Package deals across regions and parties create at least the illusion of majoritarian legitimacy: "You win some and you lose some."

The German model of political interlocking, on the other hand, has been based on careful intergovernmental bargaining and compromise all along. Because of a relatively high degree of regional homogeneity in the old West German republic and because of a highly centralized national party system, bargaining and compromise did not so much take place between regional interests as between the major parties of the right and left, and especially so when one side held a majority in the lower Bundestag (currently, for example, the conservative-liberal coalition of Chancellor Kohl) while the other side held a majority in the upper Bundesrat (currently dominated by a de facto social democratic–Green alliance of various Länder government coalitions).

What appeared to be politically interlocked in West German federalism were not just the interests of politicians and bureaucrats but essentially those of capital and labor as well. In other words, political interlocking included a social dimension that alone made it legitimate for a German electorate that understood this dimension very well, typically by voting differently in federal and *Land* elections. The system worked because it created at least the illusion of social partnership and co-determination and because the constitutionally prescribed "equality of living conditions" was relatively easy to achieve through fiscal equalization in a system dominated, at least before reunification, by a majority of rich Länder.

Political interlocking among national governments in the EU almost entirely lacks this social dimension. To be sure, there may be a number of social democratic or nominally socialist governments in the EU, but they have for the most part avoided demanding social control or co-determination *over* the Community agenda. Instead, they have typically emphasized social control *within* that agenda once the parameters of market integration are set and the "community train can no longer be stopped." Even the most powerful German unions seem to have acquiesced to that fact, resigning themselves to a strategy of market integration now and social control—perhaps—later.[3] As a consequence, the EU on January 1, 1993, became a single market with "capital, goods, services and people free to roam where they will."[4]

It is effectively a market for transnational corporate control over production capacities, market shares, new technologies, and labor forces. Because it is transnational it has been largely removed from national social control. In the much-watered-down social policy agreement added to the Maastricht Treaty, however, future possibilities for social regulation at the Community level have been severely limited. A European regulation of strike law, for instance, particularly important in an environment of transnational corporate control, has been excluded altogether and is therefore not even subject to considerations of subsidiarity any longer. Social interlocking, if at all, will likely have to take place within individual European corporations but not as part of the European process of political bargaining.[5]

In other words, the German model of political interlocking has found only restricted application in the European Community. The social dimension, upon which much of the stability and legitimacy of the German model rested, has for the most part been eclipsed. The legitimacy of the European model of interlocking federalism is therefore questionable, not a priori because it is an alternative model of political bargaining among elected representatives of national constituencies but because it is a model of restricted or limited interlocking. The politicians and bureaucrats in the European policy process may or may not pursue strategies of self-interest, but even when they do not, they are not acting on behalf of the entirety of the European peoples they claim to represent.

The subsidiarity principle may further increase the social restrictiveness of European political interlocking. The social policy agreement contained in the Maastricht Treaty, for example, states that unanimity in Council of Ministers decisions is required with regard to Community regulations of collective bargaining and co-determination. Invoking the subsidiarity principle, a member-state government may declare that it considers the matter "sufficiently achieved" at the national level (Britain already did just that by opting out of the agreement altogether). The issue or objective will be presented in purely functionalist (and hence socially neutral) terms. In reality, however, social interests opposed to national regulation will be excluded from the European decisionmaking arena.

This weighs all the heavier because it is precisely in this arena that the socioeconomic environment is being created within which industrial relations then have to take place. If it can be safely assumed that a double power transfer has taken place in the EU, namely of economic powers from the nation-state to the Union and more generally from the state to the market,[6] then this exclusion of social control from the European arena becomes outright un-democratic. Governments collectively divest themselves of economic powers yet retain national social control over those presumably most affected by a market over which control has been given up. Perhaps this has been the purpose of the completed European market all along, allowing capital to roam freely while containing labor in national straightjackets.

One might of course argue that subsidiarity plays both ways. It may allow Britain (or any other government so inclined) to avoid becoming sub-servient to the kind of social regulation at the European level it has tried to avoid (or has dismantled) on the domestic front. It may also allow a small and socially more progressive country like Denmark to preserve its level of social regulation without danger of becoming dragged down to the lowest common (European) denominator. As is well known, Denmark voted down Maastricht in a national referendum and only changed its national mind after the other Community leaders issued a rather "folksy" interpretation of subsidiarity as citizen "nearness" to European decisionmaking and after Denmark had been granted substantive opt-outs from the Treaty.[7]

General doubts must be raised, however, as to whether the subsidiarity principle will ever work according to the "rationale and philosophy of feder-alism," as a "principle of political equality among unequal partners regardless of size, economic strength, and political clout." As an opting-out strategy, subsidiarity will obviously exclude member states taking this route from fur-ther input into policy decisions that will have an impact upon their own pol-icy flexibility nevertheless. Because of these dangers of two-tiered Community development, subsidiarity will increase consensus pressures. Precisely because a potential majority vote could sideline their interests alto-gether, weaker member states in particular can hardly risk being left out of decisions by which their dominant partners want to forge ahead. They have to go along with whatever the dominant nations decide or face the danger of being left behind.

Subsidiarity therefore may well become a privilege of the big and pow-erful nation-states (and their governments). In its name, they can either press for Community regulations if that is the way their objectives can be better achieved, or they can block such regulation by claiming that they are capable of "sufficiently achieving" whatever policy objective is at stake. For all others, the choice may be a far more restricted one.

In other words, subsidiarity may turn out to be a vague decisionmaking principle allowing some nation-states to retain full sovereignty over their own policy priorities while leaving possible external costs to the Community.[8] Instead of mobilizing consent for a European political community on the basis of democratic cooperation and socioeconomic fairness, it may facilitate a self-centered retreat from universal Community goals. Within the old West German state, federalism included a vision of collectively organized social solidarity. Within the new European Union, that vision and logic of redistributive solidarity were to be extended to regional and national actors as well. As it stands, neither is possible in a European Union of free trade and corporate control. Instead, subsidiarity within a renewed *Europe des patries* may allow each level of government to use the other level as an excuse for its own selfishness. This may not only lead to increased socioeconomic polarization in the European Union, but it might also reopen the doors to fundamentalist nationalism.[9]

WINNERS AND LOSERS

If post-Maastricht Europe is not enfolding as a federal system among equal partners, there must be obvious winners and losers. At first glance, an obvious candidate for the role of winner can be identified easily: In 1992, as in all other years, Germany not only was the Community's greatest net payer per person, but it paid more into the Community budget than the other three net payers (Britain, France, and the Netherlands) combined.[10] Without German payments, there would be no Community. "Who pays also calls the shots," may be too fast a conclusion, but the evidence abounds that Germany has been the overwhelming beneficiary of the Community's economic development and success:

- A 1984 study of regional wealth and productivity differentials found that "twenty-two of the thirty regions with least intense income and unemployment problems were located in West Germany" and that except for urban core areas such as Copenhagen, Amsterdam, Rotterdam, Antwerp, Brussels, and Paris, all European regions with above-average rates of productivity and growth were to be found in West Germany.[11]
- By 1990, Germany, already the single largest Community investor by far, was said to be preparing to increase its investment in Europe by some 56 percent within the next two years.[12]

- Together with France and Britain, Germany also leads European industrial norm standardization, which is crucially important in a competitive export market. Eighty-five percent of all new norms in any year are produced by these three countries (and then have to be adopted by all others).
- German banks, with their legendary control over industrial policy,[13] were by 1988 well on their way to achieving the same status throughout the Community.[14]
- By 1993, two years after reunification, *all* of the new Germany still constituted the only Community country with a per capita gross domestic product (GDP) above 20,000 dollars.[15]

These are just some indicators, and not meant to constitute final evidence. But they underscore the kind of analysis that critics of German economic hegemony over the EC have provided over the years: "European capitalism is a hierarchical system with the Federal Republic of Germany at its apex." Supplied with a "monetary reserve generated by three decades of trade surpluses," Germany is not only able to determine integration policy "via control over financial resources" but moreover to "instrumentalize" the Community as a regional arena for West German (industrial) expansion: During the oil crisis years of the 1970s, for example, West Germany pursued a policy of strengthening the deutsche mark (DM) in order to ensure the continuation of cheap resource imports for its export industry. When this threatened German exports to other Community members with depreciating currencies, German policymakers pressed for a precarious monetary union with stable exchange rates. Because of their dependence on West German investment goods, the other members had to comply even though this meant a further weakening of their own export positions.[16]

Thus Germany succeeded in implementing a hegemonic regime of monetary stabilization at the behest of its own export industries and against most interests elsewhere in the Community.[17] The German-led push for a Economic and Monetary Union (EMU) and a European Central Bank more recently has demonstrated that Europe has become a DM-Club with West German monetary policy written into its statutes.[18]

Two main types of arguments have been raised against this assessment of Germany's hegemonic role in shaping Community development. One contends that German policymakers are not likely able to impose a coherent accumulation strategy upon the EC because of the fragmented and incrementalist nature of Germany's European policy style.[19] This argument does not reveal much analytical novelty: It describes nothing other than crisis management strategies in all advanced industrial systems—national or international—which may be adopted precisely in order to improve the overall conditions of capital valorization under conditions of sectoral and regional fragmentation.[20]

In light of Germany's overall economic success in the European arena, its capacity of interlocked policy cohesion ought not to be underestimated. What needs to be considered further is the crucial role of the German Federal Bank (significantly removed from whatever may be the fragmented hassles of German policy formation) as well as the coordinating role of the banking sector in industrial policy formation. Given the economically senseless Maastricht II convergence criteria imposed on the rest of Europe, it comes as no surprise that the European role of the German Federal Bank and its major clients is already likened to the authoritarian role the World Bank and International Monetary Fund play globally—even before the German bank's monetary rationale has been incorporated into the operational statutes of a European Central Bank.

That the end result will be more the "Germanization of Europe" than a "Europeanization of Germany" may be a somewhat overdrawn assessment. But that export economies (such as Germany) are driven by an open international market (such as the EU) to "impose their own internal structures on the surrounding world"[21] cannot be doubted seriously. None other than the former German President Richard von Weizsäcker wrote during the ratification crisis of the Maastricht Treaty that "it is no exaggeration to say that it is our currency concept that has become the European constitution, and our social market economy that has been made the basic law of European economic policy."[22]

The other argument has to do with German unification. Some hoped (mostly Britain and France) and others feared (mostly the southern recipients of Germany's EC transfer payments) that Germany's dominant role in the Community might become diminished because the German political economy would have to refocus inwardly on the new challenge of integrating East Germany, or because German investment attention would turn to the other post-Communist countries of eastern and central Europe with their market potential and cheap reservoir of labor. While both are doubtless factors the other member states have to take into account when dealing with Germany, they will hardly diminish the dominant German position within the EU. The fiscal dimensions alone reveal that Germany's superior economic reserves can cope with keeping the EU afloat financially. Consider, for example, how the meager EC budget managed to set aside DM4–6 billion for structural development in East Germany when West Germany itself anticipated pouring DM100 billion annually into restructuring its impoverished eastern annex.[23] Or consider how Germany remained deaf to French and British pleas on interest rates in 1992 and 1993, once again using monetary policy to its own advantage.[24] The fact that the German government has begun thinking loudly about whether it is paying too much into the EU budget may signal not so much a threat of withdrawal as one of intensified bullying. And Chancellor Helmut Kohl's recent efforts to stem the rising tide of German unemployment with a new round of corporatist crisis management likewise indicates that Germany will continue to defend its European position in a coherent rather than disjointed fashion.

One puzzling question remains: Why has a dominant or even hegemonic Germany become the most ardent promoter of a supranational European Union and of increased use of qualified majority voting in particular? After all, such majority voting would diminish Germany's bullying capacities at the intergovernmental bargaining table and especially so when ever more (eastern European and mostly impoverished) countries gain access to that table — a development that Germany champions as well.

There can be only a tentative answer to this complex question. In part, a Germany whose inner stability remains tied to sustained export success needs that larger European market at almost any cost. There is some evidence that Germany's share in the world's export markets has in fact declined over the years and that it has been able to compensate for that decline by strengthening its market position in the Community. The larger that Community and the more harmonized and open its economies under smooth regulation from Brussels, the better for the Community's most powerful exporter. Qualified majority decisions under the continued weight of German economic leadership might appear preferable to continued impasses in a system that requires unanimity.

In part, there may also be confidence that a more majoritarian Europe simply would have to adopt the German concept, just as Weizsäcker suggested. As in the North American free trade area, the strongest economy can be expected to impose its policy preferences, such as interest rates, for example, on the weaker members. It is hard to imagine that European member states that are dependent on German investment, transfers, and general commitment would systematically use the majority principle against the hand that feeds them.

However, German strategists may be fooling themselves to a certain degree here. Too greedy for the expansion into easily accessible markets, and assuming that monetary or political union will not happen before the end of the century in any case, Kohl and the new Federal Bank president Tietmeyer seem to have postponed thinking seriously about what will happen when a majority of poor new member states, mainly from southern and eastern Europe (Malta, Cyprus, Turkey, Poland, etc.), may be in a numerical position to gang up on them. Tietmeyer at least thought aloud about how Germany might cope with what would inevitably amount to "a certain disintegration": Enlargement is necessary, he explained, but not at the cost of always moving with the "slowest boat"; hence his revival, once again, of the idea of a "multispeed Europe," implying that the strong would forge ahead with policy coordination, while the weak merely buy and sell in a completed internal market.[25]

A brief look at those poorer countries and regions that have been Community members for some time already only confirms that they may have been experiencing the consequences of a de facto two- or multispeed Europe all along. Structural policies of regional development and cohesion came late. The Community had been founded on the faith that the common market's invisible hand would suffice. Only when subsequent rounds of enlargement increased socioeconomic disparity, mostly along the lines of a north-south divide with Ireland as part of the poorer Mediterranean fringe, did Community policy turn more seriously to the question of regional development. Increasing proportions of the Community budget were set aside, culminating in two major five-year packages in the aftermath of the SEA and the Maastricht Treaty in 1988 and 1993. It cannot be surprising, given the overall logic of this section, that the content of the second package, at the December 1992 summit in Edinburgh, should have been decided mainly as a showdown between the spokesperson of the south, Spain's Felipe González, and the paymaster of the north, Germany's Helmut Kohl.[26]

Clearly, these packages were designed to sustain peripheral support for the post-Maastricht path of political and economic integration most desired and spearheaded by Germany. González knew full well that with eastern and central Europe at the gates, the 1992 summit was probably the last chance of a major structural budget improvement for the south.[27] Kohl, on the other hand, "conceded most," knowing that Germany had to pay a price for a sustained commitment to EMU and EPU, especially so after having irked most partner governments by its unilateral reunification strategy. But even though the second package once again "more than doubled Community assistance for the least prosperous countries,"[28] and the structural funds now make up 30 percent of the Community budget, that budget still amounts to a paltry 1.5 percent of the member states' combined GDPs.

It is difficult to assess how exactly the existence of the EC has contributed to the socioeconomic development of the peripheral member states. According to one careful analysis,[29] they have all suffered similarly from considerable trade deficits, which were in part offset by fiscal transfers. Nevertheless, a certain overall trend toward the convergence of major economic indicators in all EU states cannot be denied. The productivity gap, for example, seems to have narrowed since the mid-1980s. However, even the most optimistic scenario would indicate that the overall prosperity gap will not be closed for at least another thirty years.

The problem with this and other similar analyses is that they compare countries, not regions. According to a 1990 Commission report, structural policy has not succeeded in reducing regional disparities: The GDP of the richest EC region (in the Netherlands) was four-and-a-half times that of the poorest (in Greece). The income level of the top ten regions was more than three times higher than that of the bottom ten. While national unemployment levels had converged somewhat, regional unemployment differences had increased. The report pointed out that in order to increase a per capita GDP from 50 to 70 percent of the Community average, a region would have to sustain growth 1.25 percent higher than the Community average for twenty years.[30] In other words, unless radical Community policies would begin to restrain the kind of "merciless competition" that the "neoliberal paradise" of the single market has created, the main result of post-Maastricht Europe will be the "pauperization of the south."[31]

What the Commission report reveals quite clearly is that the invisible hand of the market does not work and that Community efforts of reducing (never mind eliminating) regional disparities have remained (and will remain) insufficient. Several explanations can be given immediately: First of all, structural policy may be initiated by the Community and especially by the Commission with its more pan-European orientation, but the actual policy-making and implementation fall to the powers of national, regional, and local government. Without a strong EU commitment to predetermined policy goals and instruments, these governmental and intergovernmental actors remain largely exposed to the pressures of market and private investment. Structural policy, therefore, is weak because it can typically come into play only after the invisible hand of the market has already set the parameters. It has little or no agenda-setting power over those parameters themselves.[32]

Second, insofar as national governments bargain for Community policy packages favorable to their economies, they are driven by the interests of their strongest, rather than weakest, regions. The blocking of an overdue and long-promised agricultural reform in Andalucía by the Madrid government en route to EC membership, in order to alleviate fears of further EC agricultural overproduction, may be a case in point.[33] Cataluña's push for a Committee of the Regions at the EC level may have been likewise motivated more by the potential for collaboration with other rich regions than the promotion of regional equality. Such collaboration already exists under the Four Motors of Europe agreement aiming at the harmonization of a variety of policy fields crucial for economic growth among Cataluña, Lombardy, Baden-Württemberg, and Rhône-Alps.[34] Having been regarded as a leader in the post-1975 democratization process of Spain, Cataluña is today more likely perceived by other regions as a selfish promoter of its own interests only.[35] More explicitly, the socialist president of the poor region of Extremadura accused Cataluña of being rich because it has robbed other regions with full hands.[36]

Third, structural policies that follow the pressures of Eurocapital inevitably favor large over small projects, even in those sectors that sustain the poorest regions in particular. In the case of Greece, for example, the influx of European corporate business led to massive job losses in the agricultural and handicraft sectors soon after its entry into the Community.[37] As a consequence, high structural unemployment and the eventual exodus of the best segments of their work force further weaken poor regions. Intranational regional behavior may exacerbate this pattern. The sentiments championed in Umberto Bossi's *Lega*, for example, reflect northern Italian desires to push out the large migrant work forces from the south. No longer needed in the wake of an intensive process of economic restructuring toward "flexible production," these workers, already referred to by bigoted northerners as "Africans," further increase unemployment when they return to their southern regions of origin.

In short, the European Community presents itself not only as a capitalist hierarchy with (West) Germany as its apex but also as a dependency system of concentric circles with stronger and weaker countries as well as stronger and weaker regions within countries. It must, moreover, be seen as a stabilized regional economy within the context of the globalizing political economy. The Community was designed to meet the problems of "mature" capitalist political economies on "national, regional, and international levels." The European core economies, under German leadership, needed a transnationally integrated regional market in order to consolidate themselves nationally, at the expense of their internal peripheries, for global competition. Peter Cocks explains, "The creation of the EC, therefore, provided the means for reconciling the exigencies of the economies of scale with adherence to the ideology of competition."[38]

This critical account of a hierarchical rather than equal European system of organized market capitalism is not meant to denounce Germany as the villain or to denounce structural policy as a conspiracy of exploitation and dependence. Without Germany and without a firm German commitment the undisputed success of the Community in contributing to a peaceful and prosperous Europe hardly would have been possible, and without structural policy efforts at least some regions may not have developed further at all. The point here is merely to give some evidence for the theoretical claim in the previous section that although the European house has been built, quite legitimately, on a different fundament and model of federalism, it has not been built in such a way as to grant to or even facilitate for all members equal partnership and equal opportunity.

Federalism, it turns out, either one model or the other, is neither the panacea that Euro-enthusiasts hope it is nor the villainous "f-word" standing for Eurocratic inefficiency and the erosion of national sovereignty, as Euroskeptics see it. Federalism is first of all a broad social philosophy of mutual sharing and cooperation among spatial[39] as well as social[40] collectivities; it is nothing but a noble idea in search of a practical form of realization. Second, however, federalism as such a practical form is a rather narrow institutional device with a few variations that does not embody any commitment or value per se. In this latter sense, it is a tool of political organization that can be used or abused for whatever purpose the dominant powers may decide.

In the context of the European Community, it seems clear that the record is mixed. On the one hand, interlocking federalism has created an intergovernmental policymaking network that not only is capable of initiative but also possesses at least a limited capacity of European problem solving. On the other hand, the same system of interlocking federalism has also provided the dominant political-economic elites with a convenient smoke screen of "systemic constraints" and political buck-passing. While capital roams freely, responsibility for the social costs can be dodged by pointing the finger from one level of government to the other and back. The subsidiarity principle may only sanction what has been practice all along. At least one high-ranking Brussels official conceded in a confidential interview that social deregulation was at least part of the SEA and Maastricht calculus.

Will it be Americanization in the end? The European move from national regulation to Community deregulation roughly corresponds to the United States' condition of government "balkanization"[41] as a shield against social responsibility. One can also see the North American Free Trade Agreement (NAFTA) in much the same vein. Dominant segments of the Canadian business elite supported it not only because a higher degree of multinational capital mobility would free them from Canadian welfare constraints on capital valorization but also because a more direct exposure to the deregulated U.S. market would eventually put the thumbscrews on the Canadian welfare state itself.

Within the European Community, welfare commitment and social responsibility are (still) carried and defended by powerful social democratic parties, unions, and, increasingly, social and regional movements. Consequently, the continued exclusion from or at least marginalization of their concerns in European political interlocking constitutes a considerable legitimation deficit. Post-Maastricht Europe will undoubtedly be haunted by new rounds of consensus versus conflict, acceptance versus oppositon.

NEW CONFLICT LINES

In conceptual terms, the European Community still can be perceived as a somewhat federal response to the increasingly complex reality of Europe. As an advanced industrial system producing interdependence *and* fragmentation within and across borders, the Community offers a multilayered system of conflict regulation and accommodation, from the local and regional to the national, transnational-regional, and finally the global sphere. As long as nation-states continue to be perceived as the main legitimate nodal points of politics, it is certainly appropriate that the process of policy formation and decisionmaking remains centered on intergovernmental negotiations and agreements. With its peculiar mix of nationally based supranational policy formation and administration, the EC constitutes a novel type of political system, neither a federal state nor a mere confederation of sovereign states. It also offers a far more complex—and hence more legitimate—response to transnational trade and production than the North American free trade zone, for example.

From the perspective of federalism as a balanced system of power distribution among two (or more) levels of government, however, the EC falls short of standing the test as a federal system in design and dynamics. Its economic dynamic in particular runs counter to the goal of establishing and maintaining equitable opportunity structures. Transnational economic elites, national politicians, and European bureaucrats have unleashed an irreversible market dynamic without clearly informing the European populations about its social consequences.

Thus the SEA has stripped down the program of European integration to one core idea, the "removal of national barriers to capital movement." Attempts to replace indigenous mechanisms of national market regulation with a "similar EC structure organized from Brussels" have been stalled or at least slowed down. As a consequence, a "bacchanal" of "cost-cutting, mergers and rationalization" will likely take place that cannot be controlled any more by national governments, organized labor, or the European public at large.[42] Maastricht has not really accomplished anything that would clearly refute this stark assessment. Most of all, it has elevated the obfuscation over goals and strategies, subsidiarity, opting-out, unanimity, and qualified majority voting to the status of a treaty language that is for all practical purposes "illegible."[43]

As argued before, the widely deplored democratic deficit of the EU is not so much a matter of (inferior) parliamentary versus (superior) intergovernmental power as it is a matter of how and for what purposes that intergovernmental power has been and can be used. As the evidence at least strongly suggests, while the European intergovernmental arena has been used to *deregulate* markets, it has also been used to *re-regulate* social control. A good example is the European steel crisis of the 1970s: Community regulations (price and quota controls) provided the external framework for the national restructuring of capital at the cost of politically administered job losses. A convenient side effect (if not part and parcel of the entire strategy itself) was the weakening of labor, which remained nationally organized but increasingly confronted the elusiveness of transnationally operating capital.[44] In other words, limited political interlocking at the European level has created an additional arena for "domestic problem-solving."[45]

Post-Maastricht Europe is at the crossroads of social *and* economic credibility. Its disjointed policies toward the former Yugoslavia signal the demise of EPU. Its main two criteria for EMU may be met by only two countries: Germany and Luxembourg.[46] Its per capita GDP is far below that of the United States or Japan. It spends less on education than the United States (and about the same as Japan). Its unemployment rate is an embarrassment among industrialized nations as well.[47]

Under such circumstances, neither satisfying criteria of political legitimacy and social or regional fairness nor living up to the expectations raised by the promises of a larger market, it cannot be surprising that the era of post-Maastricht Europe has not exactly been greeted with enthusiasm. Wherever referendums were held over Maastricht, nearly half of the populations voting were against it. A poll taken shortly after the Maastricht ratification crisis was over revealed that across the Union, only 32 percent of respondents were in favor of a federal Europe, with 49 percent against it. Worse, the negative verdict was particularly high in the net payer countries.[48] And shortly after, the European election of June 1994 produced the lowest voter turnout ever.[49]

To some, such abysmal numbers clearly indicate that the "permissive consensus" that has accompanied European integration thus far is crumbling. Instead of a "Europe of citizens," it is "citizens against Europe" that have come to the fore.[50] Nevertheless, most of these citizens will get stuck with an already existing Europe of freely roaming capital, standardized mass production assembled in the low-wage niches of peripheral regions, and the elusive dream of a standard of living and lifestyle modeled before their eyes by a new European business class jetting back and forth between Paris, Stuttgart, Milan, Barcelona, and a few other places. These urban centers of growth, productivity, and prosperity begin to have more in common with one another than with the countries they happen to be located in: indeed, Americanization in the end.

Some national governments will listen carefully to their citizens' apathy and indignation, refraining from consenting to any decisive step toward a political union unless it is one that can be held responsible and accountable for the discrepancy between market myth and social reality. It is not surprising that British Prime Minister John Major, desperately trying to sell to his party's Euroskeptics the kind of European market British capital wants and needs without giving away the kind of domestic control over social issues that British capital also wants, once again conjured up, during the days before the European election, the image of a European "variable geometry." That is an old image, of a two-tiered or multitiered Europe, of Europe "des deux vitesses" or à la carte, "concentric circles" of integration around an inner core or "directorate," or, in the end, of subsidiarity.[51] It is the image of a Europe in which the powerful pick and choose while the powerless take it or leave it. Given that the completed internal market is no longer open for reconsideration, most will have to take. Oil-rich Norway may be able to live on for perhaps another twenty-two years with the illusion that it can sustain national independence. Without offshore oil wells, Poland or Turkey cannot. Once inside the EU, citizens will have to choose between apathy and opposition.

Given the outspoken neoliberal agenda of the Community today, the most natural form of opposition ought to come from unions. However, the most powerful labor organization in Europe, the West German Federation of Unions, as well as the European Federation of Unions, seems to have already made peace with the inevitable.[52] Stating that the internal market "will come," union leaders emphasized early on the necessity of building a European system of social security and democratization alongside the inevitable marketization, which may not be much more than wishful thinking. It is based on the same idea of social democratic compromise that within nation-states helped stabilize capitalist growth economies through formalized or informal corporatist arrangements, that is, by supporting accumulation strategies in return for growth-indexed wage developments and a generally improving social safety net.

The previous breakdown of most of these national arrangements after the global economic crisis of the mid-1970s is well documented.[53] If the SEA is the response of European capital to that crisis, and if there is no legitimate European framework for the pursuit or even articulation of workers' interests, a strategy of transnational social solidarity tied to the neoliberal agenda of European "anarcho-capitalism"[54] is a very long shot at best. In fact, as Kohl's renewed corporatist crisis management strategy indicates, unions in a core country like Germany may well be inclined to abandon all European solidarity. As in the past, they may become accomplices of national strategies against unemployment at the expense of colleagues elsewhere.

Outside the core, the situation may develop differently. In Spain, the socialist government appears committed to a "draconian" convergence plan securing immediate EMU access rather than "second division status within the EU" and including such economic deregulation as the elimination of past corporatist structures and practices. In a country with the second highest rate of working days lost through strikes (1986–1990), the costs of convergence may well lead to a further increase in social unrest.[55] In a quasi-federal system of European governance and regulation lacking an organized social dimension, one must fear that new conflict lines will develop or intensify between organized work forces at the core and increasingly disparate as well as desperate work forces outside that core.

The process of concentrated restructuring and reallocation and the relocation of production that penalizes local workers may in the end more openly lead to the kind of rejection of "Europe Inc." that the polls currently indicate only in a rather muted way. For the reasons given previously, this kind of opposition will not be primarily carried by an organized European labor movement, neither will it likely be carried by a European electorate uncertain of its aspirations and life chances. But it may be carried by a new sense of community that appears on the rise in many quarters of Europe, uniting regions and social movements within them.

Ironically, it may see its beginnings in Germany, the country that stands to benefit most from Europe Inc. There a federal system with a significant social dimension is still in place. The new "Europe Article" (Article 23) of the Basic Law, while reaffirming Germany's commitment to European unity, requires that all power transfers to the Union are contingent on a two-thirds majority in the upper house (Bundesrat) as well as the lower Bundestag. It proscribes violations of the "social state clause" (Article 79/3) by any European power transfer. Because majority power in the Bundesrat is currently dominated by various coalition configurations among social democrats, liberals, and Greens in the Länder governments, important control mechanisms against a further erosion of Europe's social dimension are built into the system.

Party and majority configurations can change, of course, and other member states are lacking a formally federal dimension. Still it is highly unlikely that Kohl's neoliberal agenda will find majority support before Maastricht II, and it seems clear that the German Länder are spearheading what may amount to a more general socio-regional rebellion against the further streamlining of Europe Inc. Michael Keating points out how regionalism and social democracy in Scotland have more recently coalesced in order to stem the neoliberal tide in Britain (see Chapter 8). Similar arguments apply to Ireland and the Nordic countries (see Chapters 9 and 10). In the long run, at least, federalism without a strengthened social dimension may not be a European option after all, as Cafruny argues (Chapter 5). However, as Lankowski suggests (see Chapter 7), Europe's constitutional future will depend mainly on the persistence of social forces of opposition in Germany.

CONCLUSION: CHANCES OF FEDERAL RENEWAL

In this chapter I argued that the European Union can be analyzed and understood as a nascent federal order without a fully developed social dimension, producing winners and losers in violation of the federal principle of structural social balance. As a consequence, new lines of conflict and opposition emerge, cutting across nation-states, regions, parties, and unions. What I do not claim is that federalism per se, as a system of multilevel governance among a plurality of actors (see Chapter 1), will automatically produce structural balance and social equality. Like all other institutionalized systems of governance, it can be used or abused.

To some, European federalization in the name of subsidiarity may indeed carry the promise of an open "community of communities" balancing joint solidarity with protection against corporate encroachment and German monetary domination. But, as Pia Christina Wood shows (see Chapter 6), nationalist encapsulation may often be the other side of the same coin, for the French right as much as for British Euroskeptics or Bossi's northern Italian League. Instead of promoting federal openness and diversity in a European Community of choice, these nationalist or regionalist forces seek to manipulate their respective constituencies into strategically malleable "communities of fate."[56]

On a global scale, this Janus-faced quality of integration has been described as "Jihad vs. McWorld": As "common markets demand a common language, as well as a common currency, and . . . produce common behaviors of the kind bred by cosmopolitan city life everywhere," they are, at the same time, faced with "permanent rebellion against uniformity and integration" from nation-states, subnational factions, cultures, and religions. Only a federal option of democratic balance, it is suggested, can save us from a "brave new McWorld" permanently rocked by tribalist outbreaks.[57]

Worldwide, such an option is nowhere in sight. The European Union, however, has gone a long way toward securing a flexible system of political accommodation that may yet prevent an outbreak of Jihad vs. Europe Inc. But it seems clear that without a European social dimension securing equal opportunity and equitable living conditions for all Europeans, the federal option remains incomplete and precarious.

NOTES

The first version of this essay was originally presented at the Conference on Comparative Constitutional Federalism in Salvador, Bahia, Brazil, in August 1988. Extended and revised versions were discussed at the ECSA Conference in Fairfax, Va., in May 1989, and an ECSA-sponsored workshop in Saratoga Springs, N.Y., October 1989. By 1995, large segments obviously had to be rewritten entirely. Thanks go to various commentators and reviewers who helped in preparing this extended and revised version. This research was undertaken with support from the Social Science and Humanities Council of Canada.

1. Alois Riklin, *Die Europaeische Gemeinschaft im System der Staatenverbindungen* (Bern: Staempfli, 1972).

2. Fritz W. Scharpf, "Die Politikverflechtungs-Falle: Europaeische Integration und deutscher Foederalismus im Vergleich," *Politische Vierteljahresschrift* 26, no.4 (1985), pp. 324–350.

3. Franz Steinkuehler, ed., *Europa '92* (Hamburg: VSA, 1989).

4. *Economist*, "Not the Union They Meant," November 6, 1993, p. 56.

5. Paul Windolf, "Mitbestimmung und 'corporate control' in der europaeischen Gemeinschaft," *Politische Vierteljahresschrift*, Sonderheft 23 (1992), pp. 120–142.

6. Loukas Tsoukalis, "The European Union and Global Economic Interdependence" (paper presented at the sixteenth World Congress of the International Political Science Association, Berlin, August, 1994).

7. Desmond Dinan, *Ever Closer Union?* (London: Macmillan, 1994), pp. 183–193.

8. Thomas O. Hueglin, "Federalism, Subsidiarity, and the European Tradition," *Telos* 100 (Summer 1994), pp. 37–55.

9. David Marquand, "Reinventing Federalism: Europe and the Left," *New Left Review* 203 (1994), p. 19.

10. *Economist*, "A Survey of the European Union," October 22, 1994, Survey, p. 21.

11. Hugh Clout, *Regional Variations in the European Community* (Cambridge: Cambridge University Press, 1986), pp. 31–32.

12. *Sueddeutsche Zeitung*, August 18, 1990, p. 31.

13. Peter A. Hall, "Patterns of Economic Policy: An Organizational Approach," in Stephen Bornstein, David Held, and Joel Krieger, eds., *The State in Capitalist Europe* (London: Allen and Unwin, 1984), p. 25.

14. *Economist*, "Survey: Europe's Internal Market," July 9, 1988, Survey, pp. 5–44.

15. *Economist*, "Voting Together, Pulling Apart?" June 4, 1994, p. 49.

16. Carl Lankowski, "'Modell Deutschland' and the International Regionalization of the West German State in the 1970s," in Andrei S. Markovits, ed., *The Political Economy of West Germany* (New York: Praeger, 1982), pp. 94–114.

17. Alain Lipietz, *Towards a New Economic Order* (Oxford: Oxford University Press, 1992), pp. 48–49.

18. Elmar Altvater and Kurt Huebner, "Das Geld einer mittleren Hegemonialmacht—Ein kleiner Streifzug durch die oekonomische Geschichte der BRD," *Prokla* 18,4 (1988), pp. 26–36.

19. Simon Bulmer and William Paterson, *The Federal Republic of Germany and the European Community* (London: Allen and Unwin, 1987).

20. Thomas O. Hueglin, "The Politics of Fragmentation in an Age of Scarcity: A Synthetic View and Critical Analysis of Welfare State Crisis," *Canadian Journal of Political Science* 20, no. 2 (1987), pp. 235–264.

21. William D. Graf, "Introduction," in W. D. Graf, ed., *The Internationalization of the German Political Economy* (New York: St. Martin's Press, 1992), p. 6.

22. Michael Kreile, "Einleitung," *Politische Vierteljahresschrift*, Sonderheft 23 (1992), pp. 7–8.

23. *Sueddeutsche Zeitung*, June 10, 1990, p. 17.

24. *Economist*, "Germany's Europe," June 11, 1994, p. 45.

25. Ibid.

26. Dinan, *Ever Closer Union?* pp. 403–411.

27. Ibid., p. 411.

28. Ibid.

29. Heinz-Juergen Axt, "Modernisierung durch EG-Mitgliedschaft? Portugal, Spanien und Griechenland im Vergleich," *Politische Vierteljahresschrift*, Sonderheft 23 (1992), pp. 209–233.

30. Dinan, *Ever Closer Union?* pp. 411–412.

31. Scharpf, "Die Politikverfletungs-Falle," pp. 13–16, 41.

32. Toemmel, "System-Entwicklung und Politikgestaltung in der europaeischen Gemeinschaft am Beispiel der Regionalpolitik," *Politische Vierteljahresschrift*, Sonderheft 23 (1992), pp. 185–208.

33. Ulrike Liebert, *Neue Autonomiebewegungen und Dezentralisierung in Spanien* (Frankfurt: Campus, 1986), pp. 295–297.

34. *Toronto Star*, "Four Motors Are Remaking Map of Europe," June 4, 1994.

35. Jordi Solé Tura, "Una lectura autonomista y federal del modelo de Estado constitucional," in Luis Armet, ed., *Federalismo y Estado de las Autonomias*

(Barcelona: Planeta, 1988), pp. 131–137.

36. See Spanish press.

37. Heinz-Juergen Axt, "Griechenland in der Europaeischen Gemeinschaft," *Oesterreichische Zeitschrift fuer Politikwissenschaft* 87, no. 2 (1987), pp. 169–187.

38. Peter Cocks, "Towards a Marxist Theory of European Integration," *International Organization* 34, no. 1 (1980), pp. 26–27.

39. Daniel J. Elazar, *Exploring Federalism* (Tuscaloosa: University of Alabama Press, 1987).

40. Thomas O. Hueglin, *Sozietaler Foederalismus* (Berlin: Walter de Gruyter, 1991).

41. Theodore Lowi, "Why Is There No Socialism in the United States?" *International Political Science Review* 5, no. 4. (1984), pp. 375–378.

42. Patrick Camiller, "Beyond 1992: The Left and Europe," *New Left Review* 175 (1989), pp. 7–9.

43. Kreile, "Einleitung," p. 7.

44. Josef Esser, Wolfgang Fach, and Werner Vaeth, *Krisenregulierung* (Frankfurt: Suhrkamp, 1983), pp. 100–101.

45. Miles Kahler, "The Survival of the State in European International Relations," in Charles S. Maier, ed., *Changing Boundaries of the Political* (Cambridge: Cambridge University Press, 1987), p. 301.

46. *Economist*, "Helmut Kohl, Housebuilder," July 9, 1994, p. 50.

47. *Economist*, "A Survey of the European Union," October 22, 1994, European Survey, p. 4.

48. *Economist*, "Europe Is in the Gutter," May 21, 1994, p. 14.

49. *Economist*, "Apathy Within, Enthusiasm Without," June 18, 1994, p. 55.

50. Kreile, "Einleitung," p. 7.

51. Helen Wallace, *Europe: The Challenge of Diversity* (London: Routledge and Kegan, 1985).

52. Steinkuehler, *Europa '92*.

53. Leo Panitch, "The Tripartite Experience," in Keith Banting, ed., *The State and Economic Interests* (Toronto: University of Toronto Press,1986), pp. 69–70.

54. Camiller, "Beyond 1992," p. 7.

55. Paul Heywood, *The Government and Politics of Spain* (New York: St. Martin's Press, 1995), pp. 230–240.

56. Hueglin, "Federalism," pp. 54–55.

57. Benjamin R. Barber, "Jihad Vs. McWorld," *Atlantic* 269, no. 3. (1992), pp. 53–65.

3

The Internal Legitimacy Crisis of the European Union

Michael Shackleton

Since its inception the European Community (EC), or European Union (EU), as it is now known, has been strongly marked by arguments over institutional design. It has been recognized that the shape of institutions affects policy outcomes. Using unanimity or majorities in voting in the Council of Ministers, giving the European Commission the final say in management committees, or allowing the European Parliament to adopt amendments that the Council can only overrule by unanimity are all institutional issues that derive their importance from the impact they have on the policy that emerges as a result.

However, this institutional debate was essentially limited to the balance of power and influence among the European institutions themselves. More recently, we have witnessed the emergence of a broader institutional argument that is not primarily concerned with the mechanics of particular bodies but rather has raised the issue of whether the existing institutional framework as a whole can provide an adequate system of governance for the European Union. The underlying principles of the entire structure have come under scrutiny in a way that was never the case before.

Uncertainty as to the adequacy of the present system generated a crisis of legitimacy, marked notably by the emergence of the ideas of popular participation and popular consent as necessary ingredients for the success of the European Union. How can the public take part in European decisions? And how can support of the public be won for the furtherance of integration? These questions were rarely asked until recently because elites generally assumed that they could rely on a passive public consensus. This is no longer true. The consensus broke down conspicuously during the ratification of the Treaty on European Union (Maastricht Treaty). In particular, the rejection of the Treaty in the first Danish referendum in June 1992 provoked a widespread feeling that the European enterprise did not enjoy popular consent and that therefore it was necessary to find ways to extend popular participation, if the European Union were to advance.

The search for a broader base of support for European integration generated the desire to make the 1996 intergovernmental conference (IGC) different from its Maastricht predecessor. All participants argue that a central aim of this next revision of the Treaty must be to create a system of government at the level of the Union that enjoys democratic legitimacy, but they do not agree on what that new system should look like. In particular, they disagree over how or indeed whether it is possible to reproduce at the European level a system of representative democracy that permits the views of citizens to be reflected in representative institutions comparable to those to be found in the nation-state.

I begin this chapter by considering why we are faced with this new crisis of legitimacy, arguing that the ambitious aims laid down in the Maastricht Treaty served to change the character of the Union in an irrevocable manner. I will then examine the issue of legitimacy from three perspectives, each offering different visions of how a representative system of government can be developed at the European level. First, I will look at the extension of the role of the European Parliament as a way of giving the electorate a say in European decisions; I will then ask whether the further involvement of national parliaments in the activities of the Union can provide a more representative base for decisions; and finally, I will go beyond a narrow institutional focus to see how a European political space can be created that revolves around competing conceptions of the European public interest. These approaches are not necessarily incompatible, but they do imply different kinds of reform of the existing structure as ways to deal with the issue of legitimacy. Hence they provide a means for judging the direction of change during the 1996 IGC. In the final section I will consider briefly how likely it is that this IGC will be able to find an adequate answer to the problem of representation.

THE ORIGINS OF THE CRISIS

Why is there a crisis of governance or legitimacy within the Union? It is a product of the realization that we do not yet have the means to move from a system essentially concerned with the *administration of things* to one concerned with the *governance of people*. Administration can have consequences, often important ones, for individuals: No fisherman or farmer in the Union could be persuaded otherwise. Nevertheless, it is a process that is essentially justified by reference to criteria of effectiveness, efficiency, or fairness. Governance, on the other hand, needs to meet more stringent conditions in order to be considered acceptable. It needs broader support within society, a support that can only be acquired through some form of democratic legitimation.

The reason the Union finds itself in this no-man's-land between the mechanisms of administration and those of governance comes from the enormous gap between the single market program and the goals announced in the

Maastricht Treaty. The single market was established as an economic goal that would promote growth through the lifting of trade barriers. It was generally agreed that it could be achieved by the traditional Community mechanisms: the slicing up of policy by sector, the resolution of differences through trade-offs negotiated by officials and ministers, and a passive consensus in the broader public. The Maastricht Treaty goes much farther: It sets out policy goals that touch the very heart of the sovereign concerns of individual states in terms of both economic and foreign policy. It has become clear that these goals cannot be achieved using the traditional tools of the Community as they have been developed over the last forty years.

The more administrative approach that predominated before Maastricht undoubtedly had its advantages: It refrained from addressing the question of political authority head-on. To do so was to risk the kind of defeat that was suffered in 1954 when the European Defense Community (EDC) project came to grief in the French Assembly. Instead there was a conscious attempt to establish the Community by stealth, without addressing the underlying issues of governance that have always been implicit within the texts of the treaties.[1] This strategy, so beloved of academic writers of the neofunctionalist persuasion, can no longer work if the transfer of responsibilities foreseen under the Treaty on European Union takes place; it does not offer the means necessary for the Union to move beyond the administration of things.

Helen Wallace has argued that the Single European Act (SEA) was more federalist in approach than the Maastricht Treaty, claiming that the latter reinforced intergovernmental modes of operation through the establishment of the pillar structure.[2] However, such a judgment underestimates the significant institutional developments in Maastricht, not least the mechanisms designed to achieve Economic and Monetary Union (EMU), including a European Central Bank, and the new powers accorded to the European Parliament, in particular, the power of co-decision. It also does not give sufficient weight to the cumulative impact of the policy goals laid down in the Treaty on European Union on the imagination of the wider public. It did not and does not matter that the Treaty is written in an opaque, bureaucratic way. Publics have realized that it does more than broaden the single market framework, which elites tried to persuade them was all that had been agreed. To argue, for example, that a single currency is a necessary corollary of a single market is to forget the fundamental change involved in moving toward EMU. Recognition of this potential change partly explains the extreme difficulty experienced in France and Denmark in obtaining popular support for the Treaty.

The level of opposition was doubtless also affected by the recession at the beginning of the 1990s, which contrasted sharply with the economic situation in the middle 1980s when the single market was agreed upon. However, the importance of economic downturn needs to be seen in terms of its link to the goals laid down in the Maastricht Treaty. EMU implies that the Union should take major responsibility for the management of the European economy. The question remains whether it should be entrusted with this responsibility, particularly when some of the more extravagant claims made for the impact of the single market on levels of employment were not substantiated.

The issue of governance is therefore central to the future of the Union. It cannot simply be ignored because of the obstacles that lie in the way of achieving ambitious objectives such as economic and monetary union or a common foreign and security policy. The Treaty has not just created broader areas of responsibility, but it has also put on the agenda new concepts and ideas, the most obvious of these being European citizenship. Despite its narrow application in the Treaty, the very idea obliges everyone to consider how far it should extend. The fear expressed in the Danish referendum that Danes might have to serve in a European army under German officers might seem far-fetched, but it corresponded with a perfectly imaginable conception of the future development of the Union. After all, is it not one mark of citizenship that those who hold it are prepared to defend the political entity of which they are citizens?

Two further factors impounded the difficulty of convincing skeptical publics of the value of the Treaty. First, the debate took place after the collapse of communism in Central and Eastern Europe. The democratic legitimacy of the Community had at least in part been assured by the contrast in political forms between the two parts of Europe. Once that contrast disappeared, there was much more room for questioning the democratic credentials of the Community. This was particularly so in view of the second element, namely the declining confidence among publics as to the democratic character of their own national societies. The Commission-sponsored gauge of public opinion, *Eurobarometer*, noted in 1993 that the level of dissatisfaction with the way democracy works at national level was greater than the level of dissatisfaction with its workings at Community level. Indeed, for the first time since the question had first been asked in 1973, the proportion of citizens dissatisfied with the operation of democracy nationally exceeded those who were satisfied. Together these two factors helped to create an environment in which defenders of the Maastricht model were put very much on the defensive.

THE QUESTION OF DEMOCRATIC LEGITIMATION

If Maastricht changed the character of the argument about the nature of the Union from one about the "administration of things" to a debate about "the governance of people," then the relationship between the governors and the governed becomes of central importance. In particular, we need to ask what it is that can legitimize that relationship in democratic terms. Why should the governed accept the decisions of the governors?

The challenge in finding an answer to this question is considerable. As Jürgen Habermas points out: "democratic processes have hitherto only functioned within national borders. So far, the political public sphere is fragmented into national units."[3] This fragmentation appeared in the debates on the ratification of the Maastricht Treaty; they took place at different times and followed national rather than European rhythms. And the 1994 European elections, although they more or less coincided, offered an equivalent spectacle. Are we therefore condemned to look in vain for a democratic European Union? To seek to answer this question, we need to turn to the three perspectives on representation outlined earlier.

Legitimation Through the European Parliament

On the one hand, the obvious place to start is the European Parliament. Directly elected since 1979, it surely is the institution for creating significant links between the governors and the governed. It meets in public, unlike the Council of Ministers, represents a very wide range of political opinions within the Union, again unlike the Council, and has acquired significant powers since its inception, notably in the budgetary field.

On the other hand, although in the legislative field the Parliament has the power to adopt amendments, the Council has relatively little difficulty in ignoring them. Hence, why should electorates pay much attention to what the Parliament does, even if it does stand for a broad public debate at the European level? And without such attention how could the Parliament hope to succeed in improving the legitimacy of the activities of the Union?

This latter argument was partially undermined by the Single European Act, which made it more difficult for the Council to overrule the Parliament within the legislative procedure. Under the cooperation procedure, the Council could only reject Parliament amendments to proposals by unanimity if the Commission accepted them. This proved to be an important provision, particularly on issues that divided the Council. Nevertheless, the possibility of overruling the Parliament still existed, so the Council learned to use all its various skills of brokerage to overcome internal divisions and achieve unanimity.

Hence the importance for the Parliament of the Maastricht provisions and, in particular, Article 189b, which is now generally described as the co-decision procedure.[4] That procedure is important for three main reasons: First, it makes it possible for the Parliament to *reject* a piece of legislation, even if there is unanimity in the Council of Ministers; second, it establishes a means of *direct negotiation* between the Council and the Parliament in the form of a conciliation committee, which has the specific task of seeking to overcome differences between the two bodies; and third, it makes the Parliament *jointly responsible* for the legislation adopted under this article— the president of the Parliament co-signs the legislation with the president of the Council.[5]

Although restricted in scope to about one-quarter of the legislation submitted to the Parliament, the co-decision procedure had led to the adoption of thirty-three proposals and the rejection of two by the early summer of 1995.[6] As a result, it has been possible to see the kind of impact that the Parliament can now have. The locus classicus so far has been the case of motorbikes and the Commission proposal that there should be a ban, on safety grounds, on bikes whose power exceeds 74 kilowatts. The Parliament found itself at the head of an unlikely coalition of motorbike manufacturers and leather-clad bikers seeking to overturn the Commission point of view, particularly when the Council proved able to reach agreement on a position that effectively endorsed the Commission view. The Parliament made clear that it would reject the proposal if the Council did not back down.

Here was an opportunity for the Parliament to show not only that it could adopt a coherent political stance but also that its voice could make a difference in the outcome of intergovernmental bargaining. However, the issue was not resolved easily. The Parliament failed in April 1994 to reject the text definitively. Needing 260 votes (i.e., half the number of members of the European Parliament [MEPs] plus one) to carry out its threat, it succeeded in mustering only 252, 8 short. In part, this was due to the approach of the European elections, but also it was the result of considerable pressure on the MEPs not to act against the position adopted by their governments in the Council. However, the story did not end there. The procedure allowed the Parliament to adopt amendments to the text, and this in turn led to conciliation with the Council of Ministers in the autumn of 1994. During these negotiations the Council agreed to drop power limits on motorbikes, and a joint text was signed in December 1994.[7]

What does this story tell us about the role of the Parliament in its quest for reinforcing democratic legitimacy? First, it shows the difficulty for the Parliament in finding the absolute majority of its members necessary to force the Council into negotiations, not least when members can, as in this case, be subject to considerable pressure from their governments not to put legislation at risk. And yet the Parliament's credibility as a co-decider, representing the European electorate against the member states, may depend on its ability to do precisely this—to show that it can make a difference in outcomes.

Second, the conciliation procedure's lack of transparency is at odds with the traditional rhetoric of openness of the institution. The formal conciliation meetings are preceded by much smaller informal meetings in which the Council president, in discussions with one or two of the Parliament's delegation, seeks to ascertain what the Parliament will accept. Perhaps this is an inevitable part of the search for agreement in the Union, but as one academic observer has recently commented, it has a price. "Co-decision appears to make informal, backroom bargaining and deal-making more important features of the EU's decision-making process."[8] This may serve to make it more difficult for the Parliament to establish its distinctive role as a representative of the people in the legislative process: It risks being incorporated into a structure dominated by the modus operandi of the Council and losing its distinctive face. It is, therefore, by no means self-evident that even if the Parliament achieves during the 1996 IGC its goal of broader co-decisional rights beyond the fifteen areas to which it at present applies,[9] this will by itself generate greater legitimacy within the Union. This change may be necessary, but it will certainly not be sufficient.

Legitimation Through National Parliaments

If the European Parliament is to achieve wider rights, this will necessarily have to be accepted by national parliaments, which will be called upon to ratify the outcome of the 1996 IGC. Hence their attitudes are not unimportant, all the more so because the Maastricht Treaty includes for the first time, even if in declarations rather than the main text, references to national parliaments, calling in particular for their "greater involvement . . . in the activities of the European Union."[10]

Hence national parliaments offer a second perspective on legitimation. After all, is it not they that through the links between electorates and their representatives legitimize the activities of governments at all levels, including the level of the European Union? Are they not the bedrock of representative democracy in Western Europe, and should they not therefore determine more precisely the direction of change in the Union?

There are good arguments to challenge such a point of view. However well-informed a national parliament is, it has no specific rights in the legislative process of the Union and can only seek to chase an ever more complex set of procedures in the search for better information from its government. However strong the control of a single parliament over its government, that control is of limited use in a Union that uses (or threatens to use) qualified majorities on an ever broader basis so as to make decisions possible. Certainly both of these constraints could be eliminated, but not without fundamentally altering the character of the Union.

What then is to be done? This was precisely the question that the German Constitutional Court faced in 1993, when it considered whether the Maastricht Treaty was compatible with the Basic Law. The Court ruled against the complainants but in so doing used a particular form of argumentation of relevance to the issue of democratic legitimacy. The Court considered the Treaty in terms of the ceding of powers by the German government and asked whether "the minimum requirements of democratic legitimation . . . for the sovereign power exercised towards the citizen are no longer fulfilled." It answered that the requirements were still fulfilled because the transfer of powers under the Treaty was strictly limited. The member states remained the "masters of the Treaties" in a *Staatenverbund*, a compound of states, not a proto-federal arrangement. The Union does not have a *Kompetenz-Kompetenz*, that is to say, the ability to decide for itself the extent of its own powers. Nor does the European Court of Justice (ECJ) enjoy an unlimited right to apply and interpret Community law; it is obliged to exercise its rights in a relationship of cooperation with the German Constitutional Court.

This conception of a Union exercising restricted powers was seen as having important implications for the conditions under which the German government can move to the third stage of European Monetary Union (EMU). The Court denied that the Treaty imposed an automaticity in the process over which Germany had no control. In particular, it supported the need for the German Parliament to play a vital role. The new Article 23 of the German Basic Law says that any further transfer of powers to the Union affecting the structure of the German Basic Law will require the approval of the Bundestag and the Bundesrat, and, in both cases, a two-thirds majority in favor of the change will be needed. However, it was the ruling of the Court and the government's submission to it that confirmed that this article also applied to the move to a single currency, which was not something that had been decided definitively at Maastricht and could no longer be reviewed.

The importance of this ruling for the future of the Union cannot be underestimated. It will undoubtedly set a benchmark against which the results of the 1996 IGC will be judged in Germany. However, the ruling raised as many questions as it answered about the future of democratic legitimacy in the Union. Consider for a moment the prospect that the German parliament has voted in favor of the third stage of EMU, that Germany has given up the deutsche mark, and that there is a single currency managed by a European Central Bank (ECB). What is the role of the national parliament in such a structure? The Court argued that the independence of a European Central Bank will be as legitimate as that of the Bundesbank in Germany because it will enable an institution dedicated to a long-term interest, namely stability of the currency, to avoid being made subject to short-term political interests.

This argument is difficult to sustain for at least two reasons. First, it ignores the fact that unlike the Bundesbank, the ECB will not be subject to a democratic authority that can change its role should it wish to do so: Only the unanimous agreement of the governments of the Union will suffice. Although the German parliament can be given a say in determining whether the move to the third stage takes place, once it has happened it will no longer have control over the operation of the ECB. Second, the argument supposes that a doctrine of legitimacy for the Union as a whole can be built on assumptions drawn from a particular domestic experience. It ignores the widely held fear that Europe will be run by an unaccountable committee of governors of central banks. It offers no view about how the priorities of the ECB can be balanced by the pursuit of the wider set of economic objectives laid down in Article 2 of the Maastricht Treaty, in particular, "a high level of employment and of social protection, the raising of the standard of living and the quality of life and economic and social cohesion and solidarity among Member States."

This in turn brings us back to the role of the European Parliament in the legislative process. The Court did not address the issue of the extent to which the European Parliament could go beyond a "supportive function" in relation to the European Union. The German government and parliament have traditionally supported strengthening the role of the Parliament, but how far could this extend without unraveling the idea of a Union of limited powers with legitimation coming from the national level? Giving ever greater powers to a democratically elected body at the European level calls into question the role of national parliaments in the legitimation process. In this sense, the first and second perspectives are incompatible and lay down a severe challenge to the European Parliament and national parliaments to find a means that ensures adequate parliamentary control over the development of the Union.

Legitimation from Beyond the Formal Institutions

To establish a third perspective on legitimacy, we need to step back and to ask how far parliaments, whether European or national, can offer a solution to the issue of representative democracy at the European level. We need to look more carefully at the criteria that a democratic system at the European level needs to meet. The fulfilment of these criteria requires more than institutional fine-tuning.

The importance of looking beyond formal institutional frameworks was underlined by Czech president Václav Havel when he spoke at the European Parliament. He identified the heavily mechanistic character of the Maastricht edifice in the following terms:

> When I first looked at the Maastricht Treaty, I thought it was a remarkable piece of work. I was full of admiration, even enthusiastic. But as I started thinking about it a bit more, I became less exuberant. I felt that I was looking into the inner workings of an absolutely perfect and immensely ingenious modern machine. To study such a machine must be a great joy, to an admirer of technical components. But for me, a human whose interest in the world is not satisfied by admiration for well-oiled machines, something was seriously missing. Perhaps it could be called, in a rather simplified way, a spiritual or moral or emotional dimension. My reason had been spoken to but not my heart.[11]

This statement underlines the usefulness of the distinction between formal and social legitimacy.[12] A political system can enjoy formal legitimacy in that the operation of its institutions takes place within rules laid down by democratically authorized laws. However, that system may still not be able to win the full assent of the population by speaking to their hearts. No one can contest that Maastricht was agreed to and ratified in accordance with all the necessary constitutional procedures, but these are not enough to guarantee the social legitimacy of the Union. This might not have mattered if the Treaty's goals were not so far-reaching; as it is, the achievement of the broadest possible level of legitimacy becomes an essential requirement for the survival of the whole polity.

The achievement of formal and social legitimacy requires a twofold change in the way that citizens perceive the political process at the European level. First, they must perceive their identity and involvement in the political process as extending beyond the frontiers of the nation-state. Second, they must feel at ease with and accept the rules operating within that process that determine how majorities can take decisions. It is a feature of democratic systems at national levels that people accept that majorities can decide, even if they do not like the decisions that are made. There is confidence that certain basic rules will be respected and that today's minority can become tomorrow's majority. To quote Joseph Weiler, "people accept the majoritarian principle of democracy within a polity to which they see themselves as belonging."[13]

For the time being, it is clear that the conditions that apply at the national level do not apply at the European level. Debate is very compartmentalized in each member state, and all of them display great reluctance to extend the powers that majorities can exert over minorities. Despite the existence of the qualified majority voting system in the Council of Ministers, the acceptance of systematic majority rule remains very limited. The necessary agreement on the overall rules of the game is lacking.

So what is to be done? For some the problem is insoluble. John Stuart Mill, for example, argued that there is a direct link between the possibility of representative institutions and the sharing of a single language. He put the point thus: "Free institutions are next to impossible in a country made up of different nationalities. Among a people without fellow-feeling, especially if they read and speak different languages, the united public opinion necessary to the working of representative government cannot exist."[14] However, if one is prepared to accept that the idea of transnational democracy is not a contradiction in terms, then two possible solutions can be suggested, one designed to broaden the territorial base of decisions, the other intended to generate a public debate across frontiers.

The first takes as its starting point the subsidiarity principle laid down in Article A of the Maastricht Treaty that decisions should be taken "as closely as possible to the citizens." Hence what is required is to develop decision-making structures at the local and regional levels that can be brought together at the level of the Union in the Committee of the Regions.[15] However, it is not clear that this can answer the need for a democratic framework across the Community as a whole. It is essentially directed to the articulation of a wider set of interests in the hope that this very process will make it easier to aggregate those interests. This is an optimistic assumption, given the level of heterogeneity across the Union.

On the contrary, in the second view, the development of a democratic system at the European level enjoying social as well as formal legitimacy requires structures that cut across national boundaries and allow a public debate to develop that is not confined to the concerns of a particular member state. In the words of the German Constitutional Court, it is necessary to develop "a continuous free debate between opposing social forces, interests and ideas, in which political goals become clarified and change course and out of which a public opinion emerges which starts to shape a political will."[16] A debate of this kind may take place outside the traditional political framework: The successful campaigns of Greenpeace spring to mind. However, if the debate is to extend beyond sectoral concerns and offer competing visions of the European public space, it will need to be organized. Such organization is difficult to conceive without the development of some form of party political system at the European level.

It would be rash in the extreme to argue that such a system will be easy to create. Quite apart from the difficulties of establishing a political discourse across linguistic boundaries in the face of strong national feelings, political parties are themselves widely perceived to be in crisis at the national level, with declining memberships and weakening ideological cohesion. So why imagine that parties can be developed that are sufficiently powerful to legitimize the activities of the European Union?

However, one should not exaggerate the extent to which European parties will need to match the role of national parties in aggregating the wishes of the electorate. European political parties are likely to be much less ambitious than their national counterparts. They are not, and are unlikely to be, concerned with the establishment of governing majorities and so do not and will not require the same degree of cohesion.

It would also be a mistake to overlook the potential that already exists for them to develop a role at the European level. The Treaty on European Union offers an interesting pointer in this direction. Article 138a declares that "political parties at European level are important as a factor for integration within the Union. They contribute to forming a European awareness and to expressing the political will of the citizens of the Union." These apparently anodyne words open the way to a future in which the nonpartisan character of much of the political debate among supporters of the Community is challenged. As

Weiler points out, this would represent a major break with the past: "neutralization of ideology has conditioned . . . the belief that an agenda could be set for the Community, and the Community could be led toward an ever closer union among its peoples without having to face the normal political cleavages present in the member states."[17]

Opportunities for creating such cleavages at the European level are certainly emerging. In organizational terms, we are witnessing the slow development of European political parties independent of the political groups in the European Parliament. The European Peoples Party (EPP) has existed since the 1970s, the Party of European Socialists (PES) was created in November 1992, and the Liberals are organized within the European Liberal Democrat and Reformist Party (ELDR). Moreover, they are assuming the ability to operate with a degree of autonomy within the European political system. Their preparation for the European elections in 1994, when all three parties adopted pan-European manifestos, was a good example of this. Much was made in 1994 of the differences between the British Labour Party and the European Socialists over the question of the validity of reducing working hours as a way of reducing unemployment.[18] More impressive was the difference between the 1994 elections and those in 1989, when the attempt to agree on a common platform was much less successful, the text being peppered with reservations from different national parties.

Manifestos of the competing parties continue to lack the degree of precision that can be found at the national level, but this in part reflects the limited opportunities that these parties have to vent their differences. This situation, too, is in the process of changing. The creation of new institutions widens the arena of activity for such parties: The Committee of the Regions, for example, has created a political group structure linked to the groups in the European Parliament. More important, the changing powers of the Parliament have also offered extra scope for parties to develop their role.

The most obvious example of this extra scope arose as a result of the Parliament's new rights under the Treaty on European Union—to be consulted on the nomination of the president of the Commission and to approve the nomination of the new Commission. The proposed nomination of Santer, the Luxembourg prime minister, as president of the Commission provoked considerable opposition. This was partly due to the particular circumstances surrounding his nomination, notably the opposition of the British government to the initial nominee, Dehaene, prime minister of Belgium. However, there was also an ideological element reflected in the fact that the majority of the Socialist Group voted against Santer, whereas Christian Democrats voted for him. The Socialists were less than sanguine as to what the Christian Democratic candidate for the presidency was going to do in the areas of most concern to them.

This politicization extended beyond the choice of the Commission president. Before the 1989–1994 Parliament was dissolved, it supported a report that urged governments to take account of the outcome of the European elections in their nominations for individual commissioners.[19] The clear implication was that the new Parliament, before it gave a vote of approval, would be looking for a college of commissioners that reflected the relative political strengths of the groups in the Parliament. This made the public hearings on commissioner nominations that took place in January 1995 of particular importance in the development of the "normal political cleavages" of which Weiler speaks. They provided an opportunity not just to assess the knowledge of the individuals concerned about their areas of competence but also to judge their political credentials. The idea of the Commission as a group of powerful officials was severely dented in the process, as the political responsibility of the Commission to the Parliament was strongly underlined.

The further development of this process will not be without its difficulties. Traditionally the Parliament has operated on the basis of what is sometimes called the "technical majority," that is to say, collaboration between the Socialists and the Christian Democrats. Without it, obtaining the absolute majority of votes[20] necessary to adopt amendments that can influence the shape of legislation would be impossible. If European political parties do succeed in achieving clearer definition, then this hurdle may prove more difficult to jump in the future.

At the same time, we are seeing the eruption onto the political scene of parties that wish to limit the scope of activity of the Union and to renationalize many of its activities. After the European elections a new group was formed in the Parliament with precisely such an aim. The Europe of Nations Group, chaired by Sir James Goldsmith, brings together members from the left and the right of the political spectrum with the express aim of blocking the development of European integration. It is a development that reflects the wider discussion about what kind of Union Europeans want to achieve. There can hardly be a debate on what makes citizens of the Union want to live together without enabling those opposed to the traditional European ideals to enter the political fray. Hence the importance of the development of political parties that can serve to generate a debate as to the nature of the public sphere at the European level. Such a debate is a necessary condition for the generation of a political culture marked by social as well as formal legitimacy, where minorities, however composed, can accept the decisions of majorities within a system that provides for the representation of the views of the electorate.

PERSPECTIVES FOR THE FUTURE

It is one thing to posit a set of perspectives, but another to argue that they can serve to channel the debate in the European Union toward a new system of governance that respects the principles of representative governance and enjoys popular legitimacy. In this last section I will consider the chances of the 1996 IGC leading to the successful conclusion of such a debate.

For some, such a success is a chimera. Representative government was, from this point of view, a system linked to a particular historical period during which the nation-state played a dominant role. That period is now drawing to a close as the nation-state loses much of its strength within a new global system. The result can only be atrophy of the trappings of representative democracy. One French writer argues that the age of institutions is at an end and that we are entering *l'âge relationnel*, the age of networks, which will bring about the end of democracy.[21] If this thesis is correct, then all the discussions surrounding the 1996 IGC can only lead into a dead end. From my point of view, this seems an overly determinist position that exaggerates the power of structure over human agency. The great efforts that are being expended to devise a new system of governance may not by themselves guarantee success, but equally one cannot assume in advance that they will have no impact on outcomes. Moreover, this thesis assumes that one feature of the structure of the international system will necessarily constrain behavior more than other features. The 1996 IGC will be taking place in a particular political environment in which the costs of agreement for the participants have to be set against those of failing to agree. In particular, the conference will be overshadowed by the prospect of a Union of more than twenty-five states. Such enlargement can only be envisaged if the existing decisionmaking mechanisms are substantially revised.

Already in 1994, in the debate on the accession of the states of the European Free Trade Association (EFTA), Europeans were offered a precursor of the difficulty of such a revision. The United Kingdom was very reluctant to accept the proposed raising of the threshold for a blocking minority from twenty-four to twenty-seven votes. After difficult negotiations, the so-called Ioannina Compromise served to patch up the differences, pending a review in 1996. The issue presented the British government with choices with important potential consequences for the future. An editorial in the *Financial Times* noted the temptation of a solution that would make decisions subject to the hurdle of member-state population strength as well as the traditional allocation of votes to each state.[22] In other words, qualified majorities would need the support of governments representing a certain percentage of the people living in the Union. The *Financial Times* also pointed out that this would be a significant concession to the federalist argument that the Union is composed of peoples as well as governments. The British government did not follow this direction and was successful in winning breathing space until 1996. In the IGC all governments are faced with the need to find a broader base for the structure of the operation of the Council of Ministers than that provided by the present system. They are being forced to address the issue of how peoples should be represented in decisions taken at the European level.

If the prospect of enlargement will necessarily force a revision of existing structures, can one also suggest that the revision will necessarily involve moving toward a more representative system at the European level? I suggest that it is the very large space generated by my three perspectives that gives reason to suppose there will be some movement in that direction; they offer sufficient scope to generate a set of reforms that take account of the different sensitivities of the member states. Those countries, like Germany, that support an increase in the powers of the European Parliament will have the chance to press for an extension of the co-decision procedure; those, like Britain and France, that are more concerned about preserving the prerogatives of national parliaments can seek ways of reinforcing their impact on the activities of the Union; and those, like the Scandinavians, who are more interested in generating broader public involvement in the process can press for the greater degree of openness that a true public debate at the European level requires.

It would be rash to exaggerate the likely impact of the changes emerging from the IGC. There is no reason to suppose that it will escape the pressure for compromise that has been the mark of previous IGCs. Hence we are unlikely to see the Union suddenly become a "huge fuzzy sponge of democratic forms, breathing the water of liberty in and out" referred to by Neal Ascherson.[23] And yet the conference may well mark the moment when the terms of the debate about the character of the Union changed. There are those who are still prepared to argue that it can remain a partial polity, with the essential questions of governance unresolved. If the argument of this chapter is correct, then they must be wrong.

NOTES

This article is a revised version of a public lecture given by the author at the University of Edinburgh during the time he spent at the Europa Institute in May 1994 as the Sir Edward Health Fellow. The views expressed herein are strictly personal and are not intended to represent the official view of the European Parliament.

1. For an extended discussion of this issue, see Kevin Featherstone, "Jean Monnet and the 'Democratic Deficit' in the European Union," *Journal of Common Market Studies* 32, no. 2 (1994), pp.149–170.

2. Helen Wallace "European Governance in Turbulent Times," *Journal of Common Market Studies* 31, no. 3 (1993), p. 295.

3. Hobermas is quoted by Brigid Laffan, in Simon Bulmer and Andrew Scott, eds., *Economic and Political Integration in Europe* (Oxford: Blackwells, 1994), p. 100.

4. For a considerable period the British government referred to the procedure as "negative assent"; this rather nebulous phrase seems now to be falling into disuse.

5. For more details, see Francis Jacobs, Richard Corbett, and Michael Shackleton, *The European Parliament* (Harlow: Longman, 1992), pp. 190–194.

6. Commission of the European Communities, *Report on the Operation of the Treaty on European Union* (Brussels: Commission of the European Communities, 1995), SEC(95) 731 final, p. 19.

7. For a more detailed discussion, see Richard Corbett, Francis Jacobs, and Michael Shackleton, *The European Parliament* (London: Cartermill, 1995), pp. 203–204.

8. John Peterson, "Playing the Transparency Game," "Decision-making in the European Union: Towards a Framework for Analysis," *Journal of European Public Policy* 2, no. 1 (March 1995), pp. 69–93.

9. For details, see Richard Corbett, *The Treaty of Maastricht* (Harlow: Longman, 1993), p. 88.

10. Declaration 13 of the Treaty on European Union. See Richard Corbett, "Treaty of Maastricht," p. 473.

11. Speech by Václav Havel, President of the Czech Republic, to the European Parliament, in Strasbourg, March 8, 1994.

12. See, in particular, Joseph Weiler, "After Maastricht: Community Legitimacy in Post-1992 Europe," in William James Adams, ed., *Singular Europe: Economy and Polity of the European Community After 1992* (Ann Arbor: University of Michigan Press, 1993), pp. 19–20.

13. Ibid, p. 22.

14. John Stuart Mill, *Considerations on Representative Government* (1861, reprint, Prometheus Books, 1991), p. 310.

15. See, for example, Andrew Scott, John Peterson, and David Millar, "Subsidiarity: A 'Europe of the Regions' versus the British Constitution?" *Journal of Common Market Studies*. 32, no. 1 (1994), pp.47–67.

16. Judgment of the German Constitutional Court on the Treaty on European Union, October 12, 1993.

17. Weiler, "After Maastricht," p. 34.

18. See, for example, David Butler and Martin Westlake, *British Politics and European Elections 1994* (London: Macmillan, 1995), pp. 126–128.

19. Report of the Committee on Institutional Affairs on the Investiture of the Commission. Rapporteur: Mr. Froment-Meurice, A3-0240/94, adopted on April 21, 1994.

20. Before the direct elections of 1994 this majority was 260. Since January 1995 it has risen to 314 (or half of the membership of the Parliament plus one).

21. Jean-Marie Guéhenno, *La Fin de la Démocratie* (Flammarion, 1993).

22. "Stupide Albion," *Financial Times*, March 14, 1994, p. 13.

23. Neal Ascherson, "Fuzzy Democracy," *New Statesman and Society*, March 11, 1994, pp. 24–26.

4

The Information Society in Europe: The Passing of the Public Service Paradigm of European Democracy

Shalini Venturelli

The political future of the European Union (EU) will in large part become a product of its approach to the information society and to the emerging framework of European public space. This integration of European communications is being shaped by information liberalization pressures from the global economy and from bilateral and multilateral trade agreements. The EU's initiatives indicate the information society for European citizens essentially constitutes a systematic dismantling of the public service paradigm of democratic development. This historic political change can be examined in the context of competing conceptions of European public space, in two areas significant to the future basis of integration: audiovisual policy, and the constitutional foundation of communication rights. As construction of a European information society is advanced on the basis of the decline of the public service social model, these two elements of EU communication policy raise profound questions about the possibilities of cultural self-determination and political self-determination in future processes of integration.

In this chapter, I discuss the relationship among liberal, public service, and nationalist conceptions of integration and analyze the conflict in the EU's audiovisual policies and freedom of communication policies in order to explore the role of cultural and political self-determination in the project of European construction.

PARADIGMS OF INTEGRATION

Liberalism Versus Public Service

Since the early 1980s, the growing integration of the global economy and the liberal political arrangements that sustain it have challenged the very essence of the public service paradigm of democracy. Within the EU, audiovisual policy, for instance, has evolved as a powerful site of conflict not only between rival political and social interests but also between three rival paradigms of how the European Union ought to develop: the liberal, the nationalist (or the culturalist), and the public service. The worldwide acceleration of the social form of liberal internationalism has overwhelmed communist totalitarianism and now also threatens to engulf the public service or republican basis of political community. By providing no basis for identity other than proprietary relations, liberalism challenges the foundation of civil society, which springs from a universality of participatory public freedoms among citizens, and replaces civil society with the monetarization of political society.

The emergence of liberalization, that is to say, the application of liberal policies to most areas of economy and society, and its political uses of competition as a concrete collective movement on a world scale, invokes the notion of an unprecedented transfer of knowledge through modern communication networks to individuals worldwide.[1] Yet the movement of information liberalization points to a significant redistribution of power from the public to the private sector brought about, enforced, and extended by the instruments of state action, that is, by public policy. The debate over liberalizing information space within Europe can be understood, therefore, as a debate over the terms of the transnational social order—as a struggle over the fundamental terms of reconstituting civil society on a pan-European scale.

R. Collins as well as K. Morgan characterize the audiovisual problem, for instance, as a conflict over two views of the role of the state, one advocating intervention (*dirigisme*) in the market and the other eschewing it (liberalism).[2] However, this construction of the problem does not consider that liberalization may have been mischaracterized as a noninterventionist conceptual system just as it is often misapprehended as a theory of open and perfect competition. Just as liberalism has been oversimplified as a minimal theory of the state, as I have addressed elsewhere,[3] dirigisme is frequently reduced to a peculiarity of French history, a caricature that obscures and obstructs a serious examination of the arguments advanced and of the nature of resistance to liberalization. Consequently, the debate over the role of the state in the audiovisual sector cannot be what Collins or Morgan describe, a choice between intervention and nonintervention; rather it is a debate between forms of intervention and which social interests ought to benefit. The public service idea that competes against liberalism's political assumptions in the European Community is far more useful to understanding European differences over the role of the state than the simplistic explanation of dirigisme.

The conflict over deepening the union of European states through a framework of laws and regulations can be understood as a contrast between Montesquieu's theory that the sole route to individual liberty is by way of a republic based on public service, on the one hand, and both liberal and nationalist models of social organization, on the other. This contrast better describes the political problems of European integration than the false presumption of conflict between dirigisme and liberalism with respect to state intervention. The conceptualization of civil society under public service emphasizes the principle of public freedom and the autonomy of civil society secured by differentiation from the state—not solely through the liberation of private competitiveness—and premised on institutional guarantees. G. W. F. Hegel, too, sees clearly that the central principle of modern civil society is not merely the private sphere of property and private conscience but also the public realm of associational conditions and the structure of public institutions.[4]

This public service approach to democracy best describes not only the French political tradition but also that of several other states including, for example, Belgium, Italy, and Germany.[5] The concept has evolved since the French Revolution, but especially in the period from the end of the nineteenth century to the 1930s as embodied in the corporatist organization of social sectors, such as railroads and utilities, that are held to be basic to the common interest. The principle of public service is not merely a policy convention but is constitutionally grounded in the French Constitution (1946), as in those of other member states, and more significantly in constitutional provisions of the Community (Article 2 of the Treaty of Rome; Title 1, Article B of the Treaty on European Union [Maastricht Treaty]), which underscore the role of Community law in guaranteeing the conditions of the general welfare.[6]

The idea of public service, as P. Bauby and J. Boual reiterate, rests on the recognition that certain social sectors must be exempt from sole governance by market logic in order to permit universal access to certain public goods and services that contribute to the minimum basis of equality in economic, social, and cultural relations.[7] It is grounded in Montesquieu's cornerstone principle of equality under republican law whereby the associational conditions of civil society, its self-regulatory conditions, are possible only if the law guarantees the minimum threshold of human need.[8] The republican constitution requires, therefore, that the state maintain access to basic goods and services, or else "inequality will enter at the point not protected by the laws, and the republic will be lost."[9] Civil society or associational conditions can only escape destruction by being incorporated in the political organization of society.[10] This is a fundamental departure from liberalism, which assumes civil society requires no political basis whatsoever, thus casting the individual onto his or her own resources for every aspect of human need, even the most basic.[11]

In the public service theory, the common interest in fragmentation and diversification of power in civil society, and the empowering of citizens to foster their participation in the public realm, requires that minimum needs for health, education, and basic utilities like water, electricity, and communication not be determined by proprietary social power but be equally available to all. The criterion for application of public service arises if a collectivity, whether local, regional, national, or European, determines that a public good or essential service for all, either existing or new, cannot be realized in an adequate or satisfactory manner by the private market.[12] The essential characteristic of this good could proceed from a strategic common interest, a fundamental condition of equity, or social cohesion and is mandated for all by an act of law or through processes of regulation.

Thus the attribution of governmental despotism that inheres in the accusation of dirigisme barely hints at the reality of an alternative conceptualization of democratic society based on a theory of political rights and public service and with well-developed political foundations that stands in dramatic opposition to the premises of liberalism and to its contemporary expression in the processes of liberalization. The depiction of differences between the *dirigistes* and liberals in the European Union obscures, therefore, the true underlying debate over the actual objectives of liberalization and the paradigms that oppose it. These competing conceptions of the role of the state and the basis of union among peoples and nations in the EU that bear profoundly on the struggle over policies of the information age can be identified as nationalism, liberalism, and republicanism or public service. The first two are private modes of organizing public space,[13] whereas the last bears many of the elements of a participatory concept of public space and democratic relations. The difference between a public service conception and the nationalist or culturalist approach to communication and democracy is fairly significant, not only for the distinctly opposed set of fundamental assumptions regarding the identity of the body politic with an exclusive cultural form, but also for the ironic convergence between liberalism and nationalism that this difference reveals. Despite the ostensible chasm between cultural and liberal conceptions of audiovisual production and distribution in the multimedia age, the forms of intervention identified by cultural theories of regulation create a paradoxical convergence with liberalization, thus further intensifying historical pressures on the public service paradigm.

The Convergence of Nationalism and Liberalism

Although the notion of cultural collectivism as a basis for regulating public communications may be opposed to market-based criteria, it cannot easily provide the constitutionally guaranteed participatory structures and public freedoms for citizens that form the essence of the public service tradition. The cultural-nationalist model emphasizes communication content celebrating the exclusivity of the cultural bonds of the collective at the expense of substantive participation and representation from a range of social interests, as required by the universal service conditions of the public service approach. A cultural argument for public space is not necessarily a democratic one, for both a nationalist and a liberal or market choice argument for public space can threaten the central requirements of political society. The relation between these two private modes of public space in the politically sensitive sector of audiovisual policy is addressed not only by the struggle between liberalism and nationalism but in concrete embodiments of the struggle advanced by the respective positions of the United States and France for influence over the policy framework of the European Union.

Modern nationalism takes Johann Herder's notion of the *Volk* as the conceptual origin of modern nationalism.[14] This thought advocates the community as an expressive, not a political, unity with a peculiar manner of expression that is unique, irreplaceable, frequently "pure," and that needs to be sustained and handed down in some untainted, uncontaminated form. The expressivist conception of human association as articulated by Herder[15] thus defends the idea of culture as its own "form" driven to some realization, which must be freed from external constraint—such as competing or alternative cultures—in order to discover the indefinable thread that guides it. The logic of this view of the public realm therefore suggests a purity of descent that must be defended against polluting cultural strains, which are to be excluded and on occasion exterminated or stamped out in order to release the forces of cultural self-realization or the unique form embedded within the expressive unity. This was precisely the reasoning articulated in the early stages of the European Community's justification for a transnational public realm in audiovisual production and distribution: "The audiovisual sector is of great importance to the cultural identity of peoples, regions and nations. It is also a rapidly growing sector of the world economy, significant in its own right and with considerable multiplier effects on other cultural sectors."[16] Nationalist reasoning earlier formed the political premise of the "television without frontiers" green paper in this classical cultural syllogism: "European unification will only be achieved if Europeans want it. Europeans will only want it if there is such a thing as a European identity. A European identity will only develop if Europeans are adequately informed. At present, information via the mass media is controlled at national level."[17] The "unquestionable cultural significance"[18] of program production and distribution has also been pointedly stressed by Jacques Delors, former president of the European Commission:

> The culture industry will tomorrow be one of the biggest industries, a creator of wealth and jobs. Under the terms of the Treaty we do not have the resources to implement a cultural policy; but we are going to try to tackle it along economic lines. It is not simply a question of television programmes. We have to build a powerful European culture industry that will enable us to be in control of both the medium and its content, maintaining our standards of civilization, and encouraging the creative people amongst us.[19]

The Community's emphasis on creation of a European cultural identity that transcends national cultural borders has been translated into a series of communication policy initiatives advocating creation of a shared culture through audiovisual forms. Such policies "will strengthen the Europeans' sense of belonging to one and the same Community."[20] Ministers of culture of member states have gone even further to propose expansion of transfrontier audiovisual distribution networks as "one of the top priorities of a European cultural policy . . . part of the concept of a 'people's Europe.'"[21] The communication dimension of the single market later became a key rationale in the development of a European cultural policy, and to this extent, as K. Robins and D. Morley and Collins argue, EU policy has increasingly recognized that questions of culture, politics, and identity are at the heart of the European project.[22]

The momentum behind the expressivist conception of transnational association has been strong enough to cause a significant change in the Community's narrow economic mandate: the granting of constitutional authority to shape the public realm as a cultural realm. Article 128 of the Maastricht Treaty provides legal grounds for the European Commission and other institutions of the EU, including the European Court of Justice, to intervene in the cultural domain. The political and regulatory significance makes this provision worth quoting in its entirety:

Title IX
Culture

1. The Community shall contribute to the flowering of the cultures of the Member States, while respecting their national and regional diversity and at the same time bringing the *common cultural heritage* to the fore.
2. Action by the Community shall be aimed at encouraging cooperation between Member States and, if necessary, supporting and supplementing their action in the following areas:
   • improvement of the knowledge and dissemination of the *culture and history of the European peoples;*
   • conservation and *safeguarding of cultural heritage* of European significance;
   • non-commercial cultural exchanges;
   • artistic and literary creation, including the *audiovisual sector.*
3. The Community and the Member States shall foster cooperation with third countries and the competent international organizations in the sphere of culture, in particular the Council of Europe.
4. The Community shall take cultural aspects into account in its action under other provisions of this Treaty.
5. In order to contribute to the achievement of the objectives referred to in this Article, the Council:
   • acting in accordance with the procedure referred to in Article 189b and after consulting the Committee of the Regions, shall

adopt incentive measures, excluding any harmonization of the laws and regulations of the Member States. The Council shall act unanimously throughout the procedures referred to in Article 189b.

* acting unanimously on a proposal from the Commission, shall adopt recommendations.[23]

These stipulations testify to the importance the EU attributes to the audiovisual sector as the most important of the cultural industries, an importance perceived relevant not only to the idea of audiovisual production and distribution as an agency of social cohesion but also to the perception that program production and the information industry can regenerate economic growth.[24] It is evident here that D. Bell's liberal expression of the economic power of an "information revolution" to recreate a new industrial age— "postindustrialism"—has been conjoined with the Community's notion of audiovisual creation as a way to cross-stitch self-proclaimed, exclusive national cultures into a unitary European identity.[25] The Community's synthesis of liberalism and nationalism is best summed up in the declaration: "The audiovisual sector has enormous potential to generate wealth and create jobs, as well as being essential to Europe's cultural life."[26]

According to E. Gellner the argument for the cohesive power of culture is classically nationalist, especially when it presupposes that the body politic and an exclusive cultural form are congruent. That is to say, the formulation of cultural uniqueness employed to fuse the collective into a nation serves to legitimate social and political institutions, thereby replacing a participatory, deliberative sphere where common consensus is achieved by democratic means. As Herder suggests, each collectivity constructed on the basis of cultural affinities must express its own inimitable path to humanness.[27]

The idea of European cohesion is embedded in a nationalist matrix, ascribing to the circulation of audiovisual forms the strategic function of forging a sense of Europeanness as unique identity. The development of European audiovisual policy touches on the question of union as it touches on economic enlargement. Yet these separate aims obscure the profound difficulty in reconciling the Union's jurisdiction in enhancing the conditions of transnational commerce with its construction of pan-European nationalism. Delors may be credited with discovering a working concept that allows the tools of economic jurisdiction to be applied to the cultural sphere. In his speeches and policy proposals (the "Delors White Paper") Delors has identified the economic basis of cultural production, specifically audiovisual production, as a justification for Commission intervention.[28]

Now while the 1957 Treaty of Rome provides no specific grounds for Commission action in support of cultural policy, it could be construed as a basis for regulating cultural forms as commodities or services—as activities conducted for a remuneration—thus rendering legal any Commission instruments designed to create a common market in audiovisual products.[29] This was the approach in 1989 to adoption of a Commission statute establishing a single market in broadcasting, the "Television without Frontiers" Directive, which regulated an economic activity whose form was judged to be cultural.[30] A green paper on broadcasting, which preceded the directive by several years, justified erecting Community authority over communication networks that are dominant content or programming carriers in the public realm: "Contrary to what is widely imagined, the EEC Treaty applies not only to economic activities but, as a rule to all activities carried out for remuneration, regardless of whether they take place in the economic, social, cultural (including in particular information, creative or artistic activities and entertainment), sporting or any other sphere."[31]

EUROPEAN CONSTRUCTION AND
THE AUDIOVISUAL BATTLEGROUND

The information industries are central to the debate among these competing models of European construction. Divisions in policy over the audiovisual sector exemplify the deep struggle at the heart of the political organization of the European Union. Proponents of cultural arguments and public service arguments, each with their own justifications, are united against application of purely commercial criteria to audiovisual production and distribution, instead preferring the promotion of particular forms of the role of the state and of integrating the Union. This dynamic characterizes the audiovisual battle as a "debate over the paradigm of [a] European system of organization—can there be a common European Society?"[32]

The relationship between audiovisual policy and advocacy for a particular mode of civil society is true for liberalism as well, according to which public policy in the European Union is aimed purely at securing the free circulation of proprietary assets, or a free market. According to a U.S. critic of the EU's audiovisual policy, the EEC is above all an economic community and hence, the directive's objectives are mainly economic.[33]

The contrast between competing visions of community is captured with unusual poignancy in the debate over the television directive.[34] Liberal objections to the cultural sovereignty argument have been introduced already. It is also necessary to establish that the directive is criticized equally by nationalists and supporters of the public service model. It has been fiercely resisted by member states that perceive their languages and cultures to be threatened by the internationalization of audiovisual markets and the integration of

Community markets.[35] The directive, which was advocated and designed on grounds of cultural policy, has been rejected on the same grounds by countries such as France, Belgium, and Spain who view it as an instrument of the transnational audiovisual industry and propose that the Community undertake revised forms of intervention.[36] The Community has in turn responded with policies designed to promote diversity and fragmentation of culture as a protection against the unifying cultural forces unleashed by a directive originally supported for that very purpose. These counterunification policies include, for instance, the MEDIA Programme, an audiovisual production subsidy for individual producers in member states that turned into the cornerstone of Community action to support indigenous cultural forms.[37]

Thus Community audiovisual policy is marked by conflict among three rival conceptions over the meaning of transnational community. However, its development is also marked by shifts in emphasis between rival cultural policy goals: notably between the promotion of cultural unity and the promotion of cultural diversity. The opposition between unity and diversity is not wholly identical to the argument between public service and liberalization because the ultimate ends of each and the approach to forms of state action to achieve those ends differ considerably. The single element they do hold in common is a need for intervention, even in the liberalization model, which ultimately seeks simply to reconstruct the role of the state by shifting public policy from noncommercial aims to entirely commercial aims. For instance, the television directive has achieved the cultural integrative function it set out to create, but only by facilitating much greater domination of the audiovisual and broadcast markets by the multinational audiovisual industry originating primarily in the United States.[38] Though this was not the form of common culture originally envisioned by the television initiative, a liberalized content production sector structured in favor of the international audiovisual industry was the only type of "unity" the directive could deliver.

Predictably, this result has drawn the support of liberal internationalists in the EU and alienated both nationalists and public service supporters; it has also produced responses that obscure how the expansion of liberalization is an experiment in integration. To compensate for the decline in diversity of programming content, Community intervention in the audiovisual market has grown. The question of diversity of creative forms serves both the nationalist and the public service agendas by guaranteeing the spread of ideas, information, and representations of social reality that may not be available in a commercially governed public realm.

When MEDIA was established in 1988, its mission was to promote production and dissemination of audiovisual works throughout the Community with a specific focus on training, preproduction, multilingualism of programs, and easier access to venture capital, among other goals.[39] Thus

MEDIA has supported, in a limited sense owing to modest funding, the circulation of films and television programs made in the Community for the purpose of safeguarding cultural pluralism, which is perceived to be threatened by the integration of markets, that is, by information liberalization. MEDIA can be said, therefore, to stand as a modest veto, ineffectual though it may be, over cultural policies whose consequences are the Americanization of audiovisual production and distribution and the growing governance of the public realm by large-scale private proprietors.

The significance of MEDIA has increased in recent years for nationalist and public service forces in member governments and societies that pressure the Community to contain the ever widening cultural gap between U.S. and European productions distributed through programming networks.[40] These effects of the information society led to proposal of a new initiative for the European program industry, MEDIA II, with a budget twice the size, to be disbursed in the form of loans to support training, "develop programs with a European dimension," or programs "to help preserve and enhance cultural identity"[41] and further the transnational distribution of European programs.[42] The new proposal places greater emphasis on developing pan-European distribution networks to compete with the integrated distribution networks for Hollywood films, as suggested by the European audiovisual industry in evaluating EU policy in this sector.[43]

Though the revised initiative will address some of the weaknesses of fragmentation of production and distribution in Europe and attempts to circumvent the constraints and controversies of the broadcast quota through direct public investment, MEDIA II nevertheless continues to replicate and extend the problems of the television directive.[44] For instance, the conceptualization of MEDIA is nationalist, as is the television directive, calling for safeguards to "re-establish cultural identity in the Member States,"[45] "to help preserve and enhance cultural identity,"[46] or "promote Europe's cultural diversity."[47] As argued earlier, this type of policy rationale results only in establishing boundaries of exclusivity, further isolating various groups. Thus, remarkably, the initiative strengthens the position of large-scale international audiovisual producers and distributors who can demonstrate that their particular creative forms are the only ones that can travel across such boundaries. In the absence of a constitutionally grounded, public service right of citizens to knowledge, information, and participation in the public realm of the information society, only a liberalization logic can possibly prevail.

Moreover, the MEDIA II initiative explicitly promotes concentration and consolidation in European audiovisual production and distribution while simultaneously objecting to such a structure in the U.S. audiovisual industry. A policy that holds that "cooperation between European producers . . . should be encouraged and reinforced,"[48] thereby creating incentives for collaboration and integration, ultimately produces the same consequences as the television directive. The latter unleashed the forces of liberalization by allowing consolidation of distribution networks along transnational lines and crippling the legal authority of member states to regulate this growing form of domination of the public realm by a handful of broadcasters and program suppliers. Since only the international film producers and broadcasters were organized along transnational lines, they were able to take immediate advantage of the favorable regulatory environment. In the case of the new MEDIA II initiative, policies are undoubtedly tilted toward European-based consolidation through a program of direct subsidy, despite the irony of the charge that the U.S. "concentration in film distribution raises competition-policy questions."[49] Yet the policy support for European vertical integration is nevertheless still a support for an environment of proprietary consolidation in the audiovisual market.

Under liberalization, the competitive order tends to favor the largest property holders, national origin notwithstanding. Thus MEDIA II, as well as the television directive, is liable to generate powerful liberalization effects introduced paradoxically on grounds of cultural policy. Consequently, the real deficit remains in the participatory domain of societal and political need, suggesting diminished opportunities for further development in the European Union of Hegel's or Montesquieu's nonnationalist, nonmarket, public service model for public space and for the terms of common association among peoples and social groups.

Hence the debate over audiovisual policy is not a contest between dirigistes and liberals, that is, between interventionists and noninterventionists. Each of the three contending models of audiovisual regulation—nationalist, liberal, and public service—regards state action as central to the achievement of certain social and political ends. The real question is what kind of intervention is promoted by their distinctive and opposed formulations of the problems of an information society.

COMMUNICATION RIGHTS IN THE INFORMATION AGE: THE PROBLEM OF EUROPEAN POLITICAL RIGHTS

The second aspect of the information society in the EU I examine in this chapter is the development of constitutional guarantees of communication rights by which individuals can gain knowledge and information and can enlarge and use their capacities to transform their social contexts. The question to be addressed here is, in what sense do the communication rights of the information society in the European Union provide avenues for democratic transformation? The issue is central to the public service theory of democracy, which, as discussed earlier, stresses that the public grounds of reason (i.e., arguments concerning the common interest and general welfare and not derived from reasoning on private interests and preferences) are possible only in a public realm that institutionalizes universal guarantees of access to participation in collective political judgment.[50] First, I consider the problem of communication rights as a basis for regulating the multimedia network, using the U.S. standard as an international reference point, and second, I reveal how this standard defines the central dilemma in the development of communication, and therefore political, rights in the information society of the EU.

The right of expression in the United States is a negative right, with a twofold guarantee bestowed by the First Amendment to the U.S. Constitution: It applies to the transmission of information content as well as to its reception.[51] The negative guarantee of both transmitters' and receivers' rights establishes a restraint on or political barrier to state action and has the same function, according to J. Simon, in the area of political intervention as the antitrust laws have in the field of economic intervention, that is, to provide the implicit regulatory norm to the courts.[52] As interpreted in jurisprudence and in the policies of the state, the function of the constitutional constraint on government is to stimulate the "marketplace of ideas" by submitting ideas to the test of acceptability in the market.[53] At the outset, therefore, the right of communication in the United States is handicapped in three ways: First, it is a negative right and consequently does not allow the state to account in policy and law for conditions governing participation and communication practice, except by defaulting to governance by the market, thereby reinforcing the inequalities of existing conditions. The restraint on the state would thus logically privilege private social interests with the power to exercise the right.

Second, and this is obviously an aspect of the first, releasing the conditions of political practice to the market, that is, to the "natural" or private sphere, allows communication practice and access to public space to be determined by proprietary criteria alone. This eliminates from consideration other necessary standards of determination to maintain the liberties of a civil society, for example, criteria of content, ownership, and production representing the broad range of social and economic interests, or criteria of conditions conducive to deliberative rather than subjective and noncommercial rather than commercial expression.

Third, the default to the market, meaning the governance of public space by proprietary factors alone, sets the stage for the final absorption of public freedoms by the contractual and precedent-based common law tradition. This tradition is narrowly drawn to recognize economic rights of media owners operating in a market that regulates asset transfers and extractive agreements, and it is narrowly drawn to incorporate the precedent of prevailing proprietary holdings. Obviously, then, contractually centered common law prevents the judiciary and the state from considering citizens' rights to sufficiency of content and adequacy of access.

The inherent tendencies of the First Amendment are further compounded by the historical context of its institutionalization. Because its conceptual and political logic privileges prevailing conditions in the marketplace, the proprietary structures in communication benefit from the prohibition on government to guarantee structures of public space in the common interest. The result of this political limitation on communication rights has been particularly detrimental with respect to the rights of viewers and listeners in broadcasting.

The difficulty is illustrated in new information society laws and policies proposed in the United States under which the telecommunications industry is likely to gain the same First Amendment rights granted to broadcasters, giving them freedom from noncommercial obligations in the provision of video services.[54] Although the U.S. cable industry, fearing competition from telecommunications, initially opposed this move, the fear of competition is now irrelevant given regulatory signals favoring consolidation across industry sectors.[55] Thus the move away from the common carrier model of regulating telecommunications and cable, whereby a nondiscriminatory access obligation is imposed in order to further the political intent of the First Amendment for multiplying the diversity of information sources, is also being set aside by information liberalization.[56] If information society policies succeed in allowing communications industries, such as cable and telecommunications, to join the category of audiovisual producers, broadcasters, and the print media through reclassification from common carrier status to program content provider status, liberalization's political uses of the First Amendment to deny the application of political rights of communication to the structure of public space bring about a definitive end to the promise of modern democracy, which was to enable individuals to judge politically and play an active role in the creation and maintenance of their freedom in a self-managed democratic system.

The development of free expression rights under information liberalization in the European Union, although similar in some ways, is less determined and suggests the emergence of opposite tensions. In this chapter I have already demonstrated the extension of private dominion over the public realm in areas of information liberalization that affect audiovisual policy and intellectual property, which together indicate the transformation of freedom of information from the problem of participatory and information needs of individuals, into the ownership growth and control needs of private entities. Protestations of "human enrichment" nothwithstanding,[57] in terms of actual policy provisions, the regulatory boundaries for the multimedia age preclude development of the network for public applications at the same time that they give full license to development for commercial applications. It remains to be seen whether the emerging grounds for a legal foundation or constitutional guarantee of communication rights in the European Union offers the basis for a countertrend.

It would seem incongruous, at first glance, to associate the principle of liberty of expression with that of free flow of services. The first liberty has evolved in the domain of human rights, the second in that of free trade. The linking of the two in the European Union has occurred from the absorption of transnational communication regulation by Community trade law. Insofar as communication networks are now authorized at the Community level "to receive and impart information and ideas . . . regardless of frontiers," they constitute a support of liberty of expression.[58] And to the extent the EU legal and policy regime ensures the free circulation of information services and distribution structures, the principle of free trade has come to constitute an essential component of the liberty of expression.

The Commission's green paper on "television without frontiers," which preceded the television directive, first assessed the relationship between principles of free expression and free trade while attempting to develop a rationale for some link. The green paper concluded that human rights form an integral part of the Community's central mission to create a single market, and that far from this being a coincidental correspondence, relations between Article 59 on free movement of services in the Treaty of Rome and Article 10 of the European Convention for the Protection of Human Rights and Fundamental Freedoms (ECHR) constitute a source for enriched development of both human rights protection and the normative grounding of European trade law.[59] Defending the Community's authority in the area of public communications, the green paper maintains that liberty of expression and the market can mutually enrich each other, thus rendering more effective the principle of communication rights.

It is evident, then, that the EU has strategically identified free expression as a desirable legal foundation for trade in information services even while simultaneously applying competition and liberalization policies whose logic places actual control of expression within a consolidating proprietary sector. Further, in recent years, the European Commission, the European Parliament, and the European Court of Justice have each moved to assimilate human rights into the EU's constitutional foundations by adopting the ECHR, international human rights treaties and conventions, common constitutional principles drawn from member states, and precedents from human rights case law.[60]

At the EU level, therefore, the principal legal protection for communication rights derives from an appeal to Article 10 of the ECHR. This has been upheld in several cases in which the Court has emphasized "the pre-eminent role of the press in a State governed by the rule of law."[61] The role of public communication, according to the Court, is to be both "purveyor of information and public watchdog."[62] Indeed, the Court has gone further to emphasize that it is "incumbent on the press to impart information and ideas on matters of public interest. . . . Not only does the press have the task of imparting such information and ideas: the public also has a right to receive them. Were it otherwise, the press would be unable to play its vital role of 'public watchdog.'"[63]

Analyzing a recent decision of the European Court of Human Rights, P. Duffy observes that few expected it, the second major court in Europe, to allow parties to utilize Article 10 of the ECHR to redress grievances of monopoly, yet "this is exactly what happened successfully in *Informationsverein Lentia* [1994, 17 European Human Rights Report 93]."[64] In this 1994 case, Duffy notes the Court of Human Rights condemned the de facto monopoly enjoyed by the Austrian Broadcasting Company as contrary to Article 10:

> The court has frequently stressed the fundamental role of freedom of expression in a democratic society, in particular where, through the press, it serves to impart information and ideas of general interest, which the public is entitled to receive. Such an undertaking cannot be successfully accomplished unless it is grounded in the principle of pluralism, of which the state is the ultimate guarantor. This observation is especially valid in relation to audio-visual media, whose programmes are often broadcast very widely.[65]

The differences both in formulation and interpretation between Article 10 and the First Amendment are substantive in many respects. The most significant distinction, it is argued here, is that Article 10 of the ECHR grants a positive communication right and, to that extent, is a better protection than the First Amendment guarantee. It states: "Everyone has the right to freedom of expression. This right shall include freedom to hold opinions and to receive and impart information and ideas without interference by public authority and regardless of frontiers. This Article shall not prevent States from requiring the licensing of broadcasting, television or cinema enterprises."[66] By granting not only the rights of conscience and speech but also the right to "receive . . . information," Article 10 generates a positive claim that citizens can exercise on lawgivers to guarantee their rights against the competing claim of freedom from obligation asserted by information content providers. Thus European law confers a more extensive right to listeners, viewers, and users; it provides the state with a positive legal foundation for regulation with the aim of advancing a noncommercial common good and not merely proprietary and contractual goods; and it imposes a constitutional obligation on producers, providers, and distributors of communication content by holding these entities to standards of adequacy, sufficiency, and plurality of information forms in their exploitation of the public realm.

As I argued earlier, in order for a free society to maintain the conditions of public freedom and of political rights so that the common good and processes of collective will formation may be identified and arise by democratic means, it is essential for the body politic to consider how the right of individuals to receive information and to participate in the public arena, which is not reducible to the market, may be prescribed by law. The EU has succeeded in establishing that human rights, in particular, rights of communication, are now fused into the existing constitutional framework of the Union. The EU has also succeeded in legalizing a higher level of protection for freedom of information than is provided by the First Amendment. Yet two issues central to the actualization of the right remain undetermined.

First, the very fact of the legal guarantee of liberty of expression existing in conjunction with the guarantee of market freedoms says very little, if anything. As is evident in the case of the United States, the institutionalization of communication rights within liberalism's competitive order effectively effaces the political—though not the private/subjective—right of individual citizens and transfers the protection to proprietors of the public realm. Thus the question that ought to be asked, it seems, is not if the right is codified but rather, what is its political relation to other rights? No legal code of free expression can answer the question of how the state in a specific historical context, confronting a particular social order, should act politically. A code gives an idea of the responsibility of the state to help members of a political association realize their citizenship in a certain way, as well as some indication of how the character of the democratic state and citizens' relationship to it is best interpreted; and it also clarifies the legal grounds on which a democratic conception of social and political life differs from a nondemocratic conception.

However, the question of what actions ought to be taken to further a democratic transformation of social life and create relations of public freedom (i.e., deliberative relations) between citizens can be answered only by the extent to which state action or public policy can secure a public space for information, knowledge, deliberation, and judgment. Members of political society have to arrive at common decisions, not just hold private opinions, and no free expression code can provide the political knowledge and experience that is derived from the conditions and experience of actual political participation. This requires that public space be reserved for noncommercial, associative development even though it cannot be forbidden to proprietary expansion and commercial development.

One of the issues for the European Union to resolve, therefore, is whether the principle of free trade is constitutionally higher or lower than the principle of liberty of expression. If free trade is higher than the communication right, the latter's status is merely formal and negative as in the United

States, notwithstanding its more extensive positive formulation in Article 10 of the ECHR. Only when proprietary freedoms of the market are subordinated to the higher principle of a political right to speech and reception of information can the state undertake the democratic development of the public sphere. Fusing the two classes of rights into an undifferentiated group, as the television directive[67] attempts to do, works to the disadvantage of the communication rights of individuals because their political claim to this liberty can be absorbed into the communication industry claim of freedom from content regulation under the same rights.

So far I have demonstrated that liberalization's theory of property can overwhelm all other human rights. Proprietary and contractual freedoms achieve greater authority from the assimilation of the communication right, thus assigning their interests a higher constitutional status in prescribing the responsibility of the state. The Union, therefore, would need to establish which of the two rights is a first principle before the positive communication right of Article 10 of the ECHR could be realized and embodied in the institutional organization of the EU.

The second issue determining actualization of the communication right in the Community relates to the restructuring of the role of the state under information liberalization. Regardless of the strongest constitutional framework or judicial opinion, if state action has been reordered to function as a central mechanism in proprietary growth and consolidation, the possibility for the state to act upon alternative grounds and by other means is already seriously limited. The policy architecture of the information society, as shown in this chapter, imposes a fundamental limitation, not on the power of the state to act but on the form of its intervention. Thus it was seen that Community policy has been forced to ignore alternative grounds of regulation, such as public service obligations to set noncommercial, broadly representative program content production and distribution standards, and the public interest in moral rights of authors to copyright protections on the information superhighway.

The separation of a political sphere composed of procedural voting rights and representative-legislative conditions—where public freedoms can, at best, be only hypothetical—from the sphere of communication structures and practices negates the public realm as a space for universalism, freedom, equality, and justice—the components of a public service paradigm—thus making it far easier for communication structures to be overwhelmed by particularism, atomism, subjectivity, inequality, natural law, and property dominion.

No level of constitutional protection for political rights of speech, thought, and knowledge can have significant effect or meaning, other than as formal code, unless the conception and structure of the civil state can account for the political organization of its role on those terms. A democratic constitution emphasizing political rights and common interest institutionalized on grounds of private proprietary interests and of contract by the actions of a delimited liberal state will have just as much effect as the absence of a constitution would from the outset. This is most vividly illustrated in the example of the United States and in the liberalization logic of the European Union where neither the tradition of public constitutional law nor that of positive communication rights seem to influence the actual provisions of policy, due to the transformation of the state by the competitive order of information liberalization and its underlying theory of property.

CONCLUSION

In this chapter I attempted to show that at least three alternative legal and normative foundations for communication policy are currently available within the European Union: First, there exists the constitutional orientation of public law; second, the adoption of human rights, especially communication rights, within the legal framework of the union has been accomplished at all institutional levels; and third, a republican theory of public service prevails in several member states, though often in conjunction with nationalist conceptions of state and society.

Given these conditions, it should be possible to reformulate the policies of communication to facilitate rights of viewers and listeners to receive information and ideas. That is to say, if communication policies simply embodied the communications rights of citizens, the constitutional liberty of expression would most likely be ensured. But if such policies are regarded as mechanisms of a particular competitive order or proprietary enlargement, the communication right would be imprisoned in the formal principle of the constitution but not embodied in the constitution of society. Even more serious, the analysis here demonstrates that the precipitous decline of communications rights of listeners, viewers, and users of modern information networks and services points to the possibility of the systematic destruction of political rights of speech, action, and participation (the "principle of publicity") in the information age, and hence the inevitable passing of public service and its concept of public liberty from the promise of modern democracy.

This is why the ECHR's positive right to receive information and be informed could, if applied in European law, become the basis for an extraordinary advancement in the democratization of the public realm. Yet it remains only a formal right so long as the provisions of public policy are not constituted by its terms, or so long as the Community as a network of law-making institutions is reconstituted by the competitive order of information liberalization to function as guarantor of economic consolidation.

In the United States, where the positive right does not exist even as formal principle, there are no limitations on the processes of dismantling most barriers to proprietary extension through rationales of competition and individual interest. Treating policies and laws of public space as a fundamental political question rather than as an economic, competitive, technological, or cultural question remains the only approach to the information society that is likely to bring about the actualization of democracy in modernity.

Given the prevalence of negative political rights and the tradition of common law, and the absence of Montesquieu's theory of public service or the universalism of general welfare embodied in the law, this potential is no longer a historical possibility for development of the information society in the United States. It is, however, for the European Union, provided the U.S. model of information liberalization has not already reconstituted the three crucial institutions of positive rights, public law, and public service into a facade for unaccountable governance of the public sphere by liberalism's theory of property.

The IGC process may become one of the most significant turning points in the reform and historical development of democracy. Universality of thought and law embodied in republican models of public service are easily destroyed by unquestioned hegemonic logics, be they authoritarian collectivism or oligarchic liberalism. If the opportunity for serious examination of the constitution of the public realm is marginalized in the IGC agenda, the possibility for conceiving participatory structures may indeed be lost to humankind as political society disappears under the alienation of reason and the evolution of nationalist and proprietary absolutism.

NOTES

1. Commission of the European Communities, "Conclusions of Jacques Santer," chair of the G-7 Ministerial Conference on the Information Society, Brussels, February 25–26 (Brussels: Office of the President of the European Commission, 1995).

2. On dirigisme, see R. Collins, "Unity in Diversity? The European Single Market in Broadcasting and the Audiovisual, 1982–92," *Journal of Common Market Studies* 32, no. 1 (1994), pp. 89–102; on liberalism, see K. Morgan, "Telecom Strategies in Britain and France: The Scope and Limits of Neo-liberalism and Dirigisme," in M. Sharp and P. Holmes, eds., *Strategies for New Technology* (London: Philip Allan, 1989), pp. 19–55.

3. Shalini Venturelli, "Freedom and Its Mystification: The Political Thought of Public Space," in S. Braman and A. Sreberny-Mohammadi, eds., *Globalization, Communication, and the Transnational Public Sphere* (Cresskill, N.J.: Hampton Press, 1995), pp. 143–203.

4. Charles Montesquieu, *The Spirit of the Laws*, trans. and ed. A. M. Cohler et al. (1748; reprint, Cambridge: Cambridge University Press, 1989); G.W.F. Hegel, *The Philosophy of Right,* trans. T. M. Knox (1821; reprint, Oxford: Oxford University Press, 1952), pp. 122–155.

5. R. David and C. J. Spinosi, *Les grands systèmes de droit contemporains* (Padova, Italy: CEDAM, 1973); D. Lasok and P. A. Stone, *Conflict of Laws in the European Community* (Abingdon, U.K.: Professional Books, 1987); C. Taylor, "Modes of Civil Society," *Public Culture* 3, no. 1 (1990), pp. 95–118.

6. On the Treaty of Rome, see Commission of the European Communities, "Treaty Establishing the European Community (signed in Rome on March 25, 1957)," in *European Union: Selected Instruments Taken from the Treaties, book I, vol. I* (Luxembourg: Office for Official Publications of the European Communities, 1993), pp. 91–669; on the Maastricht Treaty, see "Treaty on European Union (signed in Maastricht on February 7, 1992)," in *European Union: Selected Instruments Taken from the Treaties, book I, vol. I* (Luxembourg: Office for Official Publications of the European Communities, 1993), pp. 11–89.

7. P. Bauby and J. Boual, *Pour un citoyenneté Européenne: Quels services publics?* (Paris: Les Éditions de l' Atelier, 1994), p. 11.

8. Montesquieu, *Spirit of the Laws,* pt. 1, bk. 5, chap. 5, pp. 44–47.

9. Ibid., p. 45.

10. Alexis de Tocqueville, *Democracy in America,* 2 vols., ed. P. Bradley (1834–40; reprint, New York: Vintage, 1990).

11. John Locke, *Two Treatises of Government* (1690; reprint, New York: Cambridge University Press, 1960).

12. On the evolution of "social citizenship" in Europe, see R. Dahrendorf, "The Changing Quality of Citizenship," in B. van Steenbergen, ed., *The Condition of Citizenship* (London: Sage, 1994), pp. 10–19; Dahrendorf, *The Modern Social Contract: An Essay on the Politics of Liberty* (London: Weidenfeld and Nicolson, 1988); K. Dyson, *The State Tradition in Western Europe* (Oxford: Martin Robertson, 1980); and E. Meehan, *Citizenship and the European Community* (London: Sage, 1993).

13. For a more detailed discussion, see Venturelli, "Freedom and Its Mystification."

14. For a study of Johann Herder's thought, see R. T. Clark, *Herder: His Life and Thought* (Berkeley: University of California Press, 1955). On the conceptual origins of modern nationalism, see B. Anderson, *Imagined Communities* (London: Verso, 1983); E. Gellner, *Nations and Nationalism* (Oxford: Basil Blackwell, 1983); and C. Taylor, *Hegel and Modern Society* (Cambridge: Cambridge University Press, 1979).

15. Clark, *Herder;* Taylor, *Hegel and Modern Society.*

16. European Parliament, *Report on the European Community's Film and Television Industry* (the De Vries Report), January 9, 1989, PE 119.192/final, p. 8.

17. Commission of the European Communities, "Television Without Frontiers," Green Paper on the Establishment of the Common Market for Broadcasting, Especially by Satellite and Cable, COM (84) 300 final, 1984, p. 28.

18. Commission of the European Communities, "The Challenges and Ways Forward into the 21st Century," White Paper on Growth, Competitiveness, and Employment (the "Delors White Paper"), COM (93) 700 final, 1993, p. 120.

19. European Parliament, "Jacques Delors' Address to the Opening of the European Parliament," Commission Programme for 1985, Debates of the European Parliament, March 12, 1985, p. 64.

20. Commission of the European Communities, *The Audio-visual Media in the Single European Market* (Luxembourg: Office for Official Publications of the European Communities, 1988), p. 52.

21. Ibid., p. 49.

22. On European cultural policy, see Commission of the European Communities,

The European Community Policy in the Audio-visual Field (Luxembourg: Office for Official Publications of the European Communities, 1990), p. 52; see also K. Robins and D. Morley, "What Kind of Identity for Europe?" *Intermedia* 20, nos. 4–5 (1992), pp. 23–24; and R. Collins, "Unity in Diversity?"

23. Commission of the European Communities, "Treaty on European Union," Article 128, Title IX, p. 89 (emphasis added).

24. On cultural industries and social cohesion, see Commission of the European Communities, "Challenges and Ways Forward," pp. 120–121; on economic growth, see Commission of the European Communities, "Europe and the Global Information Society," Bangemann Task Force Report to the European Council, *Cordis*, Supplement 2 (Brussels: European Commission, DG XIII/D-2, July 15, 1994), pp. 4–31, especially pp. 11–14.

25. D. Bell, *The Coming of Post-Industrial Society* (New York: Basic Books, 1973).

26. Commission of the European Communities, *Report by the Think-tank on the Audiovisual Policy in the European Union* (Luxembourg: Office for Official Publications of the European Communities, March 1994), p. 17.

27. Gellner, *Nations and Nationalism*; Herder is cited in Clark, *Herder*.

28. For Delors's speeches, see European Parliament, "Jacques Delors' Address"; for policy proposals, see Commission of the European Communities, "Challenges and Ways Forward."

29. Commission of the European Communities, "Treaty Establishing the European Community."

30. Commission of the European Communities, "Council Directive of 3 October 1989 on the Coordination of Certain Provisions Laid Down by Law, Regulation or Administrative Action in Member States Concerning the Pursuit of Television Broadcasting Activities," 89/552/EEC; OJL 298/23, 17.10.89

31. Commission of the European Communities, "Television Without Frontiers," p. 6.

32. Interview with EU negotiator in the GATT for the audiovisual sector, DGI in the European Commission, May 1994.

33. K.L. Wilkins, "Television Without Frontiers: An EEC Broadcasting Premiere," *Boston College International and Comparative Law Review* 14 (winter 1991), pp. 195–211.

34. Commission of the European Communities, "Council Directive of 3 October 1989."

35. P. Rousseau (member of the French CSA), "Will Economic Power Replace Political Power?" in C. Contamine and M. van Dusseldorp, eds., *Towards the Digital Revolution*, published proceedings of the Sixth European Television and Film Forum, Liège, Belgium, November 10–12, 1994 (Düsseldorf, Germany: European Institute for the Media, 1995), pp. 127–130; E. May, "Il était une loi . . . ," *Audiovisuel*, no. 28 (February 1994), pp. 2-6; and S. Chalvon-Demersay and D. Pasquier, "In the Name of the Audience," *Reseaux: French Journal of Communication* 1, 1 (1993), pp. 27–28.

36. Commission of the European Communities, *Report by the Think-tank*.

37. Commission of the European Communities, *MEDIA Guide for the Audiovisual Industry,* 2nd ed. (Brussels: DGX, Commission of the European Communities, 1991); Commission of the European Communities, "Council Decision Concerning the Implementation of an Action Programme to Promote the Development of the European Audiovisual Industry (MEDIA), 1991–1995," December 31, 1990, OJL 380/37, 31.12.90; Commission of the European Communities, "Commission Communication to the Council: Action Programme to Promote the Development of

the European Audiovisual Industry, 'MEDIA,' 1991–1995," May 4, 1990, COM (90) 132 final. On supporting indigenous cultural forms, see Commission of the European Communities, *MEDIA Guide for the Audiovisual Industry*, 10th ed. (Brussels: DGX, Commission of the European Communities, June 1994); and *European Report*, "Commission Unveils MEDIA II and Calls for Financial Muscle," no. 2015 (February 11, 1995), pp. 4–5.

38. J. Servaes, "Europe 1992: The Audiovisual Challenge," *Gazette* 49, nos. 1–2 (1992), pp. 75–97; Robins and Morley, "What Kind of Identity?"

39. Commission of the European Communities, *MEDIA Guide*, 2nd ed.; Commission of the European Communities, "Council Decision Concerning MEDIA."

40. See suggestions in Commission of the European Communities, *Report by the Think-tank;* Commission of the European Communities, "Green Paper on Strategy Options to Strengthen the European Programme Industry in the Context of the Audiovisual Policy of the European Union" (Luxembourg: Office for Official Publications of the European Communities, April 7, 1994).

41. Commission of the European Communities, "Opinion on the Proposal for a Council Decision Amending Council Decision 90/68/EEC Concerning the Implementation of the Action Programme to Promote the Development of the European Audiovisual Industry, MEDIA, 1991–1995," 94/C 148/02 (OJL No C 148/3 30.5.94), 1994, section 1.2.

42. Ibid., section 3.4.

43. Commission of the European Communities, *Report by the Think-tank*.

44. Commission of the European Communities, "Council Decision of 3 October 1989."

45. Commission of the European Communities, "Opinion on the Proposal," section 2.2.

46. Ibid., section 1.2.

47. Ibid., section 2.3.

48. Ibid., section 2.4.

49. Ibid., section 1.2.

50. Montesquieu, *Spirit of the Laws;* Hegel, *Philosophy of Right*.

51. The First Amendment to the U.S. Constitution reads as follows:

Congress shall make no law respecting an establishment of religion, or prohibiting the free exercise thereof; or abridging the freedom of speech, or of the press; or the right of the people peaceably to assemble, and to petition the Government for a redress of grievances.

On the First Amendment, see R. A. Smolla, *Free Speech in an Open Society* (New York: Vintage Books, 1992); and K. R. Middleton and B. F. Chamberlin, *The Law of Public Communication* (New York: Longman, 1988).

52. J. Simon, *L'esprit des règles: Réseauz et réglementation aux États Unis: Cable, électricité, télécommunications* (Paris: L'Harmattan, 1991).

53. Smolla, *Free Speech;* Simon, *L'esprit des régles*.

54. U.S. Congress, Senate, *Proposed Telecommunications Deregulation Bill*, 104th Congress, 1st sess., S.R. 652 (1995); U.S. Government, Information Infrastructure Task Force, *Global Information Infrastructure: Agenda for Cooperation* (Washington, D.C.: U.S. Government Printing Office, February 1995).

55. For a summary of conflicting industry positions over new legislation, see U.S. Congress, "The Information Superhighway and the National Information Infrastruc-

ture (NII)," *CRS Report for Congress* (Washington, D.C.: Congressional Research Service, Library of Congress, March 22, 1994).

56. For a discussion of the common carrier rule obligation, see H. Geller, "1995–2005: Regulatory Reform for Principal Electronic Media," position paper (Washington, D.C., Annenberg Washington Program, 1994); and R. B. Horwitz, *The Irony of Regulatory Reform* (Oxford: Oxford University Press, 1989).

57. Commission of the European Communities, "Conclusions of Jacques Santer," p. 1.

58. "European Convention for the Protection of Human Rights and Fundamental Freedoms, Rome, November 4, 1950," in *European Convention on Human Rights: Collected Texts* (Dordrecht, The Netherlands: Martinus Nijhoff, 1987), Article 10, para. 1. In later citations this will be referred to as "ECHR."

59. Commission of the European Communities, "Television Without Frontiers"; Commission of the European Communities, "Council Directive of 3 October 1989"; Commission of the European Communities, "Treaty Establishing the European Community"; "ECHR," Article 10.

60. See Commission of the European Communities, *The European Community and Human Rights* (Luxembourg: Office for Official Publications of the European Communities, October 1992); European Parliament, *Human Rights and the European Community: Nationality and Citizenship,* report for the European Parliament, October 1989; and European Parliament, *Human Rights and the European Community: Conference Acts* (Strasbourg, November 1989).

61. *Castells v. Spain,* judgment of April 23, 1992, Series A, no. 236, para. 43.

62. *Ligens v. Austria,* judgment of July 8, 1986, Series A, no. 103, para. 42.

63. *The Observer and Guardian v. the UK,* judgment of November 26, 1991, Series A, no. 216, para. 59(b).

64. Case cited in P. Duffy, "European Briefing," *Solicitor's Journal* 139, no. 4 (1994), p. 90.

65. European Court of Human Rights opinion, quoted in ibid.

66. "ECHR," Article 10, para. 1.

67. Council of the European Communities, "Council Directive of 3 October 1989."

5

Social Democracy in One Continent? Alternatives to a Neoliberal Europe

Alan W. Cafruny

During the last twenty-five years Western European business has become highly centralized and concentrated. It has now become commonplace to refer to a Western European "transnational economy,"[1] and some observers cited the emergence of a unified European "business elite" or even an embryonic "transnational capitalist class."[2] By contrast, the European Left parties and labor movements remained fragmented and national in outlook. Even in Germany, where Social Democratic support for the European Union (EU) has been relatively strong, attempts to develop closer transnational linkages in the form of a European Socialist movement have had a "ritual, obligatory quality."[3] Until recently, transnational trade union cooperation has been nominal and European labor has been "virtually inert and often helpless."[4] Although the Socialists now form the largest party group within the European Parliament (EP), that body continues to lack power and legitimacy despite the modest reforms of the Maastricht Treaty.

The dramatic regional and global changes since 1989 have, however, provoked a new interest in the EU among Europe's left-wing parties and trade unions. The breakup of the Soviet Union and the attendant marginalization of Western European Communist parties virtually eliminated residual hostility to the EU arising from the Cold War. At the same time, the liberalization of trade and finance and the internationalization of production deepened skepticism concerning the effectiveness of national planning. Thus, there is now considerable interest in the EU as a potential means of overcoming the problems that globalization poses for "social democracy in one country."

In this chapter I explore the constraints and opportunities that the EU represents for the European Left. The constraints of Europe's neoliberal path to integration have received a great deal of attention and are indeed formidable. They arise from fundamental differences in national systems of industrial relations, including collective bargaining practices, labor productivity, and wage differentials.[5] The intergovernmental foundations of the emerging constitutional process have also tended to insulate the process of market creation from that of social harmonization. The Social Action Programme of the early

109

1970s was limited to the promotion of equal opportunity and issues of health and safety; the "social dimension" of the late 1980s and early 1990s is essentially voluntaristic.[6]

Yet, the contradictions of neoliberalism also open up new possibilities for the Left. The EU serves as an important symbolic component of political legitimation at the national level. More tangibly, it is a crucial diplomatic instrument through which the member states attempt to counteract the destabilizing influences of U.S. foreign economic policy. If the Union is to proceed beyond the unstable compromise of the Maastricht Treaty and continue to fulfill these functions, then Europe will be compelled to reconstruct at the supranational level many of the national redistributive policies, protective mechanisms, and social commitments that have been steadily eroded during the last two decades. Such a reconstructive process, if it is to occur, is not likely to arise from a neofunctionalist logic of spillover but rather on the basis of political mobilization and the establishment of novel forms of social consensus and legitimation.

In the first section of this chapter I situate the crisis of European social democracy within the context of the internationalization of production and capital. The constraints on and opportunities for the Left result not only from this process of internationalization, but also, as I indicate in the section on Europe and the dollar, from the chronic problems for Europe that result from U.S. foreign economic policy. In the third section I discuss the failure of European national strategies in light of these problems, focusing on the British and French experiences. The limitations of national strategy have provided the motive for the establishment of a European monetary zone of stability in the form of a European currency. However, as I argue in the final section, such a zone is unlikely to succeed unless it is accompanied by much stronger forms of social and regional solidarity.

EUROPE AND THE CRISIS OF SOCIAL DEMOCRACY

The contemporary paralysis of the Left is puzzling when viewed in the context of the obvious failure of orthodox market strategies to restore Europe's competitiveness and prosperity. The fortunes of the Left have declined, ironically, in the teeth of a "permanent recession," in which at the end of 1995 more than 10 percent (20 million) of workers were officially unemployed in the EU. Nevertheless, Communist parties are disintegrating or becoming marginalized. Social democracy is slowly decomposing, albeit toward a more uncertain end. To be sure, socialist parties cling tenuously to power or pieces of it, but all have greatly reduced their distinctive commitments to full employment, redistribution of income, and workplace democracy.

Even in the former citadels of institutionalized corporatism, such as

Germany and Sweden, there is growing agreement across the political spectrum that the social market is becoming obsolete. Constrained by the internationalization of finance and production and demoralized by the failure of state-led economic development in Eastern Europe, the Left now participates actively—if not enthusiastically—in a public discourse that frames questions of social justice in terms of what the market will bear. The locus of economic decisionmaking appears to be passing from parliaments to national central banks and to the nascent European Central Bank (ECB).

Alternatives for the Left

A decade ago most leading observers of European social democracy rejected the proposition that increases in global economic interdependence had rendered national economic planning ineffective. Fritz Scharpf, for example, emphasized the salience of continuing variations in performance among national economies. The case for the continuing effectiveness of state intervention could be disproved, he believed, "only if the economies of all the Western industrial countries had run the same course and their policies had produced the same results."[7] In principle, popular Social Democratic governments, buttressed by strong trade unions and corporatist networks, could still defend the achievements of the postwar settlement even in an unfavorable international conjuncture. Peter Katzenstein, Geoffrey Garrett, and Peter Lange convincingly argue along similar lines based on evidence from the mid-1970s to mid-1980s.[8] Yet from the perspective of the mid-1990s, as unemployment rates converge within the context of a general trend toward privatization and liberalization, the burden of proof appears to be shifting to those who argue that the destinies of national economies are shaped fundamentally from within and not from without.[9]

A comprehensive explanation for the decline of social democracy would of course need to go beyond the problem of the world economy and address a range of factors, including changes in the nature of work and the shrinking of the industrial working class, the entry of women into the economy, age stratification, immigration, and the cluster of "new politics" issues that have emerged with the decline of the Fordist order.[10] Yet given the centrality of internationalization to the breakdown of the postwar social and political settlement, and especially in the conspicuous failures of Keynesian policies in Britain (1975–1976) and France (1981–1983), the discussion of alternatives for the European Left must take as its starting point the constraints imposed by the logic of an open world economy and the realities of transnational monetary conflicts.

The first and perhaps least fashionable option for Social Democrats is to reject the thesis that "social democracy in one country" has in fact been rendered obsolete by the internationalization of production and capital. A

feasible economic nationalist strategy—at least for Europe's larger nations—
would entail rejecting the fiscal and monetary constraints imposed by fixed
exchange rates or, under the terms of the Maastricht Treaty, a single currency. The freedom to devalue, to impose capital controls, and to erect protectionist barriers would make it possible to return to Keynesian policies of full
employment. A diminishing number of voices on the Left—joined by some
on the Right—argue that economic nationalism has never been pursued with
sufficient strength and commitment.[11] Even in the crucial cases of Britain in
1975–1976 and France in 1981–1983, it might be argued, the problem was
not a qualitatively higher degree of international capital mobility but rather a
deeper political crisis of social democracy: the inability or unwillingness of
party leadership to pursue a strategy of mass mobilization when faced with
the resistance of big business. As Frances Fox Piven notes, the phenomenon
of globalization has tended to promote a certain "economism" on the Left:

> Capital exit is clearly not new, and in real terms globalization may not be
> the main reality. But post-industrial changes, including internationalism,
> have prepared the way for a much more aggressive capitalist class politics.
> Put another way, capital is pyramiding the leverage gained by expanded exit
> opportunities, or perhaps the leverage gained merely by the spectre of
> expanded opportunities, in a series of vigorous political campaigns.[12]

Alternatively, the Left might seek to salvage its electoral fortunes by
turning away from distinctive class and institutional commitments and
redefining itself in liberal democratic terms. The Left would defend human
rights of "citizens" rather than "workers." With the passing of Fordist forms
of industrial organization and labor and the rise of postindustrial values, the
traditional working class is neither large enough nor sufficiently homogeneous to support, on its own, a party of government. The Socialist era has
passed, but the Left still has an important role to play in fostering equal
opportunity and redistributive justice.[13]

The third option, that of a Social Democratic European Union, has
received a great deal of attention and not a little skepticism. After all, the dramatic advances in integration over the last decade have reinforced the power
of global capital at the expense of trade unions and socialist parties. As
Wolfgang Streeck and Philippe Schmitter noted with respect to the Single
European Act (SEA):

> For some time to come, whatever will occupy the place of the supranation-
> al Single European State governing the Single European Market, will like-
> ly resemble a pre–New Deal liberal state, with, in Marshall's terms: a high
> level of civil rights . . . a low level of political rights . . . an even lower level
> of social rights . . . [and] the almost complete absence of a European system
> of industrial citizenship.[14]

Moreover, even as Social Democrats turn to Brussels, some segments of European labor have become increasingly nationalistic and hostile to further integration, as exemplified in France during the Maastricht Treaty referendum of 1992 and, most recently, in the transportation strikes of December 1995.[15] Nevertheless, the EU has reached a critical stage in its development that opens up new possibilities for social democracy: The neoliberal strategy by which higher levels of integration have been achieved would appear to have reached a point of exhaustion. In the absence of a strong social dimension, EU policy will not be able to overcome the chronic problems of uneven development and regional and structural unemployment and thereby defuse growing nationalist tensions. It is also unlikely to counteract the threats to its unity arising from U.S. monetary policy.

EUROPE AND THE DOLLAR

The norms and rules of the post–World War II international economic order were contradictory because they sought to express simultaneously the social logic of the postwar settlement and U.S. insistence on orthodox fiscal and monetary policies. The architects of the Bretton Woods system sought to promote domestic stability and full employment while demanding that deficit countries bear the burden of adjustment. Hence, in practice the system could function only as long as the United States remained powerful enough to circumvent the norms by providing a constant supply of liquidity and as long as international capital flows remained relatively low in proportion to the gross national product (GNP) of major actors, especially the United States. Despite, or perhaps because of, the constraints imposed on the International Monetary Fund (IMF), the United States unilaterally supplied Europe with liquidity through foreign investment, defense spending, and aid. In the language of public choice, the United States provided a market for distress goods, acted as a lender of last resort, and served as steward of the world's currencies.[16]

Thus the system was built on a fundamental contradiction: U.S. balance of payments deficits provided the world with liquidity, yet as the supply of dollars outraced existing gold stocks, the growing "dollar overhang" undermined confidence in the dollar. As Robert Triffin argues, a "long run shortage of liquidity," with serious deflationary consequences, would result from either the attempts of the United States to equilibrate its balance of payments or the refusal by Europe and Japan "to pile up further IOUs from them." However, the continuation of balance of payments deficits would lead to severe inflation if surplus countries were "called upon to finance indefinitely U.S. deficits through unpredictable accumulations of dollar claims."[17]

The decision to decouple the dollar from gold in 1971 as the U.S. economy weakened did not reflect the development of a more pluralistic system of international economic relations, as assumed by many U.S. scholars, but rather the more predatory use of power by the United States as policies began to reflect more narrowly defined national objectives and interests.[18] These policies not only imposed short-term economic costs on Europe, as with high interest rates during most of the 1980s, but also tended to undermine the class compromises that had emerged throughout Western Europe.

During the postwar boom Western European countries "internalized" U.S. leadership as they relied on both fixed exchange rates to provide an anchor for the price system and on external adjustment to underwrite Keynesian strategies. In France, the ability to devalue without serious cost helped to create what Michael Loriaux calls the "overdraft economy," in which firms were able to rely on unlimited credit and in which internal adjustment was unnecessary.[19] The transition to floating exchange rates eliminated these opportunities and led to the policies of financial liberalization adopted in 1983 by the Socialist government. In Norway and Sweden, similarly, the transition to floating rates ultimately made it more difficult to contain inflation.[20]

The shift to floating rates was accompanied by the progressive deregulation of national and international finance through a series of key decisions and nondecisions that reflected U.S. power and preferences, now no longer constrained by fixed exchange rates. Among the most important deregulatory reforms were Britain's reopening of the City of London and the growth of the Eurodollar market; added incentives for U.S. banks to conduct external operations as a result of the interest equalization tax of 1964; and the International Banking Act of 1980, which allowed U.S. banks parity with U.S. subsidiaries of foreign banks. The Carter and Reagan administrations effectively lifted controls on interstate banking. The Deregulation and Monetary Control Act of 1980 and the Garn–St. Germain Act allowed banks to expand beyond their traditional spheres into property development, insurance, and mortgages.[21]

As Susan Strange notes, the progressive deregulation of finance and the consolidation of the "structural power of capital" were generally facilitated by technological developments but resulted in "certain specific political decisions or non-decisions taken by the leading financial authorities, especially in the United States."[22] These decisions flowed from a logic that was as much political as economic or technological; the size and power of the U.S. economy made it possible—in the context of floating exchange rates—to pursue economic policies according to the logic of domestic politics, a privilege that no single European country enjoys. Yet actions taken by the Federal Reserve Board for largely domestic reasons have had a great impact on Europe, provoking thus far only weak and ultimately ineffective attempts to establish a rival zone of monetary stability.

The primary rationale offered for floating exchange rates was that they would relieve countries from having to pursue domestic austerity in order to fulfill international obligations. In principle, a country seeking to maintain full employment could inflate its domestic economy without having to defend the existing exchange rate by buying its own currency. Instead, the falling currency would boost exports, further stimulating growth. As noted above with respect to France, Norway, and Sweden, the problem was that floating exchange rates and international capital mobility made it increasingly difficult to reflate by any means. By 1990, the Eurodollar market contained funds equal to the United States' yearly gross domestic product (GDP). The Bank of International Settlements estimates that the exchange of one currency for another now accounts for $640 billion in transactions per day, less than 10 percent of which bears any relation to normal commercial transactions.[23] Any attempt to reflate by reducing interest rates causes higher inflation, increases the trade deficit, and provokes capital flight. The situation calls for international cooperation, but the United States and Europe have adopted very different definitions of cooperation.

U.S. policy during the late 1970s and 1980s greatly exacerbated Europe's problems. The Carter administration's attempts to stimulate growth led initially to low interest rates and a depreciating dollar. By 1980, however, U.S. inflation was in double digits, and speculation against the dollar mounted after 1978. The decline of the dollar and resulting global inflation weakened Europe's attempts to recover from the recession by increasing exports. The Franco-German bid for a stronger European Monetary System (EMS) collapsed in 1979 as European currencies appreciated at different rates and a coordinated policy was not possible. As the United States complained about free riding, the Europeans accused the United States of aggravating global inflation.

Under President Ronald Reagan, the United States dramatically reversed course, raising interest rates to unprecedented levels in order to quell inflation. This policy had its desired effect but at a cost of deep global recession. At the same time as U.S. interest rates soared the U.S. trade deficit ballooned and capital poured in from Europe and Japan.[24] Japan benefited greatly from the export stimulus to the United States; the Europeans gained much less. The Plaza deal of 1985 reduced the value of the dollar by 10 percent and central banks coordinated their support of the dollar, which gave some relief to the Europeans. By this time, it was possible to speak of a tacit U.S.-Japanese alliance against Europe.[25] Both countries grew more rapidly than the Europeans; in Europe, job creation lagged and productivity growth trailed well behind the U.S. and Japanese standards. Yet European monetary coordination once again foundered on intra-European differences. This time neither Britain nor Italy could tolerate the rise of the deutsche mark (DM), and once again the EMS came unglued. In September 1992 the central banks of Italy,

Spain, Finland, and Britain spent DM24 billion in an unsuccessful attempt to maintain the value of the lira and another £10 billion to prop up the pound. Even a five-point increase in interest rates could not save the pound, and eventually the EMS unraveled.[26] As Susan Strange observes, "the power to maintain order had been lost, but not so much to other states so much as to market forces liberated by the conscious decision of the United States and Britain."[27]

THE LIMITATIONS OF NATIONAL POLICIES IN WESTERN EUROPE

Since the mid-1970s European countries have responded both individually and collectively to the trend toward financial integration and deregulation. A central theme in European politics has been the relationship between national autonomy and global financial deregulation. The failure of individual responses has encouraged the countries of continental Europe (and Japan) to follow, albeit reluctantly, the Anglo-American lead and in many cases surpass it. The experiences of Britain in 1975–1976 and France in 1981–1983 appeared to offer decisive proof that national Keynesian strategies were no longer possible and that international financial pressures constituted the single most important barrier to full employment. In each case, reflationary policies, although modest in scope, invited massive speculative attacks on the currency. Socialist governments, however, ultimately rejected the option of capital controls, preferring to accept austerity policies as formally required by the IMF in the case of Britain, and informally demanded by international capital markets, in the French case.

The British *Labour Programme 1974* promised to implement policies of full employment and the redistribution of income and wealth. The centerpiece of the strategy, the National Enterprise Board, would extend public ownership and provide leverage for tripartite negotiations or "sector planning agreements." In exchange for wage restraint, the Labour Party promised expansionary public financing, basing its hopes on increased oil revenues to balance the external trade account. By mid-1975, however, a balance of payments crisis resulted as reflation caused a surge in imports and a run on the pound. Pressed by central bankers, including the IMF and his own Bank of England, Prime Minister Harold Wilson imposed an austerity program, rejecting the alternative of capital and import controls.[28]

The fate of the French Socialists in 1981–1983 was very similar. In the French version of the Alternative Economic Strategy, President François Mitterrand implemented a *programme commun* based on extensive nationalization, Keynesian fiscal stimulus, and modest expansion of the money supply. As with the British experience, however, the program was pursued in the teeth of a worldwide recession and was greatly influenced by France's desire to remain within the EMS. Once again, the government retreated in the face of speculative attacks. In the French case, the European dimension was central. Whereas Britain looked unsuccessfully to the United States for support, France expected its European partners to reflate in response to its growing current account deficit. Their refusal to do so reinforced the crisis of confidence of French business and finally induced the government to devalue the franc and accommodate itself to national and international finance.[29]

The British and French experiences have been repeated on a smaller scale virtually everywhere else in Europe but Germany. As noted above, even at the end of the 1980s it appeared that the smaller European countries might prove more resilient. Yet by 1986 Norway had embarked on a "turning operation" in which the commitment to full employment was abandoned and foreign exchange controls were lifted. Sweden followed suit as the Social Democrats pushed through a massive program of financial deregulation in the late 1980s. The krona was pegged to the EMS, where it became vulnerable to speculation and finally collapsed in November 1992.

These experiences seemed to confirm that national strategies were encountering progressively greater constraints, even if some room for maneuver existed with respect to sectoral policies.[30] European governments of all stripes began individually and collectively to dismantle remaining controls on capital mobility. As Susan Strange writes, "Again and again, it is possible to trace the imitation of the deregulation trend by those who have far less to gain from it in invisible exports of service industries than the Americans. . . . In pure self-defence, other financial centres are put under pressure to offer similar facilities, equal freedom to the private banking and dealing operators."[31] Having rejected economic nationalism and recognizing the costs of dependence on the United States, Europe placed its hopes on the single market and, much more significantly, on monetary union. Yet the neoliberal basis of these projects greatly limits the scope of regional integration.

Social Democracy in One Country?

The analysis of the British and French experiences helps to clarify the political and theoretical implications of the thesis of declining sovereignty. At what point is it possible to argue that national economic autonomy no longer exists and that national strategies that seek to respond to and influence international market forces are no longer feasible? In the case of Britain in 1975, for example, standard accounts cite the central role of the IMF in the collapse of the Alternative Economic Strategy. Yet as Steven Ludlam shows, the key political debates and vital political maneuvers within the cabinet took place not in the heat of the IMF crisis but at least a year before: "The IMF deal merely codified a change of political course already well underway and proceeding under the stewardship of British social democracy."[32] In France, similarly, the new policy of *rigueur* was justified with reference to the alleged necessities of international interdependence. Yet, there is no evidence that the French government ever seriously contemplated risking a sharp political confrontation with capital or that it sought to mobilize its supporters for this purpose. Marc Lombard's recent study concludes:

> The Mitterrand experiment failed not because France embarked alone on a program of expansionary policies at a time of world recession, nor because Keynesian expansionary policies were outdated in the world economic environment of the 1980s, but because of the way these policies were implemented and more importantly because of the reluctance of the French government to operate outside the EMS guidelines.[33]

In principle, of course, both governments could have resisted central bankers and international speculators. However, in provoking strong resistance from capital, this course would have pushed social democracy well beyond its historical, self-imposed limits.

Nevertheless, the thesis of declining sovereignty in the face of international production and finance should be advanced with caution and qualification. As Fred Block writes, this view

> tends to naturalize the world economy—that is, to see it as having a life of its own independent of politics. . . . The alternative view is that the particular structure of the world economy—the rules of the game that determine international economic transactions—emerges out of political negotiations and conflicts among nation-states. The balance of political forces within and among nations shapes, and can reshape, the structure of the international economy.[34]

Financial deregulation has been established and policed by nation-states and is therefore subject to political control and reversal. That capital controls and the reintroduction of financial regulation are seldom considered as serious options in medium-sized economies such as Britain and France at least partly reflects the limitations of social democracy, not simply the internationalization of production and capital. The United States, which is in some respects still quite self-contained, clearly retains a great deal of room for maneuver. Although no single European country enjoys this privilege, the EU now constitutes a larger economic bloc than that of the United States and its partners in the North American Free Trade Agreement (NAFTA).

LIMITATIONS OF THE NEOLIBERAL PATH TO INTEGRATION

The United States' hegemonic role in Europe—especially the Marshall Plan and the gold standard—facilitated the establishment of a European Community that was deeply embedded in national corporatist systems and in which steps toward financial and trade liberalization were contingent on full employment. Marshall Plan aid served both political and economic goals of reconstruction. U.S. defense and multinational investment underwrote much of Europe's technological surge, even if it provoked widespread opposition, especially in France. After the sterling crises of the late 1940s, the United States tolerated a European currency bloc throughout the 1950s and strongly encouraged both the European Coal and Steel Community and the Treaty of Rome.

Although a strong current of liberalism ran through the Community, and especially within the European Commission, its practical application was limited and subject to national veto until the late 1980s. Europeanization and liberalism were kept in check by national interests; only small portions of sovereignty were loaned out to Brussels by national capitals, especially after 1966.[35] Only agricultural markets were integrated, although not on the basis of market rationality. The liberalization of capital and trade would have been inconsistent with state-sponsored development models and the commitment to full employment. Europe's founding fathers and many U.S. political scientists dutifully searched for a logic of spillover in which progressively more aspects of state autonomy were ceded to Brussels, but the liberalization that took place beginning in the mid-1980s still proceeded from national interests[36] and emerged largely in response to external threats: the monetary shocks arising from U.S. policies; growing competition in high technology sectors from Japanese and U.S. corporations; and, more generally, the exhaustion of the postwar Fordist accumulation strategy and the search for an alternative model.

By the mid-1980s, however, it was clear that national capitalist strategies, the nurturing of national champions, and protectionism no longer offered a viable strategy for reducing Europe's declining global competitiveness. The SEA offered a politically acceptable path to further integration because it accorded with the desires of conservative governments and European big business to adopt market-based solutions to problems that were defined in terms of excessive state intervention. Changes in the composition and policy positions of the European Roundtable (ERT) indicate the growing convergence of European capital. In the early to mid-1980s the ERT was both eclectic and factionalized, with strong currents of *dirigisme* and fortress mentality, particularly among the Italians and French. By the early 1990s, the changed orientation of the ERT suggested the development of consensus in favor of neoliberal strategies.[37] Yet, the creation of the single market in itself did little to enhance Europe's competitiveness or independence. The decline of practical sovereignty at the national level has not been matched by a comparable increase in the power and legitimacy of the EU. Deregulation broke down national barriers and precluded a strategy based on national champions without reestablishing a comparable set of interventionist and protective policies at the European level. As a result, mergers and corporate restructuring take place in response to global, not regional, logic. Thus in important respects the establishment of the single market tends to conflict with the goals of regional identity and cohesion.[38]

Contradictions of Monetary Union

Beginning in the early 1970s, the community mounted a number of ultimately unsuccessful attempts to establish a "zone of stability" against the dollar. The 1972 snake, the European Monetary System of 1979, and the subsequent exchange rate mechanism (ERM) all sought to maintain a system of internal fixed exchange rates. Yet each initiative was undermined by a combination of Europe's collective vulnerability to dollar devaluations and the chronic uneven development among the nations of the Community.

As long as the dollar continues to decline, the deutsche mark will be a powerful magnet for international capital seeking a safe and noninflationary haven. The devaluation of the dollar pushes up the value of the deutsche mark, placing chronic strains on Germany's neighbors and forcing them into cycles of deflation followed by devaluation. These cycles occurred in 1992, 1993, and, on a smaller scale, in March 1995. As long as the European economy was expanding, EMS countries were able to raise their interest rates to maintain parity with the rising deutsche mark. As the politics of reunification led the German government to raise interest rates further and the recession of the early 1990s began to bite, European countries proved unable or unwilling to remain within the system. As the peso crisis of February and March 1995 once again indicated, the other European countries have great difficulty insulating their currencies from the dollar/deutsche mark rate. In some important respects the German economy plays a role in the European monetary system analogous to that played by the United States in the Bretton Woods system. Germany itself, however, has tended to pursue a national rather than hegemonic strategy. In contrast to the United States in the early years of the Bretton Woods system, it has exerted a deflationary pressure on its partners.[39] At the same time, Britain, France, and Italy are reluctant to follow Germany's lead but also unwilling to accept the concept of a two-tier Europe. Does Economic and Monetary Union (EMU), as set out in the Maastricht Treaty, have a greater chance of success than previous, less ambitious efforts?

In principle, the EMU goes far beyond the snake because it demands a much greater degree of cohesion in macroeconomic policies. Thus in contrast to previous attempts at monetary integration, EMU is potentially a policy of re-regulation and not deregulation, which explains why the Thatcherite wing of the British Conservative Party objects to it. Under the terms of the Maastricht Treaty, all member states must harmonize their fiscal policies as a condition of entry. The Treaty limits the budget deficit to 3 percent of GDP, requires the accumulated debt to be no more than 60 percent of GDP, and sets specific targets on inflation and currency stability. Only Germany (and Luxembourg) has come close to fulfilling these requirements. Although the Reflection Group charged with planning the 1996 intergovernmental conference (IGC) did not formally abandon the goal of monetary union by 1999, such a target nevertheless appears to be unrealistic. The chronic difficulties with the EMS and Europe's inability to insulate itself from the dollar make it difficult to imagine a currency union among fifteen countries—much less twenty or twenty-five—in the absence of substantially greater intervention from the center to counter uneven development. Between September 1992 and March 1995, for example, the lira fell by 35 percent against the mark, the peseta dropped 29 percent, and the pound lost 19 percent of its value.[40] Therefore, it seems more likely, if the present trend continues, that the EU will face strong pressure to fragment into various tiers. This arrangement will be highly unstable and even core states such as France might experience problems. However, the EMU does contain the potential for greater cohesion.

The present regime of monetary union clearly flows out of a neoliberal agenda, but the agenda is self-limiting because it does not provide the social and political conditions for a single currency. Budgetary targets demand harsh cuts in social spending throughout the EC. The small size of the Union budget does not allow for the extensive redistributive policies necessary to minimize uneven development by compensating weaker economies that have lost the option of devaluation. Current EU revenues are 1.3 percent of member-state GNP, much less than the 10 percent called for in the McDougall Report of 1977.

Unless the Community budget increases substantially, the realities of uneven national development will always sooner or later overwhelm efforts to fix exchange rates, much less to establish a single currency. EU social policy will remain largely rhetorical and voluntaristic. If further development at the community level is ruled out, then countries will be compelled to choose between national solutions or adaptation to the global marketplace. Yet the former choice leaves them on the treadmill of deflation/devaluation and permanent slow growth—hardly a recipe for national economic independence and social revival. A stronger political union, based on institutions designed to redistribute resources and shelter weaker groups and regions, is a necessary condition of a currency union.

Do the EMU and the European Central Bank have the potential to evolve into something more than the present halfway house in which, given the strength of the deutsche mark, most European countries face a choice every few years between devaluation or deflation? It is of course true that the economic and monetary provisions of the Maastricht Treaty are quite specific and carefully drafted, in sharp contrast to those dealing with social policy. Article

5 of the Maastricht Treaty states categorically that "the primary objective of the European Central Bank shall be to maintain price stability." Yet Article 105 also mandates that "without prejudice to the objective of price stability, the ECB shall support the general economic policies of the community with a view to contributing to the achievement of the objectives of the Community as laid down in Article 2." And Article 2 explicitly provides a social framework:

> the Community shall have as its task . . . to promote throughout the Community a harmonious and balanced development of economic activities, sustainable and non-inflationary growth respecting the environment, a high degree of convergence of economic performance, a high level of employment and of social protection, the raising of the standard of living and the quality of life, and economic and social cohesion and solidarity among member states.[41]

If Europe were seriously to contemplate the establishment of a genuine zone of stability, in which Keynesian policies might be adopted, it would require a system of fixed exchange rates and political leadership designed to support deficit countries as well as a significant increase in the community budget. Although these policies are unlikely to arise exclusively from above, they may become increasingly more attractive to important segments of the European business community, especially if the limitations of the existing Union become more evident.

Political Power in the European Union

Because the key advances in European integration over the last decade have been linked to a neoliberal agenda, the EU has progressed toward the goal of a regional marketplace, yet federal political institutions comparable in capacity and size to the internal market have not been established. Because social democracy depends on state power, it must either reassert national autonomy with all the problems entailed by this strategy or work toward a federalist system to re-regulate the economy at the level of the EU.

The present institutional architecture, which stops well short of federalism, has led to recognition of the democratic deficit and growing nationalism, as indicated by the battles over ratification of the Maastricht Treaty and the referenda on expansion. The Community developed as a highly elite club without democratic traditions; as the mass public has become more involved over the last decade there has been an increasing recognition that existing institutions are unrepresentative and remote, and that a greater degree of localized decisionmaking, or subsidiarity, is necessary.

While greater decentralization may in some respects be desirable, it may also tend to fuel nationalism while drawing attention away from the pressing need for a centralized authority to compensate for the loss of national autonomy. The experience of the former Yugoslavia provides an extreme case in point of the centrifugal tendencies and conflicts that can arise when subsidiarity operates as a regional/ethnic competition for funds that are distributed by a weak and nonlegitimate central government. Strong regional policies and mechanisms for redistribution are essential, but these need to be under central control at the federal level, making policies in the interests of the entire union. This is especially true given that national governments have been unable or unwilling to tolerate a strong regional or subnational authority and that the principle of subsidiarity has tended not only to benefit the most powerful member states but also to reinforce market solutions.[42] National competition can be limited by strengthening all federalist institutions, including the European Parliament, a step that appears virtually inevitable if the Union is to remain viable after enlargement to twenty or even twenty-five states. A crucial means to this end is the establishment of European-wide social rights and the acceptance of a social charter that is based on the concept of rights as citizens and not simply workers.

CONCLUSION

At the beginning of this chapter I presented three choices for the Left: a nationalist path toward either withdrawal from the EU or at least substantial limitations on the both the EU and the global marketplace; the defense of the values of the Enlightenment in which the Left would refocus its attention on democracy and human rights; and a strategy of European federalism and social democracy. The first option has been rendered problematic because of the internationalization of production and capital. Even if economic nationalism is feasible in principle, it would provoke massive opposition from capital, producing forms of social conflict that are alien to the Social Democratic tradition and that few Europeans would welcome.

The second option, that of emphasizing political and human rights, has much to recommend it, and by no means contradicts other options. Social Democratic parties and trade unions have become increasingly statist and economistic, remote from new social movements and, at times, chauvinistic. In most of Europe, for example, the defense of multiethnic pluralism in the face of Serbian aggression arose from outside established Left parties or even from the Right. Social Democratic parties have failed to champion consistently and vigorously the rights of immigrant workers and refugees and have protested only weakly against the imposition of "shock therapy" on the losers of the Cold War. This record might indicate that the origins of what Perry Anderson calls the "the wider moral crisis in the identity of the major organizations of the West European Left"[43] run much deeper than the alleged necessities and constraints of international economic interdependence.

Nevertheless, there are clear limitations inherent in the second program. Lacking a mass-based strategy to reduce unemployment, to redistribute income, and to establish greater workplace democracy, the European Left would be compelled to reproduce its own version of the U.S. Democratic Party, a process that is already occurring in many countries. The fragmentation of working class communities, deteriorating social and economic conditions, and weakening trade unions are not propitious for the protection of human rights and democracy, which have historically required mass mobilization from below and substantial limitations on market forces. Nor, it should be added, has the accomodationist strategy of the Left yielded much at the polls. As the Left moves toward the center, the conservative parties, along with the voters, have moved farther to the right.

The concept of a Social Democratic Europe is thus full of difficulties and contradictions. Even as much of the Left now turns to Europe, the basis of European integration over the last decade has been widespread consensus on neoliberal solutions. To push forward with integration on any other basis would require a formidable organizational and ideological leap on the part of a movement that has always viewed its goals in essentially national terms and would also require the formation of a new social consensus patterned on the postwar settlement. It would also necessitate the surrender of state power that, despite much speculation about functionalism, spillover, and declining sovereignty, has not yet occurred and is hardly likely to emerge simply as a result of intergovernmental conferences.

A neoliberal Europe of the future is, however, likely to be poorer and less competitive. Lacking strong federalist institutions and social solidarity, it will be unable to exert much influence over U.S. policy and international capital markets. European institutions will remain weak and poorly legitimized, paralyzed by a dangerous and mutually reinforcing combination of market rationality and resurgent nationalism.

NOTES

1. Wolfgang Streeck, "Neo-Voluntarism: A New European Social Policy Regime?" *European Law* Journal 1 (March 1995), p. 31.
2. For data on business concentration, see Ash Amin and Michael Dietrich, "From Hierarchy to 'Hierarchy': The Dynamics of Contemporary Corporate Restructuring in Europe," in Amin and Dietrich, eds., *Towards a New Europe? Structural Change in the European Economy?* (Aldershot, U.K.: Edward Elgar, 1993). On the concept of class formation, see Otto Holman, "Transnational Class Strategy and the New Europe," *International Journal of Political Economy* 22 (Summer 1992). On business linkages, see Maria Green, "The Politics of Big Business in the Single Market Program" (paper presented for the European Community Studies Association

Third Biennial Conference, May 27, 1993, Washington, D.C.). Wayne Sandholtz and John Zysman also note the emergence of an elite alliance of transnational business in "1992: Recasting the European Bargain," *World Politics* 42 (October 1989).

3. Simon Bulmer and William Paterson, *The Federal Republic of Germany and the European Community* (London: Allen and Unwin, 1987), p. 140.

4. Andrei Markovits and Alexander Otto, "West German Labor and Europe 92," in Carl Lankowski, ed., *Germany and the European Community: Beyond Hegemony and Containment* (New York: St Martin's, 1993), p. 46.

5. See, for example, Wolfgang Streeck and Philippe Schmitter, "From National Corporatism to Transnational Pluralism: Organized Interests in the Single European Market," *Politics and Society* 19; Robert Geyer, "Socialism and the EC after Maastricht: From Classic to New-Model European Social Democracy," in Alan Cafruny and Glenda Rosenthal, eds., *The State of the European Community: The Maastricht Debates and Beyond* (Boulder, Colo.: Lynne Rienner Publishers, 1993); Robert Ladrech, "The European Left and Political Integration: A New Stage in Social Democracy?" in Carl Lankowski, ed., *Germany in the European Community: Beyond Hegemony and Containment* (New York: St. Martin's, 1993); Wolfgang Streeck, "Neo-Voluntarism?" For more favorable prognoses, see David Marquand, "Reinventing Federalism: Europe and the Left," in David Miliband, ed., *Reinventing the Left* (Cambridge: Polity Press, 1994), and Markovits and Otto, "West German Labor."

6. Paul Teague and John Grahl, "The European Community Social Charter and Labour Market Regulation," *Journal of Public Policy* 207 (September 1991); Wolfgang Streeck, "From Market-Making to State Building? Reflections on the Political Economy of European Social Policy," in Stephen Leibfried and Paul Pierson, eds., *Prospects for Social Europe: The European Community's Social Dimension in Comparative Perspective* (Washington, D.C.: Brookings Institution, 1995).

7. *Crisis and Choice in European Social Democracy* (Ithaca, N.Y.: Cornell University Press, 1987), p. 7.

8. Peter J. Katzenstein, *Small States in World Markets: Industrial Policy in Europe* (Ithaca, N.Y.: Cornell University Press, 1985); Geoffrey Garrett and Peter Lange, "Political Responses to Interdependence: What Is 'Left' for the Left?" *International Organization* 45 (autumn 1991), pp. 539–564; see also Peter Katzenstein, ed., *Between Power and Plenty: Foreign Economic Policies of Advanced Industrialized States* (Madison: University of Wisconsin Press, 1978).

9. Paulette Kurzer, *Business and Banking: Political Change and Economic Integration in Western Europe* (Ithaca, N.Y.: Cornell University Press, 1992); John Goodman and Louis Pauly, "The Obsolescence of Capital Controls: Economic Management in an Age of Global Markets," *World Politics* 46 (1994); Kurzer, "The European Community and the Postwar Settlement: The Effect of Monetary Integration on Corporatist Arrangements," in David Smith and James Lee Ray, eds., *The 1992 Project and the Future of Integration in Europe* (Armonk, N.Y.: M. E. Sharpe, 1993).

10. See, for example, T. Koelble, *The Left Unravelled: Social Democracy and the New Left Challenge in Britain and West Germany* (Durham, N.C.: Duke University Press, 1991); Christian Lemke and Gary Marks, eds., *The Crisis of Socialism in Europe* (Durham, N.C.: Duke University Press, 1992); Francis Fox Piven, ed., *Labor Parties in Industrialized Societies* (New York: Oxford University Press, 1992); Herbert Kitshelt, *The Transformation of European Democracy* (New York: Cambridge University Press, 1994); Perry Anderson and Patrick Camiller, eds., *Mapping the West European Left: Social Democrats, Socialists, Communists, Post Communists* (London: Verso, 1994).

Mark Kesselman offers the following definition of social democracy: First, an acceptance of a capitalist economy is coupled with extensive state intervention to counteract uneven development. Second, Keynesian steering mechanisms are used to achieve economic growth, high wages, price stability and full employment. Third, state policies redistribute the economic surplus in progressive ways, through welfare programs, social insurance and tax laws. And, finally, the working class is organized in a majority-bent social democratic party closely linked to a powerful centralized, disciplined trade union movement. "Prospects for Democratic Socialism in Advanced Capitalism: Class Struggle and Compromise in Sweden and France," *Politics and Society* 11 (1982), p. 402.

11. See, for example, Tony Glyn, "Capital Flight and Exchange Controls," *New Left Review* 147 (1986).

12. Frances Fox Piven, "Is It Global Economics or Neo-Laissez-Faire?" *New Left Review* 213 (September/October 1995), pp. 110–111.

13. See, for example, Kitshelt, *Transformation of European Democracy*; see also Steven Lukes, "What Is Left? Essential Socialism and the Urge to Rectify," *Times Literary Supplement*, March 27, 1992, p. 10: "What is left is a strongly egalitarian, liberal and anti-individualist political morality that can inspire particular institutional innovations, programmes and policies and by which they can be judged."

14. Streeck and Schmitter, "National Corporatism," p. 152.

15. See, for example, Gavin Bowd, "C'est La Lutte Initiale: Steps in the Realignment of the French Left," *New Left Review* 147 (1994); and Francoise de la Serre and Christian Lequesne, "France and the EU," in Alan Cafruny and Glenda Rosenthal, eds., *The State of the European Community: The Maastricht Debates and Beyond* (Boulder, Colo.: Lynne Rienner Publishers, 1993).

16. Charles Kindleberger, *The World in Depression, 1929–39* (Berkeley: University of California Press, 1987); E. A. Brett, *The World Economy Since the War: The Politics of Uneven Development* (New York: Praeger, 1985).

17. Robert Triffin, *The World Money Maze* (New Haven, Conn.: Yale University Press, 1966), p. 288.

18. See, for example, David Calleo, *The Imperious Economy* (Cambridge, Mass.: Harvard University Press, 1982); Riccardo Parboni, *The Dollar and Its Rivals: Recession, Inflation, and International Finance* (London: Verso, 1982); Susan Strange, *Casino Capitalism* (London: Basil Blackwell, 1986); Herman Schwartz, *States vs. Markets: History, Geography, and the Development of the International Political Economy* (New York: St. Martin's Press, 1994).

19. Michael Loriaux, *France After Hegemony: International Change and Financial Reform* (Ithaca, N.Y.: Cornell University Press, 1991).

20. On Sweden, see Jonas Pontusson, *The Limits of Social Democracy: Investment Politics in Sweden* (Ithaca, N.Y.: Cornell University Press, 1993). On Norway, see Tom Notermans, "The Abdication from National Policy Autonomy: Why the Macroeconomic Policy Regime Has Become So Unfavorable to Labor," *Politics and Society* 21 (June 1993), pp. 133–167.

21. Eric Helleiner, *States and the Reemergence of Global Finance: From Bretton Woods to the 1990s* (Ithaca, N.Y.: Cornell University Press, 1994).

22. Susan Strange, *Casino Capitalism*, p. 60.

23. These figures are taken from Schwartz, *States vs. Markets*, p. 238; *Wall Street Journal*, September 18, 1992.

24. J. P. Fitoussi and E. S. Phelps, "Causes of the 1980s Slump in Europe," in William C. Brainard and George L. Perry, eds., *Brookings Papers on Economic Activity 2* (Washington, D.C.: Brookings Institution, 1986).

25. Schwartz, *States vs. Markets*, pp. 236–237.

26. The figures are taken from the *Washington Post*, September 17, 1992.

27. Susan Strange, *Casino Capitalism*, p. 55.

28. Ken Coates, ed., *What Went Wrong: Explaining the Fall of the Labour Government* (Nottingham, U.K.: Spokesman Books, 1979).

29. Daniel Singer, *The End of Socialism?* (New York: Oxford University Press, 1988).

30. See, for example, Jeffry A. Frieden, "National Economic Policies in a World of Global Finance," *International Organization* 45 (autumn 1991), pp. 425–452.

31. Susan Strange, *Casino Capitalism*, p. 55.

32. Steven Ludlam, "The Gnomes of Washington: Four Myths of the 1976 IMF Crisis," *Political Studies* 40 (1992), p. 727.

33. Marc Lombard, "A Re-examination of the Reasons for the Failure of Keynesian Expansionary Policies in France, 1981–3," *Cambridge Journal of Economics* 19 (1995), p. 371.

34. Fred Block, *Postindustrial Possibilities: A Critique of Economic Discourse* (Berkeley: University of California Press, 1991), pp. 16, 17. See also David Gordon, "The Global Economy: New Edifice or Crumbling Foundations?" *New Left Review* 168 (March/April 1988). Tom Notermans presents a similar argument: "The ability to pursue growth and full-employment policies has not been eradicated by the anonymous forces of internationally mobile capital . . . the presently dominant views in the field of political economy have rather served to conceal the potential autonomy of present-day societies by invoking what can only be called false necessities." See "The Abdication from National Policy Autonomy: Why the Macroeconomic Policy Regime Has Become So Unfavorable to Labor," *Politics and Society* 21 (June 1993), p. 160. Notermans emphasizes the importance of the changing international monetary regime in undermining full employment; the conditions for a return to full employment on the basis of national autonomy appear to involve illiberal forms of corporatism designed to limit wage increases (pp. 161–162).

35. Alan Milward, *The European Rescue of the Nation-State* (Berkeley: University of California Press, 1992).

36. Geoffrey Garrett, "International Cooperation and Institutional Choice: The European Community's Internal Market," *International Organization* 46 (spring 1992), pp. 533–560; Andrew Moravscik, "Negotiating the Single European Act: National Interests and Conventional Statecraft in the European Community," *International Organization* 45 (winter 1991), pp. 19–56.

37. Bastiaan van Apeldoorn and Otto Holman, "Transnational Class Strategy and the Relaunching of European Integration: The Role of the European Roundtable of Industrialists" (paper presented at the Annual Conference of the International Studies Association, Washington, D.C., March 28–April 1, 1994). See also Green, "Politics of Big Business," Sandholtz and Zysman, "1992: Recasting the European Bargain."

38. Paul Teague and John Grahl, *1992 — The Big Market* (London: Lawrence and Wishart, 1990), especially chapter 4. For an analysis of this issue with regard to the defense industries, see Timothy Birch and John Crotts, "European Defense Integration: National Interests, National Sensitivities," in Alan Cafruny and Glenda Rosenthal, eds., *The State of the European Community: The Maastricht Debates and Beyond* (Boulder, Colo.: Lynne Rienner Publishers, 1993). On European telecommunications policies, see Giorgio Natallichi, "The Development of European Telecommunications Policy," Ph.D. dissertation, City University of New York, 1996, especially chapter 5.

39. See, especially, Riccardo Parboni, *The Dollar and Its Rivals*, pp. 153-155. On the limitations of German leadership, see also Kathleen R. McNamara and Erik Jones,

"A Defining Power? Germany in European Monetary Affairs" (paper presented at the American Political Science Association Annual Conference, Chicago, 1995).

40. These figures are taken from *Economist*, March 11–17, 1995, p. 70.

41. Commission of the European Communities, *Treaty on European Union* (Luxembourg: Publications of the EC, 1992).

42. Streeck, "Neo-Voluntarism," pp. 48–50. See also Paul Teague, "Europe of the Regions and the Future of National Systems of Industrial Relations," in Ash Amin and John Tomaney, eds., *Behind the Myth of the European Union* (New York: Routledge, 1995).

43. Perry Anderson, "Introduction," in Perry Anderson and Patrick Camiller, *Mapping the West European Left: Social Democrats, Socialists, Communists, Post Communists* (London: Verso, 1994), p. 2.

2

EUROPE AS A
DOMESTIC POLICY ISSUE:
ALTERNATIVE VISIONS OF UNION

6

French Political Party Opposition to European Integration,1981–1996: Myth or Reality?

Pia Christina Wood

The outcome of the 1992 French referendum on the Treaty on European Union (Maastricht Treaty)—51 percent in favor to 49 percent opposed—was interpreted widely as a signal of widespread political party and public opposition to President François Mitterrand's European agenda. Numerous commentators perceived an irrevocable blow to the political consensus over Europe among the major parties, noting the growing influence of such anti-Maastricht figures as Philippe Séguin, Viscomte Philippe de Villiers, and Jean-Marie Le Pen. They made dire predictions for France's future European policy. At the same time, the tenor of the debate, the high level of interest demonstrated by the public, and the closeness of the vote appeared to support the conclusion that "Europe" had been transformed from a quasi–foreign policy issue into a domestic issue of primary importance.[1]

This interpretation, however, underestimates the strength and durability of Mitterrand's European legacy, overestimates "Europe's" importance to France's political parties vis-à-vis traditional domestic issues, and overlooks the significance of the 1995 presidential elections. The similarity of views over Europe among the three leading presidential candidates in 1995 (Lionel Jospin, Edouard Balladur, and Jacques Chirac) indicates that while Maastricht did give voice to the opposition, it did not permanently shatter the political consensus over Europe. Europe as a campaign issue hit an all-time high during the Maastricht debate, but by the 1994 European Parliament (EP) elections it was overshadowed by the twin issues of the economy and unemployment. In the 1995 presidential election campaigns, Europe, while perhaps not "superbly ignored," as claimed in *Le Monde*, certainly was low on the list of campaign issues.[2]

My aim in this chapter is threefold. First, I seek to analyze French political party opposition to Mitterrand's European agenda by examining the three EP election campaigns during Mitterrand's presidency (1984, 1989, 1994) and the 1992 Maastricht referendum debate. Excellent studies of Mitterrand's

European policies are available, but much less attention has been given to the opposition.[3] The focus is on which political parties or factions within parties disagreed with the president's policies, over what issues, and to what degree. Thus, the positions of the Rassemblement pour la République (RPR), the Union for French Democracy (UDF), the National Front (FN), the French Communist Party (PCF), and the Greens (Verts) will be analyzed in the context of Mitterrand's evolving European policies. Throughout Mitterrand's two terms, the RPR disagreed internally over the issue of Europe and, in 1992, Séguin led the fight against the Maastricht Treaty. The UDF remained strongly pro-European and pro-Maastricht under the leadership of Valéry Giscard d'Estaing, but a small dissident faction led by Philippe de Villiers did emerge. In comparison, the FN, the PCF, and the Greens were unified in their resistance to the Maastricht agenda. Due to the limitation of space, only those party/lists that gained seats in the EP will be considered. To set the stage, I explore Mitterrand's successful strategy to undermine any opposition from within the Socialist Party to his European policies and the implications of his crucial 1983 decision to remain in the European Monetary System (EMS). Second, I examine the extent to which the Maastricht referendum reflected the emergence of a persistent and influential opposition to European integration or presaged "Europe" becoming a crucial domestic issue in French politics. Third, I look at the reasons for both the consensus among the three leading presidential candidates and the lack of a viable and convincing alternative vision of France's European policy, in the context of the 1995 presidential election. I conclude with some preliminary observations concerning France's future European policy under President Jacques Chirac.

MITTERRAND AND SOCIALIST UNITY OVER EUROPE

In 1995, after fourteen years as president of France, François Mitterrand and the Socialist Party (PS) were firmly acknowledged as responsible for France's close embrace of European integration. In fact, the strong unity of the party over Europe was clearly one of the reasons for Mitterrand's success. This coherence, however, did not exist in the 1970s or even in 1981 when Mitterrand was first elected. At the 1979 PS Congress in Metz, three main positions within the party toward European policy were apparent. The Centre d'Etudes, de Recherche et d'Education Socialistes (CERES) group led by Jean-Pierre Chevènement adopted an anti-European, nationalist stand. It vigorously opposed further progress toward European integration or enlargement of the European Community (EC) and also strongly criticized conferring any additional power on the European Parliament. The party faction led by Michel Rocard and Pierre Mauroy was the most pro-European. In favor of constructing a working people's Europe, the Rocard-Mauroy faction was the most positive toward integration and attracted the most supportive Europeanists in the PS. A third faction led by Mitterrand adopted a center-compromise position that included protection of French sovereignty and independence, the reinforcement of the powers of the European Parliament without weakening national parliaments, enlargement but only with protective economic preconditions, and dislike of the EMS. The Mitterrand position was shaped by intraparty disputes and electoral ambitions. The final formulation of the Mitterrand policy on Europe resulted from two major strategies: First, Mitterrand moved closer to CERES after Rocard challenged him for the 1981 presidential nomination, and, second, the compromise position was considered essential to holding the Socialist Party together and to attracting voters away from the PCF and the UDF.[4]

Mitterrand's presidential victory in 1981 followed a campaign that widely ignored European policy to concentrate on domestic issues, primarily the economy and unemployment. Of his *110 Propositions pour la France*, the basis of his campaign, only three referred to Europe directly. After the election, Mitterrand focused domestic policy on the Socialist economic agenda and foreign policy on the North Atlantic Treaty Organization (NATO) and France's leadership role in the developing world. France's European policy was consigned primarily to the pro-integration foreign minister, Claude Cheysson. Although Pierre Mauroy as prime minister and Jacques Delors as minister of trade strengthened the pro-European position, Jean-Pierre Chevènement and the four PCF ministers represented the anti-integration position. The victory of the integrationists was not final until Mitterrand's 1983 decision to maintain the franc in the EMS.

Mitterrand took office determined to bring down the high unemployment rate in France. In contrast to the previous government's austerity policies, the Mitterrand government proceeded with Keynesian economic reflation policies.[5] At the core of these policies was the assumption that nationalizations, increased wages and social welfare benefits, and greater public spending would lead to greater consumer demand, increased growth, and finally, job creation. Moreover, the French government was determined to persuade other EC countries to reflate their economies and believed the Organization for Economic Cooperation and Development (OECD) prediction that in 1981 the Western economies would begin to pull out of the recession. Unfortunately, neither one of these two conditions materialized—1982 was a year of global recession. At the G7 summit meeting in Ottawa in July 1981 and again at the Versailles summit in June 1982, the other Western governments led by Germany and the United States made it clear that reflating their economies was out of the question.

Thus, by mid-1982, the French economy was in trouble. The reflation measures resulted in a large increase in the trade deficit, high inflation, and pressure on the French franc. Faced with a deteriorating economy, the Mitterrand government opted to reintroduce an austerity program including a devaluation of the franc. In June 1982, the franc was devalued for a second time, but the economy continued to worsen. In March 1983, Mitterrand confronted a critical decision that brought the divisions within the party to the forefront. At issue was whether or not France should withdraw from the EMS. CERES leader Chevènement and others argued that leaving the EMS and allowing the franc to float coupled with protective measures for French business and continued reflationary actions would lead to economic growth.[6] Mitterrand chose, however, to listen to Mauroy, Delors, and other pro-Europeanists who argued that pulling out of the EMS would devastate the French economy and undermine France's position in the EC. On March 21, 1983, the government announced its third devaluation of the franc, and it was clear that Mitterrand had decided that membership in the EMS was critical to French economic policy.[7]

The 1983 decision ended the Socialist experiment with reflationary, expansionist policies. Economic nationalism, nationalizations, redistributive social reforms, and the promised "break with capitalism" were rejected in favor of conservative policies of austerity and support for further European integration. Mitterrand decided that France could not go it alone but needed the collective strength of the European Community to defend her economic vitality and political "grandeur." From the decision flowed logically Mitterrand's backing for the Single European Act (SEA) and the Maastricht Treaty. The "economic disaster of 1983" became an accepted lesson, internalized not only by the PS but also by the other major political parties.

The March U-turn also had implications for Socialist unity over domestic economic policy, which, in turn, was inextricably linked to European policy. CERES remained highly critical of Mitterrand's austerity program, but Chevènement's resignation weakened its position within the government. At the October PS Congress, the government's program received 77 percent of the votes, whereas the CERES position only attained 18 percent. Despite this dissension, Mitterrand's economic choices led to a general acceptance within the Socialist Party that France would neither isolate herself nor withdraw from the EC. As Mitterrand increasingly focused his attention on Europe and began to steer European policy personally, the PS had little choice but to fall in line. The French presidency of the European Commission during the first six months of 1984 reinforced Mitterrand's control over the direction of France's Community policy, and the dissident Socialist Party factions, despite some reluctance, followed his lead. By 1986 the PS marched in step with the president. Chevènement continued to disagree with Mitterrand's policies and strongly opposed the Maastricht Treaty but he was unable to gain support either from the Socialist Party or from the public.[8] The other major political parties disagreed with Mitterrand over some of the specifics of his European policies but not over his general strategy, as would be decisively shown by the 1984 elections to the European Parliament.

THE 1984 EUROPEAN PARLIAMENT ELECTIONS

Mitterrand's European agenda moved forward in 1984. Perhaps most stunning was the president's speech in Strasbourg in May, which was interpreted widely as support for the proposed European Union Treaty (EUT). In the past, the Mitterrand government had focused exclusively on arriving at common policies while assiduously avoiding any discussion of Community institutional reform.[9] This new treaty, however, proposed numerous institutional reform measures, including strengthening the powers of the Commission and the European Parliament and increasing majority decisionmaking. Both had previously been viewed as detrimental to French national sovereignty. Neither the Genscher-Colombo Plan in 1981 nor the Spinelli project (later called the EP's Draft Treaty on European Union) in 1982 had been considered with any enthusiasm by the French government. The PS members of the European Parliament (MEPs) voted against the draft EUT in February 1984, and the Socialist European election manifesto of 1984 denounced the EUT. Thus, Mitterrand's surprising Strasbourg speech, given several weeks before the June EP elections, appeared likely to put Europe firmly on the campaign agenda of all political parties. Yet in 1984 domestic politics dominated the EP campaign.

Throughout the EP election campaign neither the European Community nor the EUT were the focus of serious attention or debate. Instead, the parties concentrated on the state of the economy and unemployment, Mitterrand's modernization plan, and the Socialist plan to increase its control over private education. The PCF was clearly the most hostile to further European integration.[10] Although the Communist Party insisted it was "pour" Europe, it strongly criticized any measures that might weaken French sovereignty. It rejected the EMS, institutional reforms and the EUT, enlargement, and majority voting. Nevertheless, the PCF leadership did not focus on European issues. Instead, Georges Marchais first attacked and then defended the government's domestic economic program as the PCF struggled to find a formula that would appeal to the French electorate. In 1984, the PCF tried to reverse its precipitous decline in public support. This drop, combined with four Communist-held ministries, albeit minor, in the Socialist government led the PCF leadership to accommodate itself to Mitterrand's policies.

The Right (the RPR and UDF) split in its attitude toward the EC and Mitterrand's policies. Simone Veil led a joint UDF-RPR list, but on European issues divergent positions were apparent. The RPR reiterated the traditional Gaullist position that the EC should never undermine French sovereignty and independence. As a result, it opposed all projects that might enhance the supranational aspects of the EC and threaten the authority of the nation-state. Jacques Chirac, leader of the RPR, had warned against these developments already in his 1978 Cochin Appeal.[11] The RPR opposed the EUT, was cautious over enlargement, supported the continued use of the Luxembourg Compromise, and was willing to consider *l'Europe à plusieurs vitesses*.[12] The UDF faced an unhappy contradiction. It constituted an important part of the opposition, but its stance on European integration closely approximated that of President Mitterrand and the PS. Former president Giscard d'Estaing's strong support for European integration, however, was decisive in shaping the positive position of the UDF. The UDF believed that France's future could not be separated from Europe's future. According to Veil, "the struggle for a free, prosperous, and strong Europe cannot be dissociated from a free, prosperous, and strong France."[13] Veil, as a member of the EP, had voted in favor of the EUT and criticized Britain's unwillingness to play by the rules, particularly Britain's complaints over its EC budgetary contributions. However, the UDF adopted a cautious attitude on other European issues in order to avoid weakening its electoral alliance with the RPR. In the final analysis, the campaigns of the RPR and UDF centered on internal issues—educational freedom, the government's economic record, and the weaknesses of socialism.

The National Front under the leadership of Jean-Marie Le Pen was the only other party that enjoyed electoral success in the 1984 EP elections. Emerging for the first time as a national political force, Le Pen concentrated on domestic issues. The core of the FN campaign focused on law and order, the absence of traditional values, and immigrants; European issues were low on its political agenda. When he addressed it at all, Europe represented a difficult issue for Le Pen. His defense of France's national identity did not sit well with his avowed support for European solidarity based on a common history and culture. In the context of a common enemy (the USSR), Le Pen supported the EC, but he condemned EC policies that threatened French sovereignty. The title of his 1984 book, *Les Français d'abord*, illustrated the contradiction in his rhetoric; a contradiction that demanded a choice in the 1992 Maastricht debate.

The 1984 EP elections confirmed that the major political parties did not consider Europe to be a prominent campaign issue. Not only did Europe remain the purview of the president, but there was also general consensus over the basic objectives of French membership in the EC. No party advocated withdrawal from or even an alternative approach to the EC. The economic lessons of 1981-1983 were too fresh in the minds of the political elite. Instead, a general consensus that rejected any alternative to deflationary economic policies and market-based solutions emerged. In 1984, the EP elections were considered to be a test of the parties' domestic political strength and a forecast for the next major election (the 1986 legislative elections).

THE 1989 EUROPEAN PARLIAMENT ELECTIONS

Between the 1984 and 1989 EP elections numerous developments (the Fontainebleau summit of 1984, the creation of the Dooge Committee, and the intergovernmental conference of 1985) marked the evolution of the European Community. However, the Single European Act, which entered into force in 1987, inaugurated a new phase of development for the Community. The SEA not only called for the completion of the single internal market by 1992 but also provided for institutional reforms and extended EC purview over the fields of technology, the environment, defense, and monetary, regional, and social policy. To be sure, the SEA depended on the strong initiative of the Commission and Jacques Delors. But it was the leadership of Germany, France, and Britain that was decisive in driving the EC forward on the basis of liberalization of trade and, eventually, capital.[14] Mitterrand did not get everything he wanted, but he did characterize the final product as a "compromis de progrès."[15] For Mitterrand, the SEA served to consolidate at the European level France's post-1983 turn toward monetary and fiscal orthodoxy and simultaneously provided an alternative to the abandoned Socialist economic project. Whether the SEA and its subsequent implementation would focus the attention of French political parties on "Europe" and, if so, whether it would upset the general consensus among the major parties toward "neoliberal Europe" remained to be seen.

The 1989 EP election campaigns began inauspiciously with a major disagreement among leaders of the Right over the necessity for one or two lists. Giscard, Balladur, and Chirac believed that one unified list would win a larger number of votes, but François Leotard, Pierre Méhaignerie, and Simone Veil supported two lists. In the view of the latter three, the RPR was not sufficiently pro-European and two lists would attract voters from the FN on the right and the newly popular Greens on the left.[16] The internal struggle then intensified as a group of mostly younger, newly elected deputies calling themselves *renovateurs* demanded substantial changes in the leadership, structure, and strategy of the Right. Their threats to present an additional list for the elections, the subsequent warnings of exclusion by the RPR and UDF leadership, and the reconciliation of the two dominated much of the Right's EP campaign. But despite the prominence of this internal dispute and the emphasis on health, housing, education, and defense, "Europe" received more attention than in 1984. The SEA transformed Europe from largely a foreign policy issue to one with greater domestic impact. The parties' campaigns reflected this shift in emphasis. Simone Veil set the tone by stating at the outset that, "In the course of this European campaign, we will talk exclusively about France and Europe."[17]

The RPR and the UDF ultimately agreed to form a joint list to contest the elections despite their differing degrees of support for the SEA. On April 5,

1989, the two parties publicized their "declaration of union" containing their position on a variety of issues. Asserting the need for "a strong France in a strong Europe," the declaration called for realizing the single market, working toward a political union of Europe, building a real monetary union based on the European Currency unit (ECU) as the common currency, strengthening EC institutions, protecting a social Europe, and defending the environment.[18] Yet the document was vague despite its rhetorical forcefulness. The RPR continued to be more cautious than the UDF over European integration in general and the SEA specifically because of its traditional support for the Gaullist principles of independence and French national sovereignty. Moreover, both parties agreed with the general direction of the SEA as well as many of its specific proposals. Giscard d'Estaing went so far as to declare that he agreed with Mitterrand's general European principles but favored a liberal, social Europe as opposed to a bureaucratic, socialist Europe.[19] In short, "Europe" was simply not highly controversial.

Simone Veil decided to lead a separate list dubbed *les centristes* based on her charge that the UDF-RPR joint list was a front for two very different conceptions of Europe. She presented her own list as being more staunchly pro-European and advocated a new treaty for a political union of Europe by the year 2000, protection of the environment by creating a community organization with independent investigative powers, a common currency based on the ECU and a European central bank, a Europe with a social dimension, a citizens' Europe, and stronger institutions.[20] Despite Veil's assertion that her list was "more authentic" and did not have the same "political profile" as the UDF-RPR list, there was little to differentiate the two. Moreover, there was equally little to differentiate the centristes from the PS on Europe.

Opposition to the SEA and more generally Mitterrand's Europe was voiced by the PCF, the FN, and the Greens. The PCF list, led by Philippe Herzog, was the most hostile despite his insistence that the Communists were not opposed to European integration. In contrast to 1984, the Communists no longer held posts in the government in 1989. As a result, the PCF had little incentive to temper its opposition to Socialist policies on Europe for domestic political reasons. The Communist campaign called for "constructing Europe differently and a different Europe" and denounced the SEA as "hampering France's liberty and sacrificing its economy to German domination."[21] According to Georges Marchais, Mitterrand's European program was characterized by social regression, the end of social security, higher taxes, lower salaries, the death of French television and cinema, overarmament of the continent, the pillaging of the Third World, and the end of French sovereignty.[22] Gaullist nuances were evident in the PCF campaign when the party proclaimed itself sole defender of French national sovereignty; the PCF opposed both additional power for the Commission and the EP and a common currency. In its view, a common European currency would result in a decline in French salaries and reinforce the hegemony of the deutsche mark and the dollar.

The FN also waved the Gaullist banner. Le Pen argued that the construction of Europe was useful but only in the context of a confederation in which the principle of subsidiarity was respected. National sovereignty and the French identity must not be sacrificed to European integration. The FN harshly criticized the provisions in the SEA that might open French borders to immigrants or give foreigners (i.e., immigrants) the right to vote in France. According to Le Pen, "a cosmopolitan and multiracial Europe" must be avoided at all costs, but he did support "a geographically, politically, and culturally defined Europe."[23] Moreover, Le Pen supported a common European defense and security policy, a common European currency, and a regulatory institute similar to the U.S. Federal Reserve Board. Thus, his support for both European solidarity and "The French First" continued. The FN paid more attention to Europe in 1989 than in 1984 because of the perceived domestic implications of the SEA. Nevertheless, its campaign still centered on those domestic issues with proven appeal—immigration, law and order, and "national moral regeneration."

In 1989, the Greens for the first time gained seats in the European Parliament. Led by Antoine Waechter, they focused on *l'Europe ecologique* and the protection of the environment. In their view, Europe had the responsibility to enforce sound ecological development in order to achieve a just society. Additional issues of concern were support for regions, social rights, solidarity with developing countries, and antinuclearism and antimilitarism. Europe was discussed merely within the context of these issues. For example, Waechter argued that the Greens favored both the SEA, if there were adequate regulations to protect social rights and the environment, and the construction of Europe, if it took into account the diversity of the regions.[24] However, because the Greens doubted that these conditions would be met, they continued to question the merits of the single market. In contrast to the German Greens, the Greens in France did not gain lasting electoral support, and internal divisions prevented them from winning seats in the 1994 EP elections. In the final analysis, the French Greens have not influenced the terms of debate over European integration.

A comparison between the 1984 and 1989 EP elections yields several conclusions. The EC in 1989 was more intrusive at the domestic level than it had been in 1984. The SEA contained provisions that promised to turn the EC into an organization that could directly affect the lives of French citizens. An uneasiness over the EC was reflected by a poll taken by SOFRES from February 18–22, 1989, where 58 percent of those asked said they were worried about Europe 1992.[25] The French political parties responded to this new state of affairs by including Europe in their 1989 EP campaigns to a degree not seen in 1979 or 1984. Domestic issues and intraparty disputes continued to dominate the campaign, but the parties did present their views, albeit vaguely, concerning the construction of Europe. The general consensus among the majority of the parties over Mitterrand's agenda for Europe endured. The RPR-UDF and the centristes clearly favored the SEA despite a variety of criticisms over specifics. The FN, the Greens, and the PCF all were anxious not to be characterized as anti-European. The PCF was the only party to wholly denounce the single market, but it had little to offer in its place. Mitterrand's European policy thus appeared unstoppable. The Maastricht referendum of 1992, however, would call into question this widely accepted conclusion.

THE MAASTRICHT REFERENDUM OF 1992

Between the 1989 EP elections and the 1992 Maastricht referendum, Europe was radically transformed. The Soviet empire collapsed, the Eastern European countries embraced democratization, Yugoslavia disintegrated into violent combat, and Germany reunified. In response to this last development, Mitterrand decided that binding Germany more tightly to Europe would best protect France's national interests. The Maastricht Treaty represented, in his view, one means to this end.[26] In December 1991, the twelve EC countries met and successfully negotiated the Maastricht Treaty, which was then signed on February 7, 1992.[27] The Union, a continuation of the SEA, comprised three main pillars: the EC treaties and the Economic and Monetary Union (EMU), the Common Foreign and Security Policy (CFSP), and Justice and Home Affairs. In brief, the major provisions of the treaty called for a European monetary union with a common currency and a central European bank by 1999 at the latest, additional powers for the European Parliament, the extension of qualified majority voting in the Council of Ministers, the introduction of dual or parallel citizenship, a new protocol on social policy, and a potential European Defense Identity linked to the Western European Union.

In the months preceding the December treaty negotiations, the Greens, the FN, and the PCF began to criticize the direction of Mitterrand's policies. They were joined by numerous members of the RPR. For example, Philippe Séguin of the RPR argued that the Maastricht Treaty would gravely compromise French sovereignty. However, the real debate did not begin until the National Assembly was asked to amend the French constitution to clear the way for ratification. This debate was then enlarged to include the French public, when Mitterrand announced on June 3, 1991, that he would call for a popular referendum on the Maastricht Treaty.[28] The government's project for the reform of the constitution was approved by a large majority in the National Assembly (398 for, 77 against, with 99 abstaining), but the referendum barely passed with 51.1 percent in favor and 48.9 percent against. Clearly there was a wide gap between the party leadership and the public.

For the RPR, dissension over European integration was nothing new. The Gaullist belief in the authority of the nation-state and the concomitant aversion to supranationalism is an integral part of the RPR's intellectual foundation. As Alain Duhamel explains: "[The Gaullist family] has the cult of the French difference, the obsessive fear for France's identity, and a terror of French obliteration."[29] In light of the RPR's difficulty in defining a common position toward the SEA, it was not surprising that the party would split over the Maastricht Treaty. However, one important new theme occupied center stage in the debate—would Maastricht lead to more or less control over the newly united and ever more powerful Germany? The RPR disagreed over this issue, among others, and a majority *Yes* and minority *No* camp emerged. Chirac wavered back and forth but finally supported the treaty, albeit "without enthusiasm." In an attempt to minimize the divisive impact of the debate, he stated that his vote was purely personal and everyone was free to decide his or her own vote. Philippe Séguin and Charles Pasqua created the *Rassemblement pour le "non" au référendum* and led the opposition to the Maastricht Treaty.

Séguin, in his campaign, articulated the concerns of a not insignificant faction of the RPR. In many ways, the RPR's debate over Séguin's proposed agenda replicated the debate that divided the Socialists in 1983. Séguin argued that the time had arrived to implement alternative policies (*l'autre politique*) to France's persistent unemployment. Mitterrand's conservative economic policies may have led to low inflation and monetary stability but at the cost of high unemployment. In 1993, he categorized Mitterrand's economic policy as "un véritable Munich social."[30] Instead Séguin believed that unemployment should be given priority. To this end, the *franc fort* should be discontinued, interest rates cut, and the government should create new jobs despite the potential negative effects on the budget.

Even worse, the Maastricht Treaty, according to Séguin, would result in the end of the nation-state in Europe and the beginning of a federal Europe. No less than France's national sovereignty and independence were at stake. The EMU with its European Central Bank (ECB) and single currency, the additional powers to the Commission and the European Parliament, and the right to vote for all citizens of the Union were all dangerous steps. The planned European Central Bank represented the worst of "technocracy" and would undermine France's control over its own national economic power. The European Parliament lacked legitimacy and threatened the decisionmaking power of national parliaments, and the Commission possessed too much power vis-à-vis the Council of Ministers. A single currency (*monnaie unique*), as opposed to a common currency (*monnaie commune*), would signal the end of French monetary sovereignty. In addition, the terms of the

Treaty would accord Germany too much power, particularly in the realm of monetary policy. The solution, according to Séguin, was to renegotiate the fundamental core (*fond*) of the Treaty.[31] The new Treaty should acknowledge the principle of community preference and give priority to social protection and employment. Séguin, however, presented himself as neither anti-EC nor against the further construction of Europe. He opposed only the Maastricht Treaty.

The UDF, although much less divided than the RPR, did contain opponents to the Maastricht Treaty. Viscomte Philippe de Villiers, leader of *Combat des valeurs*, led the fight against the Maastricht Treaty. His objections were in many respects similar to those presented by Séguin:[32] The Europe of Maastricht would lead to a "federal Super-State" with all decisionmaking authority transferred to Brussels. De Villiers condemned granting the vote to foreigners, which he said would result in civic apartheid and social instability. He also strongly criticized any further dismantling of the borders, which would lead to an influx of refugees and immigrants; additional powers to the European Parliament and the Commission, which would undermine the powers of the national governments and parliaments; and the single currency, which would both undermine French monetary sovereignty and increase unemployment. Germany also came under attack.[33] Under the federal Europe of Maastricht, Germany would be able to impose its policies on France through its control over a majority of the votes in the Council of Ministers. In addition, the EMU proposed under Maastricht would become a deutsche mark zone with the German central bank in charge.

The FN campaigned against the Maastricht Treaty. The yes or no nature of the vote in conjunction with the provisions of the treaty prohibited Le Pen from adopting his more nuanced position of 1989. At this point, Le Pen decided that his support for French nationalism was no longer even rhetorically compatible with further European integration. He categorically denounced the treaty. The FN's campaign concentrated on the loss of French sovereignty, an emphasis reflected in its slogan *Non à Maastricht, oui à l'Europe des patries*. On this and most other issues, Le Pen agreed with both Séguin and de Villiers. However, the discourse of his campaign was racist and virulent. According to Le Pen, the Maastricht Treaty was a "world-wide conspiracy" organized by "Maastricheurs" to lead France to "national suicide."[34] It would lead only to "more immigration, more insecurity, more drugs, and more AIDS," and "France will be the receptacle of all the immigrations and the garbage can for all the dregs (*déchets*)."[35] In addition to a flood of immigrants and refugees, the Treaty would permit foreign representatives of big capital, stateless bankers, and technocrats in Brussels to gain greater authority over French national decisionmaking.[36]

The opposition from the PCF to the Maastricht Treaty was expected, and its arguments followed from its 1989 EP campaign. Georges Marchais denounced the treaty with *un non resolu*, but he was quick to point out that he favored a completely different conception of European construction, which resembled neither Maastricht nor isolation. Philippe Herzog and others wanted to take a more constructive, positive approach to European integration, but they agreed that Maastricht was unacceptable. Thus, the "No to Maastricht, Yes to Europe" theme found in other parties' campaigns was also integral to that of the PCF. The PCF based its criticisms of Maastricht on four major themes rather than an in-depth discussion over the treaty's specifics. First, it denounced a supranational Europe dominated by Germany. Second, it warned against the negative domestic social impact of Maastricht: Higher unemployment, lower wages, fewer jobs from greater competition, and increased social tension accompanied by rising nationalism would result in a profound crisis.[37] Third, it criticized the obvious link between the treaty and the policies of "la grande bourgeoisie." Finally, the PCF vaguely called for a new and different construction for Europe.

IMPLICATIONS OF THE MAASTRICHT DEBATE

Maastricht represented an unmistakable wake-up call for the leadership of France's political parties, but the conclusion that the referendum debate shattered the consensus among the parties is not as clear-cut as many have assumed.[38] Certainly, the close vote must be interpreted as a sign that the French public was apprehensive about at least some of the proposals in the Maastricht Treaty. The close vote and the loud dissident voices of Séguin, Pasqua, de Villiers, Le Pen, and Marchais, however, should not obscure the strength of the Yes camp. In favor were "the president, the government, the Socialist party, the leadership of the UDF, including former President Giscard d'Estaing, and virtually all of its parliamentary personnel in both houses; the top leadership of the RPR, though little of its parliamentary strength; the business community; the Church . . . ; some unions (CFDT); and a long list of business and literary celebrities. . . ."[39] But did the debate presage the emergence of an influential opposition to the Maastricht Treaty? It is true that Séguin's following in the RPR, the FN and the PCF, and de Villiers' movement opposed much of the Maastricht agenda, but none demanded a French withdrawal from the EU. However, the advocates for "alternative policies" had significant public support. The PS, the UDF, and the Maastricht supporters in the RPR realized that the opposition to Mitterrand's Maastricht plan would have to be taken into account in future policies. For the RPR, the vote fueled the growing conviction that the Treaty would have to be renegotiated. The PS and the UDF continued to support the Maastricht Treaty but began to redefine their positions toward some of the specifics of the treaty as demonstrated by their 1994 EP campaigns. Nevertheless, by the 1995 presidential campaign, the UDF, PS, and RPR, as in the past, reestablished the general consensus that European integration must go forward while disagreeing over the timetable and some of the specifics.

The question of "Europe" as a crucial domestic issue was also raised by the Maastricht referendum. Many argued, prematurely, that with the referendum the European Union (EU) broke through the barrier of public indifference and party disinterest and emerged as a domestic issue that rivaled unemployment, the economy, education, and so on. Certainly the EU was the center of the debate during the referendum, but it could hardly have been otherwise. The very nature of a yes or no referendum, in contrast to a national election, mitigated against the discussion of other issues. Thus, although some did use the referendum vote to protest against Mitterrand's record and internal party posturing was part of the campaign,[40] the EU occupied center stage. However, the 1994 EP campaigns and the 1995 presidential campaign cast doubt on the permanence of the EU's prominence in party campaigns.

THE 1994 EUROPEAN PARLIAMENT ELECTIONS

The 1994 EP elections were considered by the parties to be, first and foremost, an early test of political strength for the upcoming 1995 presidential elections. Led by presidential hopeful Michel Rocard, the PS conducted a campaign that concentrated on traditional domestic issues. On April 16–17 at the national convention, Laurent Fabius argued that the Socialist campaign should focus on the "obsession of employment," which would determine the winners of both the EP elections and the 1995 presidential elections. "Europe" as an issue was not ignored, but the Socialist position was full of generalities in order to avoid losing any more support from the Euroskeptic portion of the electorate. Descriptions of Europe as "an unlimited horizon, a dream to be constructed" and " the last of the great utopias of this century" were commonplace.[41] At the same time, the PS with its slogan "l'Europe Oui, mais solidaire" introduced a new tone into the debate. Support for Maastricht remained strong, but there was a recognition that the PS needed to actively reassure the public that its vision of Europe would not be detrimental to French interests or sovereignty.[42]

The main concern for the leadership of the Right was once again to prevent the different European visions of the UDF and the RPR from splitting the coalition. Disagreements between the two presidential hopefuls, Edouard Balladur and Jacques Chirac, over the acceptability of the Maastricht Treaty complicated the picture. Chirac, more closely tied to the Gaullist tradition, was more critical of the terms of Maastricht. However, unity was given priority. According to Balladur, "each time that we [RPR and UDF] are divided, we are sanctioned. Each time that we are united, we win. How many times have we had this experience in the past 20 years, now?"[43] To achieve this unity, however, the joint RPR-UDF list, led by Dominique Baudis, conducted a campaign that sought to suppress any in-depth discussion of the controversial aspects of the Maastricht Treaty. No doubt the decision by Séguin, president of the National Assembly, and Pasqua, minister of the interior, not to participate in the campaign helped the unity of the two parties.[44]

Thus, the official position of the UDF-RPR joint list was ultimately hardly distinguishable from that of the PS. All three parties supported monetary union and a single currency, institutional reform, enlargement, and a European defense identity. To be sure, differences over details existed. For example, the PS declared that the EP should be given a real legislative power equal to that of the Council of Ministers and decisionmaking by majority vote in the Council should become the rule. The RPR-UDF proposed a five-year presidency for the Council, greater EP and Council control over the Commission, and an increased role for the national parliaments in EC decisionmaking. The RPR-UDF advocated the need for a "new concept of integration" that would progressively allow central and eastern European states to join. This position did not differ greatly from the Socialists' call for enlargement that would not come at the expense of "deepening" the European Union.

The campaign of de Villiers changed in emphasis from the 1992 Maastricht referendum. Along with representatives of the FN and the PCF, he paid greater attention to domestic issues, particularly unemployment. But he continued to denounced Maastricht as the harbinger of a federal Europe and "a program of euthanasia of nation-states" while shifting his campaign to emphasize the negative economic aspects of the treaty. Like Séguin, he attacked the Socialist government's orthodox economic policies and championed the cause of the unemployed. According to de Villiers, unfettered free trade had increased the monetary value of European exports, but at the price of high unemployment and the departure of large numbers of businesses.[45] The only solution was to veto agreements such as the General Agreement on Tariffs and Trade (GATT) and reintroduce protectionism and Community preference. Other themes from 1992 included the rejection of a single currency, the abolition of the Schengen accords, the reestablishment of border controls to prevent unwanted immigration, the return of greater authority to national parliaments, and unanimous decisionmaking.

The FN and the PCF campaigns also followed closely from 1992. Le Pen called for national preference, the rejection of a single currency, and a reduction of the power of the Commission. But as expected, he concentrated on denouncing the large numbers of immigrants and demanding employment preference for French citizens. The PCF also called for Community preference, decreasing the power of the Commission, increasing the power of the national parliaments and the EP, and maintaining national currencies. In contrast to Le Pen and de Villiers, the PCF's campaign did not extol French nationalism but continued to emphasize European cooperation.

Despite some expectations to the contrary, the 1994 EP elections were not a repeat of the wrenching Maastricht debate. The arguments for and against Europe were the same, but the emotionalism had largely disappeared. As in previous EP elections, the three major parties (PS, RPR, UDF) focused on domestic issues and only vaguely invoked Europe in their campaigns. There was little discussion over the specifics of institutional reform, enlargement, monetary union, federalism, or a "two or more speed Europe." Internal party posturing and the desire by the UDF-RPR leadership to demonstrate unity for the upcoming 1995 presidential elections dominated the campaign. In addition, the 1994 EP elections reaffirmed the general consensus among the three major political parties over the need for further integration. However, it was also clear that the political opposition to the Maastricht Treaty was undiminished. Candidates on the anti-Maastricht lists led by de Villiers, Le Pen, and Wurtz considered "Europe" to be a worthwhile campaign issue, albeit not important enough to overshadow or replace domestic issues. In the final analysis, the 1994 elections proved that the strength of the political opposition to the Maastricht Treaty meant that "Europe" could no longer be disregarded as a political issue, but neither could it challenge the priority given to domestic issues.

THE 1995 PRESIDENTIAL ELECTIONS

The 1995 presidential elections confirmed two important points. First, with the possible exception of Philippe de Villiers, none of the candidates focused their campaigns on Europe. Even de Villiers was careful to stress such domestic issues as corruption, family policy, and unemployment in addition to attacking the Maastricht plan for Europe. Le Pen continued to denounce the "unemployment, insecurity and immorality" of Maastricht but focused his attention on the ills brought on by the immigration "menace from the South." Chirac, Balladur, and Jospin, however, concentrated on the traditional domestic issues of unemployment, tax reform, social security, education, and law and order. As a noted political analyst observes, "Europe continues to shine by its absence in the presidential debate."[46] After the first major debate between Chirac, Balladur, and Jospin, *Le Monde* concluded "Europe is not a major stake in the presidential campaign."[47] On May 2, during a second debate between Chirac and Jospin, the candidates discussed salaries, unemployment, taxes, the budget, and defense but barely mentioned Europe. Europe, when invoked at all, was done so in only the vaguest of terms, for several reasons. First, there was little to differentiate the agendas of the two men on European integration. Second, divisions within Chirac's RPR and his need to appeal to the UDF prevented any decisive stance on the hard issues of Europe. Finally and perhaps most significant, neither Chirac nor Jospin appeared to have either clear answers to or a coherent vision of Europe's future and France's role in it.

The second major point established concretely by the 1995 presidential campaign was precisely the agreement over European integration between the three leading candidates. When discussed at all, the positions of Chirac, Balladur, and Jospin were strikingly similar. If Jacques Delors had carried the banner for the PS, greater disagreement would have ensued. For proof, one only has to consider the furor engendered by his remark that his idea of Europe was based on a "federation of states."[48] His decision not to run, however, removed one of the strongest supporters of the Maastricht vision of Europe from the political arena.

All three considered the future of France and the future of Europe to be inextricably linked together. According to Chirac, "Europe is today a necessary ambition. . . . Our capacity to influence depends on the Union." Jospin stated, "Europe has become the natural cadre of our action," while Balladur insisted that Europe was indispensable to France's future.[49] None questioned the validity of the Maastricht Treaty. Both Balladur and Jospin stated that France would respect the terms of the Treaty. Chirac, while insisting that the Treaty would have to be renegotiated, did not withdraw his 1992 support for it. He reiterated his words at the time, "the treaty of Maastricht constitutes a small step in the right direction."[50] The Franco-German alliance was given the highest priority. Balladur insisted that the reinforcement of Franco-German cooperation was essential, and Jospin declared that "Franco-German relations [are] the essential axis of European construction."[51] Chirac devoted an entire article in *Le Monde*, "Une volonté pour L'Europe," to Franco-German relations. He argued that cooperation between the two countries was indispensable to the further construction of Europe. All three candidates supported a single European currency but differed slightly over the timetable. Balladur pressed for a single currency in 1997 if at all possible. Jospin agreed but declared that France would have difficulty in meeting the convergence criteria by 1997 and that 1999 represented a more realistic date.[52] Chirac stated simply that a single currency would be appropriate when all the conditions outlined in the Treaty were met. All three endorsed enlargement, but only if preceded by institutional reform. All three candidates avowed a strong belief in a Europe of nation-states where major decisions would be made by intergovernmental cooperation and the Council would wield executive power, with the Commission remaining subordinate. Majority voting was supported by Jospin and Balladur, but Chirac avoided discussing the issue. Finally, there was agreement that EU control over the CAP, social protection, and foreign policy and defense should be strengthened.

This obvious convergence of views demonstrated that Balladur, Jospin, and even the previously skeptical Chirac rejected the alternative policies of Séguin and de Villiers. In fact, Séguin, who supported Chirac, went so far as to retract his rejection of a single currency. In an about face due in all likelihood to the imperatives of domestic politics rather than a fundamental change in beliefs, he argued that the franc fort and the reduction of unemployment were not necessarily incompatible goals.[53] Thus, the presidential candidates opposed to a Maastricht-led Europe were, surprisingly, not de Villiers, Le Pen, and Robert Hue of the PCF. Their campaigns reiterated the same major themes developed during the 1992 Maastricht referendum and the 1994 EP elections. Their elimination after the first round left two strong supporters of further European integration, Jospin and Chirac, to face off in the second round. In May 1995, Jacques Chirac was elected president of France.

In the year following his election victory, Chirac appears more pro-Europe than ever. In the run-up to the beginning of the intergovernmental conference (IGC) in late March 1996, the debate centered on the future of the EMU. Despite the crippling strikes in November–December 1995 to protest government reforms to decrease the budget deficit, the Chirac government continues to support both the convergence criteria for EMU and the timetable of a common currency in 1999. In February 1996 Chirac reiterated that "the Economic Monetary Union is . . . in progress. Certainly efforts are necessary to realize the objective of 1999. I know that the determination of the German Chancellor will not weaken. Nor will mine."[54] Within the RPR, Balladur remains highly critical of l'autre politique and has stated on numerous occasions that Europe and the EMU are inseparable.[55] Even Séguin, who railed against the "historical stupidity" of Maastricht, appeared to soften his opposition to the Treaty to achieve political acceptability. The political leadership of the PS and the UDF remain firm in their support for the EMU. Although Giscard d'Estaing proposed a "flexible" accounting of the public debt, he continued to denounce the "anti-Europeans" and demand that the 1999 EMU timetable be respected. Laurent Fabius, Jacques Delors, Lionel Jospin, and Michel Rocard all strongly voiced their support for EMU. Thus, the political elite of the major French parties continue to support a cornerstone of Mitterrand's European vision.

THE UNSUCCESSFUL ALTERNATIVE VISION OF EUROPE

The fact that Jospin, Chirac, and Balladur all supported further European integration guided by Maastricht begs the question: Why did none of the major presidential candidates favor an alternative approach to European integration? Certainly l'autre politique championed by Chevènement, Séguin, and de Villiers provided an intellectual foundation for change in French policy toward Europe. Chirac had always been skeptical of the European policies of both Giscard d'Estaing and Mitterrand. But by 1995, his conversion to European integration appeared complete.[56] A variety of reasons explain the lack of opposition among the major presidential candidates.

Mitterrand's personal and determined twelve-year support for integration after the 1983 U-turn created a logic and dynamism that would have been difficult to reverse. Despite the French government's failure to bring down the high unemployment, the lessons of 1981–1983 were seen to preclude any radical change in course. The candidates' competition to win the vote of the pro-European center (UDF and PS) served to reinforce their support for already established policies. As *Le Monde* pointed out on more than one occasion, to be a serious presidential candidate, one must necessarily be pro-Europe.

In addition to domestic political exigencies, the international and European arenas place limits on French policies. A more powerful, reunited Germany has altered the balance of power between France and Germany within the European Union. Freed from the political constraints of the Cold War, Germany is more willing to use its economic strength to press for its vision of Europe. Any French rejection of le franc fort or, more generally, a significant eschewal of the Maastricht design for Europe would not only create difficulties for the Franco-German relationship but would undermine an accepted tenet of French foreign policy—use the EU to bind Germany more closely to France and Western Europe. In addition, the French elite believes that any weakening of support for the *franc stable* would result in currency crises that, in turn, will negatively affect the French economy. Finally, French influence in the world is being more closely linked to its membership in the EU. Both Chirac and Jospin ascribe to this position.[57] Thus, an alternative approach to Europe resonates within some sections of the French public and political elite but not within the leadership of the major parties.

CONCLUSION

Mitterrand's strong support for the SEA and the Maastricht Treaty fundamentally shaped France's European policy in keeping with the dramatic change in domestic economic policy after the debacle of 1983. France, together with Germany, would lead the EC and later the EU, an organization now espousing an economic strategy of free market competition and giving priority to monetary stability rather than full employment. Until 1992, the RPR and the UDF accepted this vision with little debate. The smaller opposition parties (PCF, FN, Greens), although more critical of the details, nevertheless also fell in line with Mitterrand and did not issue a fundamental challenge over Europe. The general consensus across the political spectrum, coupled with Mitterrand's personal control over France's EC policy and the public's relative disinterest in the Community, meant that "Europe" never became a salient or contentious domestic political issue. As a result, the political parties seldom focused any significant attention on Europe in their political campaigns.

In this context, the passions unleashed by the public and party debate over the Maastricht Treaty and Europe were quite remarkable. In contrast to the SEA, the Maastricht Treaty, with its plan for monetary union, was clearly perceived by many as a direct threat to French national interests. The referendum meant that the discussion over Europe could no longer be confined to the political and business elite. Opponents of the consensus were quick to seize on the opportunity offered by the referendum. Séguin, de Villiers, Chevènement, Le Pen, and the PCF attacked not just specific policies but the European project in its totality. Séguin, in particular, demanded an alternative vision for France and the EU. To varying degrees, these dissidents campaigned for the protection of French national interests, community preference and protectionism, monetary policies to defend employment, and social priorities.

Although the emotionalism of the Maastricht referendum subsided rather quickly, its long-range impact cannot be dismissed. It is true that "Europe" in the 1994 EP and 1995 presidential campaigns was not an issue of high priority. The leadership of the PS, the RPR, and the UDF concentrated on domestic issues and internal party politics. However, the anti-Maastricht political parties (FN, PCF, de Villiers' party) continued their attack on both the general vision and specific plans of the treaty. Thus, "Europe" was more salient in the 1994 than in the 1984 EP elections, and it is likely that Europe will continue to be a more contentious issue than it was in the 1980s.

The 1995 presidential elections nevertheless suggest that in the short to medium term the debate in France will not be over the viability of European integration but over timing, speed, and specific policies. Alternative policies are not without appeal, but the platforms of Chirac, Balladur, and Jospin indicate that a return to economic nationalism continues to be rejected. The post-1983 consensus remains in place—at least among the large majority of business and political elites.

Jacques Chirac, elected president in June 1995, faces the difficult task of negotiating the next stage of European integration. The French agenda at the ongoing IGC conference that began in March 1996 includes support for reducing the size and power of the Commission, increasing the authority of the Council of Ministers, and rejecting qualified majority voting over defense and security issues. The decision at the June 1995 meeting in Corfu to postpone the third stage of the monetary union until 1999 already reflects the understanding that the terms of the Maastricht Treaty are negotiable. Chirac continues firmly to support the EMU and the introduction of the Euro but the persistence of high unemployment may lead to further delays. The French government will have to undertake major real cuts in government spending if it is to reduce the public sector deficit to no more than 3 percent of GDP by 1997 as called for in the Maastricht Treaty. However, strict adherence to the criteria may be modified at future IGC meetings. In the final analysis, the determination of Jacques Chirac and Helmut Kohl to implement the Maastricht vision will be decisive for its success.

NOTES

1. See for example: *Le Monde*, September 5 and 18, 1995; *L'Express*, September 11 and October 2, 1992.

2. *Le Monde*, May 4, 1995.

3. See for example: Ronald Tiersky, *France in the New Europe: Changing Yet Steadfast* (Belmont, Calif.: Wadsworth, 1994); Alistair Cole; *François Mitterrand: A Study in Political Leadership* (New York: Routledge, 1994); Elizabeth Haywood, "The European Policy of François Mitterrand," *Journal of Common Market Studies* 32 no. 2 (June 1993), pp. 269–282.

4. Wayne Northcutt, *Mitterrand: A Political Biography* (New York: Holmes and Meier, 1994), pp. 70–71.

5. For a detailed examination of Mitterrand's economic program see Volkmar Lauber, "Economic Policy," in Patrick McCarthy, *The French Socialists in Power, 1981–1986* (New York: Greenwood Press, 1987), pp. 23–44; Peter A. Hall, "The Evolution of Economic Policy Under Mitterrand," in George Ross et al., eds., *The Mitterrand Experiment: Continuity and Change in Modern France* (Oxford: Oxford University Press, 1987), pp. 54–72.

6. Cole, *François Mitterrand*, p. 36; Lauber, "Economic Policy," p. 26.

7. The exact reason(s) for Mitterrand's decision remain unknown but for one explanation; see Hall, "Evolution of Economic Policy," pp. 56–57.

8. For his views on Europe and the Maastricht Treaty see Jean-Pierre Chevènement, *Une certain idée de la France m'amène à . . .* (Paris: Albin Michel, 1992).

9. For a detailed analysis see Elizabeth Z. Haywood, "The French Socialists and European Institutional Reform," *Journal of European Integration* 12 nos. 2–3 (1989), pp. 121–149.

10. For an analysis of the PCF position of the early 1980s see Joy Bound and Kevin Featherstone, "The French Left and the European Community," in David S. Bell, ed., *Contemporary French Political Parties* (London: Croom Helm, 1982), pp. 165–189.

11. From his hospital bed after an automobile accident, Chirac issued a statement on December 6, 1978. "Nous devons dire non . . . nous disons NON. Non à la politique de supranationalité. . . . Nous disons non à une France qui démissionne aujourd'hui pour s'effacer demain. [We must say No . . . we say No. No to the politics of supranationality. We say no to a France who resigns today to fade away tomorrow.]" *Le Monde*, December 8, 1978.

12. François Saint–Ouen, "Les Parties Politiques Français et l'Europe: Système Politique et Fonctionnement du Discours," *Revue française de science politique* 36, no. 2 (April 1986), pp. 215–217.

13. *Le Monde*, March 15, 1984.

14. Andrew Moravcsik, "Negotiating the Single European Act: National Interests

and Conventional Statecraft in the EC," *International Organization* 45 (winter 1991), pp. 19–56.

15. *Le Monde*, March 15, 1984.

16. *Le Monde*, March 21, 1989. There was a strong sentiment among the political analysts that the Right's battle over the EP lists had little to do with Europe. Instead, priority was given to internal domestic considerations such as the 1995 presidential elections.

17. *Le Monde*, May 11, 1989.

18. *Le Monde*, April 7, 1989.

19. *Le Monde*, May 23, 1989.

20. *Le Monde*, June 10, 1989.

21. Ibid. In 1989, Herzog coauthored a book with Yves Dimicoli entitled *Europe 92: Construire autrement et autre chose* (Paris: Messidor/Editions Sociales, 1989).

22. *Le Monde*, April 23–24, 1989.

23. *Le Monde*, May 3, 1989.

24. *Le Monde*, May 9, 1989.

25. *Le Monde*, March 3, 1989. The exact question was: "On parle beaucoup de grand marché unique européen de 1992–1993. Voyez-vous cette échéance avec confiance ou avec inquiétude?" Thirty-three percent responded "avec confiance" and 58 percent responded "avec inquiétude." Nine percent had no opinion.

26. See Cole, *François Mitterand*, pp. 150–163.

27. For several excellent analyses of the Maastricht Treaty see Alan W. Cafruny and Glenda G. Rosenthal., eds., *The State of the European Community: The Maastricht Debates and Beyond*, vol. 2 (Boulder, Colo.: Lynne Rienner Publishers, 1993).

28. For two in-depth analyses see: Andrew Appleton, "Maastricht and the French Party System: Domestic Implications of the Treaty Referendum," *French Politics and Society* 10, no. 4, (Fall 1992), pp. 1–18; and Bryon Criddle, "The French Referendum on the Maastricht Treaty September 1992," *Parliamentary Affairs* 46, no. 2 (April 1993), pp. 228–238.

29. *Le Monde*, June 3, 1992.

30. *Le Monde*, June 18, 1993.

31. Séguin explained: "Par mon 'non,' je demand justement une renégociation. Si je dis 'non', ce n'est pas pour mettre un terme à la construction européenne, c'est pour qu'elle revienne sur de meilleures bases. Il ne s'agit pas de renégocier uniquement sur quelque petits points de remise en cohérence juridique, mais de renégocier sur le fond. [With my No, I ask for a renegotiation. If I say No, it is not to end the construction of Europe, it is to return it to a better basis. This does not mean only renegotiating several small points for judicial coherence but a renegotiation of fundamentals.]" *Le Monde*, July 4, 1992.

32. Philippe de Villiers, *Notre Europe sans Maastricht* (Paris: Albin Michel, 1992).

33. After Kohl's remarks during the Mitterrand-Séguin debate on September 3, de Villiers stated: "L'intervention de M. Kohl m'a choqué . . . Un Allemand . . . , quand il nous dit à nous Français, faites ça, c'est bon pour vous les Français, moi, je le soupçonne de penser que c'est surtout bon pour lui. [The intervention of Mr. Kohl shocked me. A German, . . . when he tells us, do that, it is good for the French, me, I suspect that above all it is good for him.]" *Le Monde*, September 5, 1992.

34. *Le Monde*, August 25, 1992.

35. Ibid.

36. *Le Monde*, May 17–18, 1992.

37. *Le Monde*, April 16, 1992.

38. See, for example, Cole, *François Mitterrand*, p. 163.

39 Criddle, "French Referendum," p. 231.

40. Polls stated that only 12 percent of voters planned to use their referendum vote to express disapproval of President Mitterrand. *Economist,* September 12, 1992, p. 48.

41. *Le Monde*, April 19, 1994.

42. Bernard Kouchner, former PS minister of Health and Humanitarian Action, explained: "L'idée d'Europe ne séduit plus, pire elle fait peur. Elle est devenue le bouc émissaire d'un monde qui craque. . . . [The idea of Europe is no longer seductive, worse it causes fear. It has become the scapegoat for a world breaking apart.]" *Le Monde*, May 7, 1994.

43. *Le Monde*, May 18, 1994.

44. On January 4, 1994, Prime Minister Balladur stated that members of the government should not take part in EP elections. "Je me demande si le mieux ne serait pas que le gouvernement se tienne en dehors de cette affaire d'élections européenes. [I ask myself if it would not be best for the government to remain uninvolved in the European elections.]" *Le Monde*, January 6, 1994.

45. *Figaro Magazine*, May 14, 1994.

46. Laurent Cohen-Tanugi, "Les carences de l'Europe minimale," *Le Monde*, April 15, 1995. See also *Le Point*, no. 1181, May 8, 1995, p. 45, where Europe is categorized as "very absent, too absent from the presidential debate. . . . "

47. *Le Monde*, March 2, 1995.

48. See Delors's interview in *Der Spiegel*, no. 48, November 28, 1994, pp. 147–152, and in *Le Monde*, December 7, 1994.

49. For Balladur's position on Europe, see his article, "Pour un nouveau traité de l'Elysée," *Le Monde*, November 30, 1994.

50. On March 16, 1995, Chirac declared that the Maastricht treaty "a été ratifiée par le peuple français et il n'est donc nullement question de le remettre en cause. [was ratified by the French people and therefore there is no possibility of calling it into question.]" *Le Monde*, March 17, 1995.

51. *Le Monde*, December 16, 1994.

52. *Le Monde*, April 21, 1995.

53. *Le Monde*, April 22, 1995.

54. *Le Monde*, February 4–5, 1996.

55. See, for example, *Le Monde*, January 17, 1996.

56. Chirac reiterated this support throughout his campaign. *Le Monde*, March 17, 1995, and April 28, 1995.

57. *Le Monde*, May 3, 1995. According to Chirac, "an isolated France will be weakened" and "our capacity to influence depends on the Union."

7

Poetry on Palimpsest: Germany, the Greens, and European Integration

Carl Lankowski

In the introduction to this volume, three processes were said to be at work as a result of the intensification of economic integration in Europe: rationalization, regionalization, and tertiarization. "New social movements" best articulate the postindustrial politics associated with the process of tertiarization. Of all the parties on the political spectrum, Green parties best express the penetration of the movements into the parliamentary domain. The growing willingness of these parties to exercise power in government is of great relevance to European integration. Moreover, their European policies act as a kind of leading indicator of the European Union's (EU's) evolving issue agenda. For that reason, they possess a theoretical interest in equal measure to whatever practical implications their behavior has for EU politics and policymaking.

Though the German Greens were not the first Green party in Europe, Germany's size, location, and domestic political constellation insure that the German Greens present by far the most important example of the trend toward increasing Green party EU engagement. In this chapter I trace the evolution of the German Greens' vision of Europe and its translation into practical policy proposals. Because Germany is the site of Europe's densest network of social movement actors[1] and its most successful green party in electoral terms, examining the European policy of the German Greens amounts to carrying out a critical case study of the relationships between emerging social forces, represented by the social movement sector, and the processes of European regional integration.

Green reactions to Europe's unfolding constitutional process until recently have been projections of alternatives generated directly from social movement norms and visions. They have been likened to a writing project whose authors had mistakenly presumed the availability of a blank slate. But Europe is so well-used that the Greens must learn to write on the continent's historical palimpsest—a surface bearing the imprint of previous writing efforts. The history related below summarizes the episodes that led the Greens to embrace "palimpsest" in their efforts to redraw the contours of Europe.

In the section immediately following, I link social movement attitudes to

Green parties with respect to regional integration in Europe. In the second section, I describe the evolution of German Green Party attitudes toward regional integration, beginning with an overview of the first ten years of the existence of the party at the national level (1979–1989). Important episodes are discussed thereafter: the impact of German unification; the Maastricht debate; formation of the European Federation of Green Parties (EFGP); the Aachen party congress of November 1993; and the emerging European policy of the new Green Bundestag Group in 1995. I conclude the chapter with a summary of main factors responsible for producing the Greens' evolving European policy and an evaluation of the Greens' initial response to the intergovernmental conference (IGC) convened in 1996.

MOVEMENT PARTIES AND EUROPEAN INTEGRATION

The New Social Movements and European Integration

Social movements are defined by some form of opposition to prevailing cultural, social, economic, and political conditions. By "new social movements" I mean those mobilizations that challenged the Western European postwar status quo beginning in the latter part of the 1960s. In addition to the ecology (or environmental) movement, the European movement sector encompasses mobilizations around military issues, gender questions, and specific state actions or contemplated actions interpreted as threats to health or individual freedoms. Of these, the most comprehensive and persistent is undoubtedly the environmental movement. Although the temptation to reduce its critical thrust to functionalist terms is to be resisted, one can still define the environmental movement's leitmotif as the unsustainability of dominant production and consumption patterns. In this chapter I examine the fate of that opposition vis-à-vis the European Union.

Organizational traits vary across movement segment and country, as does the degree to which opposition is expressed explicitly. In the context of postwar Europe, these variations have given rise to a broad palette of actions and a profusion of collective identities. Nevertheless, a voluminous and growing literature pays tribute to the transnational empirical studies that claim to discover beneath this heterogeneity a stable complex of common attitudes and values. Ronald Inglehart developed a materialist/postmaterialist typology to describe and analyze the phenomenon. Postmaterialists value quality of life issues such as a clean environment, individual freedom, and participation in decisionmaking processes affecting them. They form the attitudinal and cognitive basis of "new politics" expressed by the movements.[2]

To the extent that citizens are rational political actors, the external configuration of power and channels of influence should be as important as value orientation in determining action. Because all effort—even collective identity-creating effort—is "economized," action will be crafted for effect. This central insight of the "resource mobilization" school helps us understand the disconnect often found between the source of a grievance and the manifestation of corresponding protest.[3] As the EU is an incomplete polity, this insight is particularly important in dealing with opposition to the EU. Movement parties such as the Greens during one phase of their development may relate to EU policymaking arenas expressively, by way of symbolic politics, rather than instrumentally.

Beyond their generally negative orientation to economic growth, the movements' critique of regional integration comes from the apparent remoteness of its institutions from European citizens. In this, attitudes toward the EU are part of the broader syndrome of mass disaffection from political establishments throughout Europe in recent years. A new critical civic awareness has been connected to the same new middle-class strata that produce most postmaterialists.[4] It is connected in turn to the preference for small-scale communities historically advocated by political ecology. Leopold Kohr's *Disunion Now!* manifesto was an important source of inspiration for eco-guru E. F. Schumacher. Schumacher acolyte Kirkpatrick Sale developed the political notion of bioregions, which ended up in German Green Party European election manifestos and program studies.[5]

In sum, for movement activists the project of European integration in whatever form—in the context of a Gaullist *l'Europe des patries*, technocratic functionalism, or the federalist notion of a "United States of Europe"— seemed to be built on the same faulty foundations. All of these variants shared the original sin of the materialist ethos of the 1950s. Against this background, what are the circumstances, if any, under which movement activists come to view the project of European regional integration in a positive light? Put the other way around, what impact are the organizational, legal, and administrative practices of the Brussels institutions having on the green project?

Movement Parties and the European Community

One of European sociology's recent contributions to social movement theory consists in resisting the Anglo-American tendency to locate the movements either in the psyche or in organizations. A totalizing, phenomenological perspective is clear in Alain Touraine's studies of May 1968 in France, the antinuclear movement, and Polish Solidarnosc (Solidarity), as it is in Alberto Melucci's work focusing on identity.[6] This perspective helps us get close to the centrality of ideologies in the European political experience. Parties have played a central role as the locus for historical agency based on ideological precepts. In that sense, as the state has become an increasingly important element in the constitution and reproduction of social life, parties have become natural conduits of totalizing movements oriented to social transformation. The apotheosis of this development comes with the deracination of movement parties from the industrial era, the freezing of the Left-Right political spectrum, and the narrowing of the universe of political discourse around questions of distribution of the economic pie. In this context, postindustrial politics was forced to become an antipolitics. Emancipation from the economistic structures that permeated the political-administrative system required their reprogramming, if not dissolution. Movement activists resisted the notion that this task could be an "inside job." No matter how diffuse and fragmented, extraparliamentary forms of action were considered the authentic expression of the common project of social transformation. In short, party formation was very problematic for many movement activists. Indeed, "parliamentarization" of the movements constituted the dominant issue of the 1980s.

Helped along by perceptions that even fewer opportunities presented themselves for exercising influence there, the antipolitical posture carried over to the European level. This is clear from the coalition behavior of the first Green delegates to the European Parliament (EP). In 1984, the eleven Greens elected to the EP (including seven Germans) joined with several successful regionalist candidates and the four Danish members of the European Parliament (MEPs) elected from the People's Movement Against the European Union to form the Green Alternative European Link (GRAEL), in order to attain the group size necessary to enjoy full benefits under internal EP rules. Consequently, to the normally high degree of political heterogeneity within EP groups, one must also factor in the effects of the historical novelty of the Greens and their coalition with others. Especially in the absence of external pressure (either from a responsible European government or a European-level party structure), the predictable result was internal fragmentation, isolation of MEPs from each other and their own national parties, and low levels of policy coherence.[7]

Contributing the largest single national delegation to GRAEL gave the German Greens decisive influence over the formation of the initial EP group. The 1989 EP elections returned a much larger Green delegation, almost equally balanced between the German (eight MEPs), Italian (seven MEPs), and French (eight MEPs) national delegations. This configuration attenuated the antipolitical, movement orientation of the first EP group and led to the formation of a "purely green" group of twenty-six MEPs. Exclusion of the regionalists led one German Green to resign from the Green Group and join the regionalists. From the point of view of the balance between national delegations, the 1994 EP elections marked a return to the 1984 pattern: The German Greens would have an absolute majority of members in the Green Group. By this time, however, a revolution in German Green attitudes toward the EU had transformed the behavior of the German delegation. A much more cohesive

EP Green Group has been the result. Overall, the group declined from twenty-six in 1989 to twenty-one MEPs in 1994. Two MEPs were added, one each from Sweden and Finland, due to enlargement in January 1995. The results of the three EP elections in which Greens have won seats are listed in Table 7.1.

Table 7.1   Green Group MEPs, by Country

	1984 MEPs		1989 MEPs		1994 MEPs	
Country/Party	%	Number	%	Number	%	Number
Belgium, Agalev	7.0	1	7.6	1	6.7	1
Belgium, Ecolo	3.9	1	6.3	2	4.8	1
Denmark, De Gronne	–	–	–	–	–	–
France, Les Verts	3.4	–	10.6	8	2.9	–
Germany B90/Greens	8.2	7	8.4	8	10.1	12
Greece, Pol. Oikol.	–	–	–	–	–	–
Ireland, Green Party	0.5	–	3.8	–	–	2
Italy, Fed. Verdi	–	–	6.2	5	3.2	3
Luxembourg, Greng	–	–	–	–	10.9	1
Netherlands, Groen.	–	–	–	–	–	–
Netherlands, G-Links	5.6	2	7.0	2	3.7	1
Spain, Las Verdes	–	–	–	–	–	–
UK, Green Party	0.55	–	14.5	–	3.2	–
Total elected MEPs		11		26		21
After enlargement (1/95)						23

The need to achieve some coordination between European Green parties was recognized at the time of the first Green EP electoral successes. After a decade of experience, Green parties all had embraced the notion of affecting policy through parliamentary participation. Eschewing the rhetoric of rejectionism, the EFGP was founded in June 1993 on the basis of guiding principles that advanced a "Pan-European strategy of ecological and social reform."[8] Grouped in three clusters—eco-development, global security, and new citizenship—the principles reflect the main thrust of movement concerns, minus the sharper and more radical profiles of constituent parties in each of these domains. By 1994, twenty-eight parties had affiliated with the EFGP, compared to the eight member parties from the Benelux, France, the United Kingdom, and Germany that established the much more loosely organized European Coordination of Green Parties in 1984. Nine EFGP parties come from countries that are not members of the EU. In addition to the twenty countries represented by single parties, two parties each represent Luxembourg and the Netherlands, and separate, regionalist parties represent Scotland, Wallonia, and Flanders.

The German Greens

In retrospect, 1989 appears to have been the high-water mark of Green electoral success in Europe. In arenas at every level, the overall trajectory of Green parties suffered a significant decline in the period after 1989. Standing out against this trend is the remarkable electoral resurgence enjoyed by the German Greens. Of the Green parties in the four largest EU member states with demonstrated Green electoral potential, only the Bündnis-90/Die Grünen (hereinafter B-90/Greens) prospered after 1990.

The scope, depth, and stability of the German Greens electoral anchoring are remarkable, especially when measured against the performance of Green parties in the other large EU member states. Green parties have enjoyed some electoral success in the UK, Italy, and France, but in only one case have Green parties done better than 3.7 percent of the vote in a national election, whether parliamentary or presidential (French parliamentary elections of 1993 yielded 8.6 percent for the Greens). In elections to the European Parliament, the 1989 vote for the French Greens (10.1 percent) and British Greens (14.5 percent) matched or exceeded the best German results, but were one-time exceptions, suddenly emerging and just as suddenly returning to electoral oblivion. Regional results are similary meager outside Germany.

A good picture of the degree to which the Greens have been able to consolidate their electoral position—particularly in the Western *Länder*—since 1990 is provided in Figure 7.1 by the curve depicting a rolling three-year average Green result for all Landtag elections contested by the Greens since 1979. From 1981 to the time of this writing the party contested all fifty-three Landtag elections; the trend line moves from 4.9 percent to 9.2 percent. With the exception of the curve for national elections, which takes a dip at the election of 1990 before recovering in 1994, the trend for performances on all other levels is similar. In addition to these data, most revealing are the figures for local Green representation. They demonstrate the deep roots struck by activists over the 1980s and suggest an essential springboard for success at regional, federal, and European levels. Thomas Scharf has one of the very few systematic accounts of local level Green activity in Germany. His summary data for West German local Green representation in 1991 are as follows: In 1991, there were 3,281 Green representatives at the *Gemeinde* (town) level and 1,249 at the *Freistadt/Kreis* (city/county) level, for a total of 4,467.[9]

Finally, the difficult relationship between West Germany and the five Eastern Länder deserves mention. The first post-Communist Landtag elections were held in March 1990, in anticipation of unification with the eleven Western Länder. Once unification was an accomplished fact, the Party of Democratic Socialism (PDS) became an attractive means to express disquiet over the often brutal hardships of system transformation. In the second round of Landtag elections, held during 1994, two trends forcefully asserted themselves: the resurgence of the PDS and the decline of B-90/Greens (by this

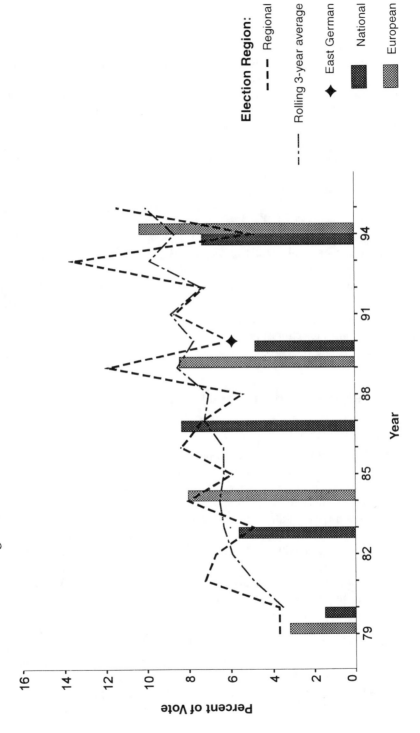

Figure 7.1 Electoral Performance of the German Greens

time a fused, all-German party), a pattern offering strong, if indirect, sub-
stantiation for the postmaterialist thesis regarding Green support mentioned
earlier. In Brandenburg, the Greens' percentage of the vote dropped from 9.2
to 2.9 percent; in Thüringen from 6.5 to 4.5 percent; in Sachsen from 5.6 to
4.1 percent; and in Sachsen-Anhalt from 5.6 to 5.1 percent (the only Eastern
Land in which B-90/Greens are still represented in the Landtag). Their support was stable in Mecklenburg-Vorpommern, at 4.2 percent. Consequently,
all the improvement in overall Green electoral performance is accounted for
by disproportionate increases in the old West German Länder. Indeed, major
breakthroughs have been achieved in Baden-Württemberg, where the Greens
received 9.4 percent of the vote; Hamburg (1993), 13.5 percent; Bremen
(1995), 13.5 percent; Hessen (1995), 11.2 percent; and in Germany's most
populous and industrial state, Nordrhein-Westfalen (1995), 10.0 percent. The
red-green (Social Democrat [SPD-B-90/Greens]) coalition in Nordrhein-
Westfalen is being heralded as the prototype of a similarly composed national governing coalition.

The general contrast between German Green entrenchment and the
evanescent Green party organizations in other EU member states is striking.
What explains the resilience of the German Greens? Why and how did a party
locked into a rejectionist posture toward the EU come to embrace a reformist
strategy?

THE HISTORY OF THE GERMAN GREENS

Formative Period: 1977–1989

With a view toward the agreeable prospect of receiving public funding under
West Germany's party finance laws to promote further citizen mobilization,
the Greens launched themselves as a national party in order to participate in
the first elections to the European Parliament in 1979. Despite their antisys-
tem posture, the political outlooks and styles of the original elements of the
party were extremely heterogeneous. Different shades of opposition to the
European Community (EC) coexisted within the party. Reflecting the integrating function of the peace movement in the social movement sector at the
time and the expectation that SPV-Die Grünen would benefit from the energy of the movement, the EC was interpreted in terms of North Atlantic Treaty
Organization (NATO) strategy.[10]

The 3.2 percent of the national vote harvested by the fledgling party was
insufficient to win seats in the European Parliament, but convinced activists
that there was space for a new party in Bonn. The Greens' 1980 constitutive
and program congresses were followed by initial electoral failure in the 1980
Bundestag elections (1.5 percent of the vote). In March 1983, they entered the
Bundestag with twenty-seven members. In June 1984 the first German

Greens entered the European Parliament. Bundestag ratification of NATO missile deployments in December 1983 encouraged the party to continue its practice of framing EC issues in terms of the military blocs. Its Peace Manifesto called for withdrawal from NATO as a way to dismantle the European bipolar bloc structure. The Greens ran against the Brussels bureaucracy, on the slogan of "Europe of the regions," that is, decentralization of authority and power to subnational communities.[11] The party's officially rejectionist posture vis-à-vis the EC can be gauged by the statements of two successful Green candidates for the European Parliament:

> We should use this fake parliament lacking legislative and executive competences mainly as a tribune [*sic*] for public relations work. The current goals of the EC . . . are to be rejected. (Brigitte Heinrich)

> This dinosaur is no longer capable of being reformed, but we must prevent it from falling on our heads when it collapses. (Jakob von Uexküll)[12]

By 1987 a pattern of deepening introspection about the party's attitude toward the EC and other regional international organizations was well under way, although the consummation of this process had to wait until the end of 1992. Several factors were at work. First, dramatic changes in the EC (ratification of the Single European Act [SEA]) and Soviet Union (Mikhail Gorbachev's glasnost and perestroika policies) demanded attention and led to differing assessments within the party. Second, the political conjuncture in West Germany looked favorable to the Greens. After the Bundestag election of 1987 almost doubled the number of Green members, the apparent weakness of the national government gave rise to speculation about possible government participation. The same event provided growing resources for policy studies, facilitating a refocusing of the attention of party elites on the EC and NATO. A Realo initiative posited that Western integration, begun under former West German Chancellor Konrad Adenauer, both encouraged democratization of German society and reassured Germany's Western neighbors.[13] Third, the first delegation of German Greens to the European Parliament had gained experience with EC institutions. As awareness of the implications of the SEA and the internal market program spread, some MEPs began campaigning for greater engagement in the Brussels institutions. By the end of their first period in the EP, Green MEPs achieved results, however modest, in dealing with the aftermath of the Chernobyl catastrophe and UK Plutonium contamination at Windscale, increasing EC budget outlays for renewable energy projects, banning beef containing growth hormones,[14] exposing a transnational nuclear waste scandal,[15] and generally encouraging the Commission to respond to the environmental agenda.[16] Despite these promising developments, GRAEL's organizational performance was under par. According to its secretary-general, "in four years of shared political work, the GRAEL has been unable to adopt a common position on its basic attitude towards the EC."[17]

Finally, partly as a reflection of intraparty conflict and partly to fulfill their regionalist aspirations in the EC, Green Länder parties in Hessen and Baden-Württemberg organized their own debates and campaign events for the coming European Parliamentary elections.[18] Despite important nuances that differentiated positions of the Länder organizations, they all moved away from a rejectionist stance toward a perspective of radical reform. The Baden-Württemberg Greens introduced their EC position at the December 1988 extraordinary federal party congress at Karlsruhe as a formal proposal for a "global alternative" to the material circulated by the party's program commission. The initiative was designed to induce the delegates to sharply focus the Greens' statement on the EC internal market program, which the initiators were promoting as the campaign's central theme. In a compromise decision, the Realo-influenced document was adopted as a platform on the internal market and circulated with other campaign materials.[19]

Despite all this activity, formidable obstacles stood in the way of policy change. First of all, strictly speaking, there had been no Green policy on most European issues apart from declarations of general attitude. Working out a policy amounted to an exercise that demanded focused expertise and time. By 1991 all that had emerged was a study organized by the Bundestag group that placed European institutions in the framework of a global ecological reform project for the international economy.[20]

Second, discussion within the party was necessary. Two factors conspired to prevent any real discussion from occurring. One was the structure of the party. Designed as a conduit for the social movements, the party's European policy reflected the view of the peace movement, the central thrust of which was a policy to dismantle the bipolar military blocs on the continent. EC affairs were seen primarily in this light, enjoying no autonomous existence as objects of party policy. The other, related factor consisted in the majorities that the Fundamentalo wing of the party routinely mobilized at the federal delegate assemblies at which such discussions would have to be aired. Proponents of policy development, even if supported by party rank and file and potential voters, might have thought better than to try to force a debate they were doomed to lose under these circumstances.

Unification

The unexpected prospect of unifying the two Germanies after the breach of the Berlin Wall in November 1989 created a contradiction in the Greens' attitude toward the EC. Deterioration in East-West relations during the early 1980s focused attention on relations between the two German states across the political spectrum, giving rise to speculation about German nationalism and the possibility of a new Rapallo—an eastward diplomatic shift. German-German cooperation in the interest of peace did emerge from time to time as a theme among the Greens, but nationalist motivations were consistently disavowed. Indeed, prior to November 1989, renunciation of unification designs of any sort increasingly defined the Greens' position with respect to the German Democratic Republic (GDR). Unlike any other West German party, the Greens persisted in advocating a two-Germany scenario as a contribution to a peaceful European order after the Wall fell, well into 1990.[21] Establishment of Green Länder affiliates in eastern Germany after unification was hesitant and late, especially in comparison to the behavior of the other West German parties. And merger with Bündnis-90, the parliamentary form adopted by citizens' movements prominent in the overthrow of the GDR neo-Stalinist regime, came in 1993 as a tardy acknowledgment that unification was permanent.

Against this background, the collapse of the Soviet empire, occurring before the fusion of B-90/Greens, at first strengthened the pacifist orientation of the party. Greens condemned military solutions to the Gulf crisis of 1990–1991 and Yugoslavia's disintegration. By the same token, it became increasingly difficult to adhere to positions of fundamental opposition to membership in the EC and NATO after the fait accompli of German unification. Under the prevailing circumstances, how else could the Greens credibly demonstrate their opposition to nationalist revivals?

Meanwhile, merger of Bündnis-90 with the Greens generated momentum for revision of the Greens' pacifist stance. Signaling its alarm over continuing ethnic cleansing in Bosnia, the newly fused B-90/Greens *Länderrat* adopted a resolution at its June 1993 meeting in Bonn advocating the principle of "active intervention in support of human rights." The resolution went on to say: "In cases such as Bosnia-Herzogovina, where an ethnocentric, imperialistic *Grossmachtpolitik* rages, any application of compelling force cannot be entirely ruled out in advance." In crossing the threshold of force so at odds with the tenaciously held principle of nonviolence, this formulation unleashed a storm of protest within the party and precipitated the first extraordinary party congress of the newly fused party, held in Bonn in October 1993.[22] Although the Greens' pacifist stance was reaffirmed, the debate turned on the concept of "civilian foreign policy." The logic of this position required the party to demonstrate their commitment in nonmilitary peacekeeping structures, above all, the EU.

Thus, nearly a year prior to the German Federal Constitutional Court decision of July 1994 allowing Bundeswehr participation in NATO "out of area" missions, events had already compelled the Greens to decouple EU policy at least partially from broader questions of foreign policy. This line of development, immanent in the Greens' ideology of nonviolence, joined a second stream of thinking that had surfaced among Realos in 1988.[23] Green

Realo leader Joschka Fischer summarizes the arguments for German *Einbindung* (tying) into European organizations in his 1994 book, *Risiko Deutschland*.[24] Not only were there practical limits to what Germany could do on its own—even a Green Germany—but especially after unification and the collapse of the Soviet Union, an independent course of action *(deutscher Sonderweg)* was disruptive and dangerous. Only a reformist course, working within extant forms of international cooperation, could reassure other states and promote stability.

The Debate over the Maastricht Treaty

A major turn in the attitude of the German Greens toward the EU involved the negotiation and ratification of the Treaty on European Union (Maastricht Treaty). The IGCs on Economic and Monetary Union (EMU) and political union that gave rise to the Maastricht Treaty convened the same month the Western Greens were punished by the electorate and their own miscalculations with dismissal from the Bundestag. Instead of succeeding in their attempt to bend public opinion to ecological issues (their slogan was, "Everyone is talking about Germany. We're talking about the weather: acid rain, the ozone hole, global warming."), they were overwhelmed by the issue salience of German unification. Owing to their efforts to create a separate electoral district out of the East German Länder, however, the Eastern Greens combined with a loose association of movement organizations to form B-90/Greens and received just enough votes to enter the Bundestag with eight members.

The loss of nearly three hundred staff positions and corresponding financial support was a major blow for the Western Greens. Along with the newness and small size of the new (Eastern) parliamentary group, which had no official links with the Western Greens, the electoral debacle deprived the party of the capacity and motivation to pay much attention to the Maastricht negotiations. European policy formulation became more reactive, but it also brought together elements of the Eastern and Western parties as the new Bundestag deputies rehired some of the old *Fraktion* (party) staff. Not surprisingly, the German delegation to the European Parliament was far more attentive to negotiations in the IGCs.

Meanwhile, rediscovering the logic of the Schuman Plan, German Chancellor Helmut Kohl was only too willing to accommodate French interests in responding to unification with more integration. But Kohl answered the French desires to control the Bundesbank (by launching a new EMU project) and German foreign policy (through some form of common framework for action) with a counterproposal to increase the powers of the European Parliament. His government also acceded to the European Commission's plans to streamline the institutional structure as well as to proposals for increasing the fields in which the EU could act.

The structure of German governance[25] ensured that domestic constituencies would extract a price for this approach. First, German federalism operated already so as to provide the Länder with a privileged observation post on EC policy.[26] Insisting that their competence not be diminished without a corresponding increase in their control capacities, the Länder pushed both federalism and the democratic agenda. Federalism also accounts for the effectiveness of pressure for democratic reform by Social Democratic Bundestag opposition. Their dominant position in the Bundesrat, Germany's lower national legislative chamber, created a de facto grand coalition. Second, the legal independence of the Bundesbank created a parameter of action for Kohl. He had to insist on the strict convergence criteria ultimately laid down in Article 109j of the Maastricht Treaty. Even there, the Kohl government insisted on a strict parallelism between EMU and European Political Union (EPU): Germany would approve EMU only on condition of a significant breakthrough in the democratization of the EC.

As it turned out, Kohl was only able to deliver what appeared to be modest gains in the area of EPU, an outcome easily blamed on limits placed on the bargaining positions of other member states. This situation placed the Greens in a curious position. In effect, their political problem—all the more pronounced in light of their removal from the national political arena—consisted of establishing an independent profile against the established parties, each of which had striven for objectives at least similar to those of the Greens.

Maastricht: so nicht! Soon after the Maastricht ratification phase opened with the official signing on February 2, 1992, a team of party activists belonging to the party's federal working group on peace and international policy (BAG-FIP) and the Bundestag group's working group on Europe (AK-Europa), which included Green MEPs, produced a policy paper destined for adoption at the Länderrat in Kassel the following October. The resulting resolution, "DIE GRÜNEN zu den Maastrichter Beschlüssen: SO NICHT!" (Maastricht: NO WAY!), is both the last in a series of major Western Green documents on Europe and the first that takes cognizance of the preferences of East German party members and colleagues from B-90.

Governed by the instinct to act as tribune of the movements, a role very much in keeping with efforts of otherwise isolated MEPs to connect with *die Basis* (Green Party constituencies), the Kassel document emphasizes rejection of the Maastricht Treaty. The text complains that the Treaty does not reduce the democratic deficit, is not oriented to ecological and social reconstruction or to "civilian policy" internally or externally, and does not address all-European structures. In sum, the Kassel Länderrat resolution is an expression of identity that summarizes what the Greens are against. No coherent vision of European policy emerges. However, it acknowledges the desirability of integration, especially in light of German unification, and the relevance of the fact of Western European integration, "which must be the starting point for any policy."[27]

Adopted in the context of several Bundestag debates on Maastricht in the autumn of 1992, the resolution calls for a renegotiation of the Treaty, accompanied by special joint parliamentary assemblies and nongovernmental organization (NGO) participation from all over Europe to lend the effort a democratic character. Finally, added to the original draft is a three-paragraph "Recommendation for a Green European Initiative" that calls for the convening of an all-European IGC in 1992, renegotiation of EMU to modify its structures and extend monetary cooperation to the rest of the continent, and provision of greater powers to the EP and NGOs. Beyond Maastricht renegotiation, the text advocates revision of the Treaty of Rome with the aims of distributing policymaking competence among levels of governance, democratizing EC decisionmaking bodies, and preparing for enlargement on the basis of respect for new members' social policies and regulatory arrangements.

Reflecting the ambivalence within the German Greens as well as other Green parties in Europe vis-à-vis Maastricht, the Kassel resolution contrasts with the remarkably cogent plea for a reformist strategy aimed at the 1996 IGC and written by another German Green MEP.[28] For its part, the Green Group in the EP could barely unite on a common strategy. In April 1992, seeking to activate an alliance between several member states and the EP (Italy, which had a referendum on the issue, Germany, and Belgium) to improve the status of the EP in the Treaty, Green MEPs voted against the Martin Report in the European Parliament Plenary, which heavily criticized the Maastricht Treaty but accepted it as the basis for further progress. The negative vote came as a result of the rejection of a Green amendment offering support in return for attaching conditions to be met by the European Council meeting in Lisbon in June 1992.[29] Back in Bonn, despite the Kassel resolution and although most arguments were supported by the members,[30] four B-90/Greens voted in favor of ratification, four against in December 1992.

Constitutional challenge.   The inspiration for a constitutional challenge to Maastricht came the same month the Kassel resolution passed, from German MEP Wilfried Telkämper, member of the Green Group since 1984. Preparations accelerated after the June referendum in Denmark. Of the six remaining German Green MEPs (two had defected to other EP groups), three besides Telkämper supported the complaint. In contrast to the West German party's federal executive board's (BuVo) accommodating response for support, the East German B-90/Greens Bundestag Fraktion was noncommittal. The courtroom proved to be just as crowded as the movement sector, as numerous constitutional challenges were also launched by elements of the

Right, including Manfred Brunner, Die Republikaner, and many right-wing *Prominenz.* Brunner had been the national-liberal head of the Bavarian FDP, before becoming EC Commissioner Martin Bangemann's *chef de cabinet,* and was fired by Bangemann in August 1992 for going public with his criticisms of the Treaty. Several weeks after the Bundestag and Bundesrat votes, in January 1993, the Federal Constitutional Court (BVG) decided to hear Brunner's and the Greens' challenges.

The Greens' case was based on the guarantee of German statehood given in Article 79/3 of the Basic Law: "Amendments of this Basic Law affecting the division of the Federation into Länder, the participation on principle of the Länder in legislation, or the basic principles laid down in Articles 1 and 20, shall be inadmissible." The relevant passage of Article 20 states: "All state authority emanates from the people. It shall be exercised by the people by means of elections and voting and by specific legislative, executive, and judicial organs" and "All Germans shall have the right to resist any person or persons seeking to abolish that constitutional order, should no other remedy be possible." Article 1 cites the duty of the state to respect and protect the dignity of individuals and refers to a catalogue of civil rights. The Greens also relied on Article 38, the first article under Basic Law Part III (the Bundestag), pertaining to elections. It establishes that elected deputies are to represent the whole people.[31]

In essence, the Greens argued that the Maastricht Treaty disrupted the relationship between the institutions of German statehood and undermined the effectiveness of the Bundestag and Bundesrat by transferring ill-defined powers to the EU Council of Ministers. Specifically, they feared that a strongly expansive functionalist logic based on the EMU mandate might lead to arrogations of authority to Brussels by way of Treaty Article F/3, the general empowering clause replacing the EC Article 235.[32]

Having heard oral arguments in July 1993, the Constitutional Court handed down its decision on October 12. Maastricht was deemed to be in compliance with the Basic Law. This finding rested on evidence that adaptation of democratic structures had so far kept pace with the process of integration. Nothing in the Treaty undermined the decisionmaking and control by the Bundestag. In particular, the Court rejected the argument that EMU escaped such control. Maastricht had created a *Staatenverbund* (federation of states) with supranational elements, not a *Bundesstaat* (federal state). Article F/3 does not authorize the EU to create its own resources, financial or otherwise, to fulfill the objectives it may set forth. The Federal Republic of Germany remained master of the EU. The Court reserved for itself the right to examine in the future whether EU organs remained within their sphere of competence.[33]

Politically more important than the legal argumentation was the public relations dilemma indirectly admitted by the Western Green Party. In virtually every public communication it made on the subject, the party was at pains to distinguish their position from that of their co-complainant, national-liberal Brunner. The discomfort was confirmed by a disparate series of events extending from June 1992 to June 1993. By the time the Court ruling came down enthusiasm had waned considerably. There was no reference to the case in the forty-eight-page Aachen European Parliament manifesto, voted less than a month after the ruling. It seems clear that the (recently fused) party wanted to dissociate itself from the case. Meanwhile, the EC further demonstrated its environmental credentials at the Earth Summit in Rio de Janeiro and with the adoption of the Fifth Environmental Action Program. Moreover, by the spring of 1993, the Danes authorized ratification of Maastricht in the second referendum on the subject, and the treaty finally cleared the British House of Commons after a year of deliberation and sailed through the House of Lords shortly thereafter. Suddenly, Germany was isolated as the sole member state that had not completed ratification.

The federal government deposited its instrument of ratification in Rome on the same day the Federal Constitutional Court spoke, thus enabling the treaty to come into force on November 1, 1993. Eleven days after that, the B-90/Greens met in Aachen to launch their campaign for the fourth direct election to the European Parliament.

Establishment of the European Federation of Green Parties

Coincident with the Maastricht ratification drama, discussions initiated by the German, French, and Benelux Green Parties led to the foundation of the EFGP in June 1993 at Majvik, Finland. The initiative was meant to improve their capacity to act at EU level and repair the studious lack of attention given to Green Party coordination in the past by national parties and MEPs. Representatives of the Green Parties were able to persuade other delegates to give priority to structure and process issues that would guide the constitutive meeting of the new EP group in June 1994 and establish a profile across Europe. A second leading motive was the concern that German preoccupation with central and eastern Europe might fatally undermine the project of regional integration, if, when the anticipated smaller Green group in the EP combined with a disproportionately larger German delegation, there were no organizational counterbalance.[34] The Germans preferred to have it both ways by advocating a pan-European entity; the Belgians preferred a group confined to EU members.[35] The compromise was a pan-European party with a standing group on EU affairs. In short, the B-90/Greens encountered an undercurrent of concern about a possible German breakout from its Western corset during the formation of the EFGP.

On June 22, 1994, in accordance with the protocol adopted by the EFGP Council in January of that year, the EFGP Standing Committee on EU Affairs recognized the elected MEPs as the Green Group. Significantly, rules of order were adopted that gave eight members a blocking minority vote (one-third + 1 = 8). Practically speaking, this device was designed to protect the group from the appearance of German hegemony (there were twelve German MEPs in the group).

In both the EFGP and the Green EP Group, German Greens adopted a reformist posture with respect to vital questions of substance. They advocated a European constitution with federal characteristics that nevertheless reinforced the subsidiarity principle as applied to subnational units.[36]

The Aachen Party Congress

With unusual clarity, cogency, and forcefulness, the recently fused party presented an entirely new agenda at its 1993 federal party congress devoted to Europe, evidenced in the speeches, the EP election manifesto adopted by an overwhelming majority of the over five hundred delegates, and the list of candidates for the EP election. Jürgen Trittin, Minister of Federal and European Affairs for the red/green government of Niedersachsen, and BuVo speaker Ludger Volmer provided the keynotes and introduced the program. Bad policy had driven the discussion of European integration into reactionary channels; the Greens needed to act against this dangerous background of nationalism. Affirmation of European political integration was a new but essential departure for the Greens, even though Maastricht was geared to Europe of the Cold War period. A pan-European strategy was now necessary. In addition, the neoliberal model of economic growth was in deep crisis. Far from consolidating the gains of integration, EMU was a recipe for fragmenting and destabilizing the continent. Only the Greens clearly articulated an alternative vision of ecological and social reconstruction. Finally, the Greens felt that people could only be won for integration by a massive, multifaceted democratic opening in the framework of a new type of federal concept.

The centerpiece of the BDV was the adoption of the EP election manifesto.[37] Utopian alternatives and easy slogans (e.g., Europe of the regions) disappeared, and the Programm Kommission (PK) dispensed with the dichotomies (e.g., *Für/Gegen*, *Traum/Alptraum*) of previous programs. Instead, the manifesto proceeded from a vision animated by strategic political considerations in the context of specific institutional arrangements. The program's most important departure consisted in its conceptualization of European policy as a species of domestic policy. This step dramatically increased the relevance of EU affairs for day-to-day politics, so it was not surprising that this program reverses the order of previous ones with respect to the presentation of policy areas. Fully twenty-six pages are devoted to "European domestic policy." Institutional questions come first, followed closely by analysis and proposals for a "radical ecological transformation" in European economics. Sections on monetary questions, social questions, and a section on the "feminization of Europe" come next. External relations (including the military dimension) and enlargement questions appear at the end of the program, comprising nine of the thirty-five pages after the thirteen-page overview.

As important as the domestication of European policy was the manifesto's consistent embrace of a reform strategy. Several weeks in advance of the Aachen congress, the chairman of the PK captured the tone of the draft text with his remark that "it would be fatefully myopic to tear down the European house built by generations in order to send out tenders for a new architect. The time when one dreamed of blank pages on which new poems could be written is long gone. Now we only have palimpsest."[38] Reform implied translation of "new politics" priorities into guidelines for action that both addressed the current concerns of the electorate and also operated predominantly within the matrix of existing EU institutions. In practice, the challenge was to tone down the utopian element while maintaining a critical edge, a purpose served by the introduction of three "master themes" that anchor the document in a recognizably Green coordinate system and advance the cause of reform. An all-European perspective functions as an implicit critique of hypostatizing the *acquis communautaire* in its current, Western European framework. The problem of democratization is a stable point of reference for challenging the diplomatic-technocratic methods and institutional design of regional integration as currently conceived. And principles of social ecology call into question the EU's policy priorities.

The resulting framework facilitated a level of specificity unprecedented in the Greens' approach to the project of regional integration. So, for example, the program approves of interregional transfers via the structural funds as long as the criteria are revised. The Committee of the Regions is embraced as a positive development whose powers should be expanded. In a theme that was to take on increasing importance over the next phase of Green European policy, the program insists upon planning integration as a common, inclusive East-West endeavor. Central and eastern European countries were to be connected to the EU from an early date according to the design concept of differentiated integration (*abgestufte Integration*). Accordingly, enlargement to the east should take precedence over establishing the exclusive deutsche mark zone implied by EMU: Central and eastern European countries should be offered a payments union modeled on the EPU of the 1950s.

Besides a credible program for reform, the program implies a political strategy to implement it. Recasting EU politics as European domestic politics points to the levers of influence that can affect the trajectory of the EU. They are found not in Brussels but in Berlin and the other national capitals. In the case of Germany, they are also found in the Länder, which control the second national legislative chamber. Consequently, national elections had to be viewed henceforth as arenas of the wider European domestic policy.

Another important change was that the program clarifies the areas of overlap with other parliamentary and nonparliamentary groups. A good example of this clarifying process, one which was to provoke further debates within the party, concerns the Greens' relationship to the military. Despite pressure from the special party congress in October 1993 called to reconsider the Länderrat's June resolution on Bosnia, the drafters maintain the Greens' pacifist stance. Thus, Common Foreign and Security Policy (CFSP) is the one area where the traditional rejectionist line persists. The current Green party majority also rejects European federalism to prevent the evolution of Europe toward military superpower status. Over and against this, the Greens insist on the civilian character of the EU:

> Whoever is ready to use military force cannot end arms production for export into crisis areas. Therefore, we reject military preventative or retaliatory actions. No exceptions can be made. In military affairs the exception always becomes the rule and the rule the exception; the "worst case scenario" governs action. We desire to hold no weapons and no soldiers. Otherwise nonviolence as utopia of the universal guarantee of human rights will be lost once and for all.[39]

The party supported its program with a candidate list that had demonstrated reformist engagement in European affairs, corresponding expertise, and personal flair. An admixture of continuity and change characterized the list, on which three of the MEPs who brought Maastricht before the Constitutional court won placement at and near the top (positions 1, 3, and 7); the only German MEP advocating Maastricht ratification also found vindication during the selection process at position 9. An enthusiastic advocate of the Maastricht Treaty, B-90 Bundestag member Wolfgang Ullmann, won the second place, and Daniel Cohn-Bendit, advocate of armed intervention in Bosnia, ended up at position 8, defeating longtime MEP and prime mover behind the Maastricht constitutional challenge Wilfried Telkämper, who was forced down to position 12. A second East German was nominated to position 5. Two members from the first EP group were renominated to positions 4 and 7.

The Aachen party congress marked a sea change in the Greens' outlook on Europe. It can be argued that the new relevance of EU policy as European domestic policy galvanized party activists, providing them with an overarching theme connecting the eighteen elections held to contest seats at every level of governance in Germany in 1994. In providing a reformist alternative to the current government, the party for the first time in its history gave the electorate an opportunity to vote for a national red/green coalition undistorted by conflicting messages. "Europe" was potentially captured as a Green issue. A new set of conceptual coordinates transcended the tired debate between federalists and antifederalists operating out of the same "old politics" paradigm. Vindication at the polls exceeded all but the most optimistic expectations.

In a resounding victory for the German Greens and a clear vindication of party strategy, they won 10.1 percent of the vote on June 12, 1994. With the exception of the small countries of Luxembourg and Ireland where Greens were elected to the EP for the first time, the returns for EFGP parties in the rest of the EU stood in stark contrast to the German Greens' gains. The Italians lost three representatives; the French all eight; the Belgians one. This left the Germans with over half of the seats in the newly constituted EP Green Group. Nationally, beginning with the September 1993 election in Hamburg, 1994 was a year of electoral triumph. The electoral cycle was completed in 1995, highlighted by the unprecedented electoral breakthrough in Germany's most populous and industrialized Land, Nordrhein-Westfalen, in May 1995, which broke the SPD Landtag absolute majority, led to a red/green governing coalition, and confirmed the installation of the Greens as Germany's third political force.

Europeanizing the Bundestag Fraktion

If Aachen was a turning point in the Greens' European policy, how far did it reach into the organizational networks that form the party? Did party strategists actually behave as if EU policy were a species of domestic policy? How, if at all, was EU policy integrated into election campaigns at other levels, particularly for the Bundestag? After the Bundestag campaign, how has the new B-90/Green Fraktion organized itself to deal with Europe? What can be said about policy development in the new Fraktion?

The party launched its Bundestag campaign at its federal delegate assembly in Mannheim on February 25–27, 1994. In sharp contrast to 1990, the Greens were determined to offer the electorate proposals that resonated with the most salient domestic issues. Equally novel was the shift of emphasis in favor of highlighting the party's willingness and capacity to govern. These priorities were clear from the prominence given to the party's economic reform agenda, the first and by far the largest section in the Mannheim program.[40] These priorities were reinforced at meetings of all Green Bundestag candidates and the Länderrat following the European elections in June.

Evidence as to the strategic relevance of "Europe" in this campaign is ambiguous. On the one hand, the reform orientation and willing engagement in governance runs through both campaigns. On the other hand, the EU is mentioned in the Mannheim program only in those places where it could not be avoided, such as in the form of a passing comment on genetic technology on page 26. It also receives mention under discussions of agriculture and immigration/asylum and figures most prominently in the concluding section on foreign policy. Except for the one page in the latter section devoted specifically to the EU, the tone of the discussion is critical. Although the EU acts both as a significant constraint on and as an opportunity for action in the key policy areas singled out by the Programm Kommission for emphasis (economics, ecological and social construction), the EU is not mentioned at all in this discussion. To take but one symbolically important example, the Delors White Paper on Growth, Competitiveness, and Employment was widely discussed during the autumn of 1993 and spring of 1994.[41] That document's concluding chapter places the entire effort at defining a medium-term development plan for the EU in the framework of environmental priorities. Prominent in the paper's analysis and policy prescriptions was the potential link between labor costs (therefore, employment) and the tax system, which also dominates in the Mannheim document. If the EU were as important as the Aachen congress suggested it was, why was such a strict separation of discussions maintained in the two documents?

It could be argued that this studied absence of cross-referencing between the Bundestag and European campaigns was strategically motivated in a European sense. Reentering the Bundestag had top priority. Attempts to raise unpopular themes in a positive light or themes perceived as irrelevant (memories of 1990!) could cause voters to turn away from the party at the polls. Public reaction to the Maastricht Treaty provided ample reason to steer clear of Europe in the Bundestag election campaign. Furthermore, there must have been some doubt as to whether the Greens could control the European issue during the crucial "hot phase" of the Bundestag election campaign after the summer holidays. In routine rotation, Germany had taken control of the EU Council presidency for the six-month period from July 1–December 31, 1994. The presidency confers upon the country infrequent but important opportunities to influence the agenda and public relations of the EU. All governments naturally seek to reap the local benefits of demonstrating international leadership. Could the Greens hope to compete with this "bully pulpit"?[42] In sum, Europe continued to be on the minds of party strategists, but their imperative was first to be elected to the Bundestag, precisely in order to exercise influence on EU policy.

While this logic could help explain the complete absence of Aachen's dominant "Europe as domestic politics" theme, it is quite likely that an organizationally based explanation of this outcome is stronger. The policy-formulating process leading to Aachen was the domain of the party's few European specialists, who were concentrated in the foreign affairs field, not diffused throughout the many internal policy development federal working groups (BAGs) of the party. The Greens simply did not (and still do not) possess a large enough cadre of party experts and activists with sufficient knowledge about the EU to carry through the links established at Aachen.

The evidence indicates that the party's EU silence was the silence of structural ignorance.

Under these circumstances, the most important source of information regarding the intentions of the party, as well as the most important locus of synergistic policy development regarding Europe and Germany, is likely to be the Green Bundestag Group elected in October 1994. With 7.3 percent of the national vote, B-90/Greens won forty-nine seats in the Bundestag, confirming the party's emergence as Germany's third political force. Combined with this showing, the party's explicit reformist orientation led to acknowledgment of its political importance by the governing parties. This took the form of making room for Green participation in the Bundestag leadership. Antje Vollmer was installed by an agreement between the Christian Democrats (CDU) and the Greens as the party's first Bundestag vice president. The outcome also gave the Greens sufficient resources to participate in all parliamentary functions and the potential to resume their pre-1990 role as programmatic dynamo of the party.[43]

As the new Bundestag began its work, rotation of Green extraparliamentary party leadership proceeded. At its December 1994 federal party congress in Babelsberg (Potsdam), Jürgen Trittin joined Krista Sager as newly elected cospeakers of the party congress's federal executive board. Trittin had served as Niedersachsen's minister for federal and European affairs in the red/green coalition from 1990–1994 and was very much aware of the relevance of the EU as an arena of European domestic politics. Sager led her party in Hamburg to the Greens' greatest electoral triumph (13.5 percent) in the September 1994 Bürgerschaft election on the basis of a firm commitment for a red/green government there. Her election was meant as a signal of the party's commitment to seeking power with the SPD in Bonn.

Along with Kerstin Müller, Josef "Joschka" Fischer, former environmental minister and vice-minister-president of Hessen, was elected to the position of parliamentary leader. Selection of their most prominent Realo figure for this role sent a clear signal about the parliamentarians' general intentions as a reformist party oriented to assuming governmental responsibility when the situation permitted. A strategy meeting in mid-January 1995 clarified the Fraktion's plans. Because the Kohl government would likely stay in power for most, if not all, of the legislative period, the Fraktion decided to accent its opposition to the government and seek to present a systematic and clear alternative to its policies.

Despite the German Council Presidency, the EU played a modest role in the Greens' early sparring in Bundestag plenary sessions. When he discussed the main government declaration of its new legislative program on November 23, 1995, Fischer did, in a general way, attempt to interleave EU and German policy processes, alluding in the main body of his remarks to the declining role of the national state in the context of economic globalization. In remarks about foreign policy, he went on to underline the value he placed on continuity with respect to German participation in the institutions of European integration. In that context he made the additional point that unity would come only if it were supported by the people through democratic participation, and he challenged Chancellor Kohl to deliver on his government's promises to advance European integration in more than a rhetorical sense.

Personnel and organization. Meanwhile, an impressive network of working groups and communications channels on European policy radiating out from the Bundestag Fraktion was being established. The party's most experienced European experts were called to Bonn to supervise the process. Fischer's personal staff aide, who had worked on foreign policy for the Fraktion between 1990 and 1994 and was clearly identified as a revisionist with respect to party policy on NATO participation and German military preparations, led a group that persisted in trying to get the party congress in Mannheim to accept German participation in NATO and UN peacekeeping missions, noting that the credibility of the party as a coalition partner in a future national government was at stake. Another Green Party activist and academically trained expert in international relations who spent 1990–1994 in charge of EU policy in Trittin's Niedersachsen federal and European affairs ministry came to head the Fraktion's EU coordination office. The person in charge of BuVo's international relations dossier from 1991–1994, after election to the Bundestag, joined two Fraktion colleagues on the EU Committee, newly created by constitutional amendment as part of the Maastricht debate.

Set up at the urging of Fischer, the EU coordination office is one of only two such offices set up by the Fraktion, the other being that for the Bundesrat, Länder, and local parliaments. In principle, all legislation or activity in every other domain relevant to the EU must be registered in the coordination office. The head of the office reports directly to Fischer, a practice that should facilitate a high degree of policy integration between the various levels touched by EU activity. In short, the Bundestag leadership has concentrated an unusual amount of attention on and political commitment to the European link. The record since early March 1995, when the coordination office effectively got up and running, demonstrates that it has used its capacity creatively and ambitiously. The available early evidence suggests that EU affairs are, indeed, being approached as if they were European domestic politics, thereby moving in the direction of fulfilling the promise of the Aachen party congress.

The functions of the coordination office include (1) creating a routine system of internal party communication on European affairs; (2) communicating with Green Party Fraktionen in other parliaments (Länder, European Parliament), the European Federation of Green Parties, and all relevant Green Party organs (BuVo, the relevant BAGs); (3) helping to set the policy agenda; and (4) taking a leading role in working out policy positions. To begin with the question of internal communication channels, in a clear departure from all previous Green parliamentary groups in both Strasbourg/Brussels and Bonn, a regular intraparty communications channel has been established. *EUROINFO*, a joint undertaking of the two groups, commenced publication in June 1995. This newsletter includes *GREENFAX* (reports from the EP plenum); Bundestag developments; reports on activities of the two groups, the German Länder, and the parties (German federal and EFGP); a calendar of coming events; and contact numbers and addresses.[44]

Program development: toward the 1996 ICG. EU preparations for the IGC mandated by the Maastricht Treaty to occur in 1996 have provided a natural orientation point for program development and liaison activity. The task was facilitated by the release of a CDU/CSU paper during the German Council presidency to express intraparty consensus as well as to provoke debate on EU reform both in Germany and in the EU at large. The paper advocated a double strategy of EU widening and deepening. The focus of deepening was the EU's Franco-German "hard core." It was recommended that the 1996 IGC work to produce a "quasi-constitutional" document oriented toward federalism. Reconciliation of the tensions between the priorities was to be achieved by a "multiple-speed" or "variable geometry" approach that allowed the core to move ahead with the integration project. The plans for EMU written into Maastricht were cited as an example of how variable speeds should work. Widening would be advanced by invitations to Poland, the Czech and Slovak republics, Hungary, and Slovenia to join the EU, but only if they could meet the acquis communautaire. (Otherwise, forms of advanced association were contemplated in different areas according to the variable geometry design.) This is particularly important for association in EU pillars II (CFSP) and III (Justice and Home Affairs). Finally, citing the waning commitment of the United States to participation in European conflicts and, specifically, differences with respect to the war in Yugoslavia, the CDU/CSU paper recommends immediate intensification of EU defense cooperation.[45]

With the Green Bundestag Fraktion acting as its central coordination point, discussion began on initial positions in the spring of 1995 on the basis of the Aachen and EFGP election manifestos. Meetings between Bundestag and Landtag groups as well as mixed party/parliamentarian meetings at the European level were staged. The party's federal working group on peace and international politics (BAG-FIP) created six project groups to focus on different aspects of EU reform. BAG-FIP's aim was to produce a unified document by mid-September that would then be adopted as a position paper by the federal party congress in December 1995. Not surprisingly, BAG-FIP defined its mandate not only as commenting on the reform proposals of others but as developing an alternative Green agenda, which envisioned a series of IGCs after the one scheduled for 1996 to accompany the process of connecting internal social-ecological reform with enlargement to the east.

Bundestag members contributed by introducing a major parliamentary inquiry (*grosse Anfrage*) on EU reform on May 19[46] and tabling a resolution during the debate in advance of the Cannes European Council meeting in June 1995. At the time of this writing, these interventions comprise the most fully developed Green response to the quasi-official EU reform vision enunciated in the Lamers paper. In their resolution the Greens identified the democratic deficit as the core pathology of European integration, and enlargement to the east as the EU's greatest challenge. They juxtaposed the concept of differentiated integration (abgestufte Integration) to the notion of variable geometry, which they rejected because it would continue and even deepen the split between the western core and the eastern and southern EU periphery. Europeans east and west would move the integration project forward together in a common strategy that left no one behind.

Overall, the European vision that emerges from these documents features a more diffuse set of organizations than the one that is reflected in the CDU/CSU paper. Expressing less allegiance to EU institutions, its pan-European dimension in effect receives higher priority than maintaining the acquis communautaire. The internal market is not only to be attenuated by broadening the general aims of the EU as an *Umweltunion* (environmental union), but also its internal coherence is to be lessened both by locally designed social and environmental regulations and by forms of monetary cooperation that are less rule-based and designed instead with comprehensive, regionally (nationally?) based development strategies in mind.

This perspective is strengthened by the documents' image of the relationship of the EU to other European organizations. Pressing the case for demilitarization of international relations generally and wishing to set the example in Europe, the documents adhere to the official party policy of pacifism, reconfirmed during the autumn 1993 debate over intervention in Bosnia to secure human rights. Joint action through the mechanisms of CFSP is welcomed if and only if a military dimension has been ruled out from the start. Thus, the Greens reject any reconstituting of the Western European Union (WEU), let alone its integration into CFSP. Instead, the documents express impressive continuity with the basic position adopted by the party in 1990: "civilianization" of foreign policy that accentuates political agreements in a pan-European setting. Thus, the Organization for Security and Cooperation in Europe (OSCE) is the preferred setting to organize Europe: Both NATO and the EU should be modified in light of whatever agreements are attained in that forum. Even the weakness of the OSCE is appealing to the Greens because it reinforces their preference for a subnational, regionally based integration design.

It comes as no surprise that this vision is at odds with those of Germany's other mainstream political parties as well as with the IGC preparatory papers offered in May 1995 by the European Commission and the European Parliament. Those actors all take the EU as the most advanced expression of European integration, one that should be used as the center of gravity for further efforts. They argue that risks may be taken for the sake of continent-wide integration, but that one should be extremely cautious about jeopardizing the acquis communautaire.

The Greens' position converges with that of the Commission with respect to the desirability of a unified decisionmaking structure and the institutional balance between the Commission (which the Greens propose to democratize) and the Council of Ministers. Notably, initial Green IGC position papers oppose the consensus position of the German Länder in the area of energy policy. Whereas the parliamentary Greens advocate the inclusion of a chapter on energy in the Maastricht Treaty (and retirement of both the European Coal and Steel Community and Euratom), the Länder prefer exclusion of EU competence in this field on grounds of subsidiarity.[47] The Greens also oppose the expressed desire of the environmental NGOs for a special "ecological council" possessing superordinate legal status to the Council of Ministers.[48] Finally, in addition to supporting increased powers for the Parliament, the Greens' documents allude to the further use of plebiscites.

The Greens' preparatory documents and Commission and Parliament positions diverge in two important ways, which concern the Treaty structure itself and its external aspect. The Greens would like to abandon EMU in the interest of avoiding a two-tier Europe. They prefer a politically generated solidarity inclusive of both the cohesion countries (Greece, Ireland, Portugal, and Spain) and the central and eastern European countries. Also in contrast to the Commission and Parliament, they reject any security component, even to the point of speculating that an increase of the Parliament's competence in this area may boomerang by indirectly legitimizing evolution of a European military superpower.

CONCLUSION

The account just given demonstrates that three sets of interacting factors have been at work in transforming the outlook and behavior of the German Greens with respect to the post–Cold War construction of Europe and the European Union in particular. The first set of factors has to do with the development of the party itself. Even prior to the dramatic events of 1989, the cumulative effect of Green participation in the Bundestag and even in government at the local, regional, and European levels was significant, strengthening the wing of the party that wanted to assume government responsibility even at the national level. German unification accelerated the exodus of many adherents of the eco-socialist and fundamentalist wings. That process facilitated further structural reform after the Bundestag defeat of 1990 and once again increased the weight of the Realos by increasing the position of the Länder organizations. Fusion of Bündnis-90 and the Western Greens strengthened the reformist orientation of the party. Electoral success in 1994–1995, particularly the reentry of the B-90/Greens into the Bundestag and the spectacular outcome in Nordrhein-Westfalen, consolidated even further the internal position of those who had been advocating reformist engagement all along.

A second cluster of factors concerns the issue salience of "Europe." The operation of the single market had already begun to point to the "domestic" character of EC decisionmaking prior to the IGCs that led to the Maastricht Treaty. German unification and collapse of the neo-Stalinist regimes of Central and Eastern Europe dramatically raised the visibility and political importance of the EC, if only in the negative sense associated with dangerous tendencies toward renationalization of European politics under the suddenly increased pressures of dislocation, unemployment, increasing fiscal demands, and migration. The ratification debate over Maastricht began even before the Treaty was signed, as intra-elite and interinstitutional positions diverged during negotiations. During the ratification phase, discontent over government in general and immigration was channeled into a popular *fronde* against the Treaty, a trend that was only reinforced by the unfolding drama surrounding the referenda in Denmark and France. The Greens played a role in this process by their Constitutional Court challenge to the Treaty. Finally, the European elections in mid-1994 maintained the European discussion at a comparatively high level. In this context, the Greens' desire to reconnect with the electorate intersected with their general critique of German society and politics. The party responded to the political imperative to pay more attention to Europe.

The third factor complex consists of the opportunities presented to the party by its policy of constructive engagement and radical reform vis-à-vis the EU. For its part, the institutions of the EU had demonstrated a certain responsiveness to key concerns of the Greens. In any event, environmental questions would be adjudicated in the EU with or without Green engagement. Party experts had been arguing for a coherent and aggressive response to the challenges and opportunities since the end of the 1980s. In Germany, after the 1990 Bundestag defeat, party strategy revolved around displacement of the Kohl government by a red/green alternative. The main roadblocks along the way to realizing that project lay in the sphere of foreign affairs generally and European policy in particular. The Aachen program and the party's subsequent preparations for the 1996 IGC have gone a long way toward establishing the Greens' credibility. Their disposition toward military force constitutes the remaining barrier toward fuller political participation.

As ever, the major issue with German Green thinking is the gap between the alternative image projected and the chances that it can actually be put into practice.[49] The underlying difficulty is the continuing organization of the international system by states whose governments exhibit high degrees of self-referentiality (that is, they will act in their own perceived short-term interests) and possess organized military force. Visionary pacifist images, no matter how internally consistent and logical, will make little headway against the classical security dilemma (and the generalized distrust associated with it that leads to prudential military preparation) that is structurally embedded in international politics. To be sure, there are mechanisms that add to this basic instability, for example, expansive economic designs, leadership atavisms, and the like. But these features only coexist with and amplify, not cause, the security dilemma and "rational" responses to it. It is, in short, a politically dubious form of idealism to believe that the intractable structure of international politics can be attacked head on. That method was tried and failed in the 1920s with the League of Nations, the Kellogg-Briand agreement, and other similar efforts whose common element consisted in the attempt to promote good behavior through legal texts.

If the Greens truly desire to reform the European system rather than merely criticize it, the central issue is how best to support those learning processes that attenuate self-referentiality and encourage nonmilitary solutions and choices motivated by higher degrees of transnational solidarity. Certainly, the process of integration itself is crucial in this respect. Thus, the problem for the Greens remains how to change the design of regional integration without undermining the effectiveness of its institutions. It seems clear that learning will occur not with radical breaks but through incremental changes.

Because of their conception of Europe, the Greens will be compelled by diplomatic and domestic political realities to confront some difficult issues. In the first place, the Greens' vision for restructuring Europe raises the question of how wise it would be to weaken the acquis communautaire, which is the result of compromises reached painfully over a long period. What would guarantee that the effect of the kind of wholesale structural change promoted by the Greens would not reinforce tendencies toward an uncontrollable European *décollage*? Moreover, given the political constellations in other EU member states and third parties, what would prevent reversion to a loose free trade zone without the social and environmental advantages of supranational institutions? Relatedly, is there sufficient political will in the member and candidate states to sanction multiplicity of local derogations from the internal market? Or is the very integrity of this market the symbol of solidarity as well as division? Questions such as these point to the quite practical problems associated with the Greens' present core concept of abgestufte Integration.

Another practical problem comes in the accustomed form of principled opposition to policies already taken and part of the institutional landscape. The Greens took a giant step in overcoming this problem with respect to the EU in the generally reformist orientation of their Aachen program. However, decisions have been made in the EU that render specific elements of their opposition beside the point, if not completely obsolete. To recall Butikofer's memorable words, in European affairs, the Greens do not have a tabula rasa, only palimpsest.[50] This observation applies to EMU, which is not on the IGC agenda. It also applies increasingly to the defense dimension of CFSP, especially since the 1994 NATO summit, which cleared the way for providing NATO-dedicated forces to the Western European Union under EU auspices. Sooner or later, the Greens must find a way to cope with an institutional matrix created by others.

On the domestic side, the pressure will be intense to revise the party's strict pacifism by acknowledging the intractable reality and demonstrable utility of the use of force. Without some movement in this area, the possibilities of a red/green government at the national level appear to be slim, as the SPD has made such change a sine qua non of national governmental cooperation. As discussed above, the Realo wing of the party has been advocating such a revision since 1988 in one form or another.

At the time of this writing, the most recent initiative came in the form of a letter addressed to the Green Bundestag Group and the party, dated July 30, 1995. Fischer argues from Green principles, indeed, from the most profound psychological sources of party identity, its antifascist complex. Fischer launches his letter with a quote from Michael Thumann's article in *Die Zeit*: "The Bosnian War is above all a battle of armed criminals against the unarmed civilian population." Fischer reasons that the pivot of the Bosnian debacle is Serb expansionist aggression combined with continuing Great Power determination to depend precisely on Serbia as their main Balkan *Ordnungsfaktor* (agent of order) after the civil war. This situation, if unanswered, would reintroduce war as a legitimate means of politics in Europe, threatening victory of the nationalist past against the common European future and wiping out fifty years of progress in peace and integration. Furthermore, the failure of Western and UN policy also applies to the Greens. When all other nonviolent policies failed, how should the Greens respond to the continuing slaughter of the civilian population? Solidarity with the innocent victims requires intervention. The war places three fundamental values of Green identity in conflict: protection of human life and freedoms versus the principle of nonviolence. Although pacifism was the correct response to the logic of nuclear exterminism, the same cannot be said for today's ethnic wars. The consequence for Green policy is clear for Fischer: Either speak out in favor of military defense of UN protection zones for civilians or advocate a UN pullout and violent determination of the outcome among the warring parties. In the latter case, the West must supply the Bosnian side weapons. No end to the war is in sight. As UN withdrawal will only intensify the violence, the least objectionable solution is military protection of UN protection zones. Above all, circumstances now demand that the Greens' position on Bosnia be thoroughly discussed and an appropriate resolution advanced.[51]

In both domains, European and German, events are pushing the Greens in the direction of exercising power. The party cannot develop in any other way into the role of a full-fledged historical agent. They are beginning to leave behind the false Manichaean dichotomy that pits ideals against action and are learning that the requirement to act often clarifies ideals. Without a presence in government, the party forgoes the major lever available in influencing outcomes. In acknowledgment of this, the Greens' appetite for governing has been growing, even in areas such as foreign policy where ambiguity and the clash of values is greatest and the outcomes most fateful. The party's experience with the EU demonstrates the complexity of this learning process.

NOTES

The author would like to thank Wade Miller and Simona Cristanetti for technical assistance with the manuscript.

1. Karl-Werner Brand, Detlef Büsser, and Dieter Rucht, *Aufbruch in eine neue Gesellschaft* (Frankfurt: Campus Verlag, 1983); Brand, ed., *Neue soziale Bewegungen in Westeuropa und den USA: Ein internationaler Vergleich* (Frankfurt: Campus Verlag, 1985); and Joachim Raschke, *Soziale Bewegungen: Ein historisch-systematischer Grundriss* (Frankfurt/Main: Campus Verlag, 1988).

2. Ronald Inglehart, *The Silent Revolution: Changing Values and Political Styles Among Western Publics* (Princeton, N.J.: Princeton University Press, 1977); Inglehart, *Culture Shift in Advanced Industrial Society* (Princeton, N.J.: Princeton University Press, 1990); see also Russell Dalton, *The Green Rainbow: Environmental Groups in Western Europe* (New Haven, Conn.: Yale University Press, 1995); and Robert Rohrschneider, "Environmental Belief Systems in Western Europe: A Hierarchical Model of Constraint," *Comparative Political Studies* 26, no. 1 (April 1993), pp. 3–29.

3. Sydney Tarrow, *Struggle, Politics, and Reform: Collective Action, Social Movements, and Cycles of Protest,* Western Societies Occasional Paper No. 21, Ithaca, N.Y.: Cornell University Center for International Studies, 1989; Charles Tilly, *From Mobilization to Revolution* (Englewood Cliffs, N.J.: Prentice-Hall, 1978).

4. Christopher Harvie, *The Rise of Regional Europe* (New York: Routledge, 1994).

5. Leopold Kohr, *The Breakdown of Nations* (London: Routledge, 1957); E. F. Schumacher, *Small Is Beautiful: Economics as If People Mattered* (New York: Harper and Row, 1973); Kirkpatrick Sale, *Dwellers in the Land: The Bioregional Vision* (San Francisco: Sierra Club Books, 1985); Group of Green Economists, *Ecological Economics: A Practical Programme for Global Reform* (London: Zed Books, 1992).

6. Alain Touraine, *The Voice and the Eye: An Analysis of Social Movements* (Cambridge: Cambridge University Press, 1981); Touraine, *Anti-nuclear Protest: The Opposition to Nuclear Energy in France* (Cambridge: Cambridge University Press, 1983); and Touraine, *Solidarity* (New York: Cambridge University Press, 1983); Alberto Melucci, "The New Social Movements: A Theoretical Approach," *Social Science Information* 199 (1980), pp. 199–226; Melucci, "Getting Involved: Identity and Mobilization in Social Movements," in Bert Klandermans, Hanspeter Kriesi,

Sidney Tarrow, eds., *From Structure to Action: Comparing Social Movement Research Across Cultures* (Greenwich, Conn.: JAI Press, 1988), pp. 329–348.

7. Interview with Leo Cox, secretary-general, European Federation of Green Parties, Antwerp, Belgium, June 6, 1994.

8. European Federation of Green Parties (hereinafter EFGP), "Guiding Principles of the European Federation of Green Parties," approved in Masala, Finland, June 20, 1993.

9. Thomas Scharf, *The German Greens: Challenging the Consensus* (Providence, R.I.: Berg, 1994), p. 77.

10. On citizen mobilization, see Werner Hülsberg, *The German Greens: A Social and Political Profile* (London: Verso, 1988), pp. 90–93; on the EC and NATO strategy, see SPV-DIE GRÜNEN, *Alternative für Europa* (Bonn: SPV-DIE GRÜNEN, 1979).

11. Die Grünen, *Global denken—for Ort handeln: Erklärung der Grünen zur Europawahl am 17 Juni 1984* (Bonn: Bundesvorstand der Grünen, March 1984).

12. Brigitte Heinrich and Jakob von Uexküll, excerpted candidate statements, Federal Green Party Congress in Karlsruhe, March 1984.

13. Wolfgang Bruckmann and Jürgen Schnappertz, "Die Vorteile der Westintegration," *Die Grünen,* Munich, February 11, 1989.

14. Jürgen Peter Esders, "Überall die grünen Nasen hineinstecken: GRAEL: 17 grüne Parteien in Europa koordinieren ihre Arbeit," *Das Parlament,* Nr.24/25 (June 9–16, 1989), p. 9.

15. GRAEL (Green-Alternative European Link in the Rainbow Group in the European Parliament), "Transnuklear Affäre: Über die Arbeit des untersuchungsausschusses im EP" (Brussels, December 1988).

16. See, for example, Task Force on the Environment and the Internal Market, *1992: The Environmental Dimensions* (Brussels: Commission of the European Communities, November 1989).

17. Ivan Behrend, quoted in GRAEL, "Green Peace Policy," GRAEL Publication Series Number 13 (Brussels, January 1988).

18. Landesvorstand NRW, "Gegen eine Wildwest-EG der Konzerne: Für eine demokratische und solidarische Gemeinschaft der ökologischen Vernunft" (October 1988); Plattform der Grünen Baden-Württemberg zu den Europawahlen 1989, "Landesdelegiertenkonferenz der Grünen Baden-Württemberg, Ergebnisse und Beschlüsse" (October 1988); and Joschka Fischer, "Sein oder Nichtsein: Entwürfe für ein realpolitisches Manifest" (June 1988).

19. Federal Executive Board (BuVo), Plattform der Grünen zur Europawahl '89, "Grüne Positionen zum EG-Binnenmarkt" (Bonn, 1989).

20. Group of Green Economists, *Ecological Economics;* interview with Claudia Dziobek, staff economist, Grüne Bundestagsfraktion, February 8, 1992.

21. Carl Lankowski, "One Step Backward, Two Steps Forward? Between Antifa and Machpolitik: Die Grünen and the German Question," *German Politics and Society* 20 (summer 1990), pp. 41–56.

22. "Der Beschluss des Länderrats der Grünen, auch mit Gewalt gegen die Serben vorzugehen, und die heftigen Reaktionen darauf," *Frankfurter Rundschau,* September 1, 1993, p. 12.

23. Bruckmann and Schnappertz, "Die Vorteile der Westintegration."

24. Joschka Fischer, "Radikale Sekte oder ökologische Reformpartei: Die Grünen am Scheideweg" (1987, mimeographed).

25. Peter Katzenstein, *Policy and Politics in West Germany: The Growth of a Semi-Sovereign State* (Philadelphia: Temple University Press, 1987).

26. Klaus Goetz, "National Governance and European Integration:

Intergovernmental Relations in Germany," *Journal of Common Market Studies* 33, no. 1 (March 1995), pp. 99–116; Charlie Jeffery and Roland Sturm, eds., *Federalism, Unification and European Integration* (London: Frank Cass, 1993).

27. Die Grünen, "Länderrat Beschluss: Die Grünen zu den Maastrichter Beschlüssen—SO NICHT!" (Kassel, October 11, 1992), p. 3.

28. Birgit Cramon-Daiber, "Maastricht und kein Ende: Einige Anfrage an grüne Politikkompetenz" (manuscript, January 1992).

29. Diana Johnstone, *Greens in the European Parliament: A New Sense of Purpose for Europe: Record and Prospects of the First Green Political Group in the European Parliament* (Brussels: Green Group, 1994), p. 44.

30. Bündnis-90/Die Grünen im Bundestag, "Zu Europa: Reden—Aufsätze—Gespräche" (Bonn: Arbeitskreis II, March 1993), pp. 21–49.

31. *Basic Law* (GG), Article 79/3; GG, Article 20; GG, Article 1; GG, Part III, Article 38.

32. Treaty on European Union, Article F/3; EEC, Article, 235.

33. BVG, "Urteil des Bundesverfassungsgerichts über die Verfassungsbeschwerden gegen den Vertrag von Maastricht, verkündet in Karlsruhe am 12. Oktober 1993." Az:2BvR, 2134/92 and 2159/92.

34. Interview with Leo Cox.

35. Helmut Lippelt, "Eine Föderation als Grüne Europapolitik," *Punkt* (Bündnis-90/Die Grünen membership magazine) 1, no. 5 (October–November 1993), p. 14; interview with Lippelt, member, Federal Executive Board, Bündnis-90/Die Grünen, responsible for relations with sister parties, Brussels, June 22, 1994.

36. EFGP, "Guiding Principles."

37. Bündnis-90/Die Grünen, "Programm zur Europawahl '94," verabschiedet auf der Bundesdelegiertenkonferenz in Aachen (Bonn, November 12–14, 1993).

38. Reinhard Butikofer, "Europa wählen!" *Punkt* 1, no. 15 (October–November 1993), pp. 12–13.

39. Bündnis-90/Die Grünen. Programm fur Europawahl 94.

40. Bündnis-90/Die Grünen, "Nur mit uns: Programm zur Bundestagswahl 1994," verabschiedet auf der Bundesdelegiertenkonferenz in Mannheim im Februar 1994.

41. Commission of the European Communities, "The Challenges and Ways Forward into the 21st Century," White Paper on Growth, Competitiveness, and Employment (the "Delors White Paper"), COM (93) 700 final, 1993.

42. Carl Lankowski, "The German EU Council Presidency: Modest Expectations Met," *ECSA Newsletter* 8, no. 1 (winter 1995), pp. 7–10.

43. E. Gene Frankland and Donald Schoonmaker, *Between Protest and Power: The Green Party in Germany* (Boulder, Colo.: Westview Press, 1992), p. 123 ff.

44. EUROINFO, "Die Grünen im Europäischen Parlament and Bundestag-sfraktion Bündnis 90/Die Grünen," Number 1, June 13, 1995.

45. Karl Lamers, "Deutschlands Aussenpolitische Verantwortung und seine Interessen: Vorlage für die Klausurtatung des Geschäftsführenden Fraktions-vorstandes der CDU/CSU Bundestagsfraktion am 23./24. August 1993 in Berlin." CDU/CSU-Fraktion des Deutschen Bundestages, "Reflections on European Policy" (September 1, 1994).

46. Deutscher Bundestag, Grosse Aufrage Abgendentan Christian Sterzing und der Frastian Bündnis 90/Die Grünen. Verbeitung der Regeirung-Konferenz 96 ("Maastricht II") Drucksache 13/1471. June 19, 1995.

47. Bundesrat, "Entschliessung des Bundesrates zur Vorbereitung der Regierungskonferenz 1996," Drucksache 169/95 (Beschluss, March 31, 1995).

48. Declaration of Heidelberg, "Revision of the Maastricht Treaty: Repre-

sentatives of European Environmental Associations Ask for a European Environmental Union" (Heidelberg: January 28, 1995).

49. See Lankowski, "One Step Backward?"

50. Butikofer, "Europa wählen!"

51. Joschka Fischer, "Die Katastrophe in Bosnien und die Konsequenzen für unsere Partei Bündnis 90/Die Grünen," ein Brief an die Bundestagsfraktion und an die Partei (Bonn, July 30, 1995).

8

Territorial Protest
and the European Union:
The Case of Scotland

Michael Keating

SCOTLAND IN THE BRITISH STATE

It is impossible to appreciate the problems that Scotland has encountered within the United Kingdom or the European Union (EU) without considering the peculiar form of the British state. Built up over centuries by a process of incremental accretion, it lacks a tradition either of absolute monarchy or of popular sovereignty. In the absence of revolutionary change, liberal democracy arrived gradually through existing institutions. Although a generation of political scientists portrayed this process and the resulting unwritten constitution as a piece of crowning genius, the limitations of the U.K. model have become increasingly clear. The central feature of the British constitution is the doctrine of parliamentary sovereignty, underpinned by a two-party system with a right-of-center and a left-of-center party alternating in power. The strength of the party system and executive government, together with a homogeneous professional bureaucracy steeped in traditions of genteel elitism and secrecy, makes British government extremely difficult to penetrate. Although the main producer groups have enjoyed stable relationships with central departments, new social movements have few points of access. They thus tend to align themselves with the major parties, their ideas, energies, and activists being absorbed by the parliamentary system. Nor has the British system always passed the test of effectiveness. Despite the efforts of successive Labour and Conservative governments, Britain has never achieved economic modernization and international trading competitiveness.[1] Since 1979, the effort has been abandoned in favor of selective integration into the global financial market. The democratic shortcomings of the U.K. constitution also became increasingly evident as the postwar political consensus broke down in the 1980s. A government with the support of barely 40 percent of the electorate was able to push through a radical redistribution of power; centralize the governmental system; curb the independence of a range of civil institutions including the trade unions, universities, and broadcasting media; and deregulate the business and financial sector. This in turn provoked a new movement for constitutional reform and forced the Left to reconsider its traditional support for strong, authoritative government.

The territorial structure of the state also came under a challenge that cannot be considered in isolation from the other crises of the governing order. The United Kingdom is a union created by conquest of four countries that have never been politically or socially assimilated. In this respect it bears comparison with Spain rather than France, where Jacobin republicanism, even more than the absolute monarchy, was committed to linguistic, cultural, and political assimilation.[2] Scotland acceded to the United Kingdom in 1707 through a negotiated parliamentary union, a century after the union of the monarchies. Controversy still surrounds the union (described as an Act in England and a Treaty in Scotland), and there was more than the usual eighteenth-century corruption about the process, but its general outlines are fairly clear. The governing classes in Scotland surrendered their state in return for access to English imperial trade and the right to retain key institutions of their own civil society. The latter included the established Church of Scotland, the educational system, and the burghs. There was also an ambiguous provision stipulating that matters of "public right" could be decided on an all-British basis, but the laws pertaining to "private right" could be decided only according to "the utility of the subjects within Scotland." Unfortunately, no mechanism was inserted to enforce these provisions, and the courts have subsequently held that although the union is binding on Parliament, they have no jurisdiction in the matter. Despite this and several violations of the union, Scotland has preserved its own civil society, oscillating between periods of assimilation and assertion. The late nineteenth-century and the years since the mid-1960s have been notable periods of assertion and differentiation.

The failure to socialize the population into a single U.K. national identity is reflected in vocabulary. Scots bridle at the insensitive North American habit of using the term *England* to apply to the whole kingdom—yet there is no adjective to describe its citizens. As Rose remarks, "nobody speaks of the Ukes as a nation."[3] Scots have a diffuse sense of dual loyalty to Scotland and to the wider entity, but defining the latter presents further difficulties. For much of the time since 1707 the wider loyalty was to the British Empire. This provided an external support system for the regime, furnishing a focus of loyalty, a trading system, military protection, and employment outlets for the middle classes. Since the demise of empire, a residual British loyalty exists alongside Scottish identity—though whether the state should encompass Northern Ireland continues to divide opinion.

In the twentieth century, Scotland was also bound to the state by class loyalties cutting across territorial divisions and a party system based on class divisions. The Labour Party in particular emphasized a universalist class discourse, attacking nationalism as divisive or petty bourgeois, but its ideology of class tended to stop at the British border and coexisted with a willingness to play territorial politics in various forms. In its early days, the Scottish labor movement was favorably disposed to nationalism and around the time of World War I went through a strongly nationalist phase calling for a high degree of independence, albeit within the framework of the British Empire.[4] By the 1930s, it had committed itself to a strategy of advance through U.K. institutions and accepted the territorial as well as other aspects of the British constitution. The party system, itself largely the product of the parliamentary constitution and electoral system, forced Scottish politics into the same bipolar mode as England's, leaving no outlet for territorial movements. After World War I, a strong element of economic calculation entered the equation. Scottish industry suffered very badly in the interwar depression, and unemployment rates were consistently higher than those in England until the early 1990s. Scottish independent capitalism collapsed as firms moved south or were taken over by non-Scottish conglomerates and economic dependency came to reinforce the political dependency on London.

Territorial Politics

Territorial politics was not suppressed but merely managed in a different form. Scotland is governed by a form of administrative devolution, that is, a separate British government department whose minister is a member of the Cabinet. In Parliament, separate committees deal with Scottish legislation. This does not, however, imply a capacity for autonomous policymaking. The secretary of state for Scotland is a member of the governing party (even where this is the minority in Scotland), and Scottish committees are subject to the will of the House of Commons as a whole. All that is possible is a modification of the details and institutional modalities of policy within the general framework laid down by the Cabinet.[5] Of greater significance are the opportunities that this presents for lobbying for Scottish interests within the unitary system of government. The secretary of state for Scotland is recognized as having a duty to lobby for Scotland in Cabinet and with the Treasury, and most Scottish members of Parliament (MPs) are absorbed in Scottish business, venturing into the U.K. arena only where Scottish material interests are at stake. Those who make their names as major figures in U.K. politics are the exception and have usually made a conscious career choice to do this.[6]

It has long been recognized in the major parties that there is a trade-off between autonomy for Scotland and access to central decisionmaking. An elected, autonomous Scottish assembly might have more independence than the secretary of state and could reflect Scottish demands more accurately, but achieving this could involve sacrificing the guaranteed representation in the

Cabinet provided by the existing system. The role of territorial intermediaries, ministers, MPs, bureaucrats, parties, and interest groups is thus critical to sustaining support for the constitutional status quo in Scotland. Polls have consistently shown majorities of the population in favor of a measure of self-government, but elites have usually been able to prevail with the argument that access to central decisionmaking is more important. A cohesive and occasionally powerful territorial lobby has thus developed in which the parties, both sides of industry, the professions, and the churches have been able to come together in support of Scottish material interests without sacrificing their ideological, class, or sectoral differences.

Politics was thus forced into the two-party Westminster mode with territory as a subordinate theme. The whole system was managed by a network of elites, with little popular input. An enlightened bureaucracy in the Scottish Office ran an administrative machine of considerable sophistication and elegance but with a minimum of popular or political input. These arrangements have periodically come under attack by autonomist forces, especially at times when the lobby has not been delivering, when the parties have been realigning, or when alternative routes to economic progress have appeared. In the late nineteenth and early twentieth centuries, the emerging labor movement challenged the constitutional status quo with strong support for Scottish Home Rule.[7] By the 1920s, however, labor had adjusted to the system. Labor's incorporation into the Westminster parliamentary regime received territorial expression after 1922 when the Scottish Labour Party made a breakthrough into the House of Commons, and this became the center of attention and career ambition. New social movements similarly were absorbed into the central strategy. In Scotland, such movements have frequently seen the union as part of the problem and adopted a pro-independence policy. This is especially true of movements for land reform in the Highlands. The earliest breakthrough in popular representation in mainland Britain came in the late nineteenth century with the election of Crofters candidates to Parliament. Committed to Home Rule as well as land reform, they gradually aligned themselves with the left wing of the Liberal Party, although some moved toward the emerging Labour Party. After World War I, a new Highland Land League (HLL) negotiated an electoral alliance with Labour but faced opposition from urban socialists who saw a landed urban peasantry as a potential bulwark of reaction and preferred the creation of a unionized rural proletariat.[8] With the failure of the Labour-HLL candidates, the Highlands came under a period of landowner–Conservative Party dominance until the 1960s.

Despite sporadic protest movements since 1945, urban social movements in Scotland have been very weak, a point obliquely conceded by Castells, whose Glasgow example dates from the World War I era.[9] Glasgow stands out as a city that managed massive transformation, including the relocation of most of its population and rebuilding a large part of the physical fabric, without any serious social upheaval.[10] Thus, apart from short-lived protest votes in the late 1960s and late 1970s, Labour has steadily increased its hold on Scotland's cities. Such protest as exists tends to be passive and disorganized, as in the insistence of many individual families in staying in condemned properties rather than accepting rehousing, or the estimated 20 percent of the population of Strathclyde Region (itself accounting for half Scotland's population) who had not yet paid their poll tax at the end of its first year of operation in 1989. In 1992, Scottish Militant candidates, some expelled from the party, ran against Labour candidates and won five seats on the Glasgow city council. A jailed poll tax protestor gained 20 percent of the vote in Glasgow Pollok at the 1992 general election. This was evidence both of large-scale discontent and a failure to channel it into anything more effective than a bizarre amalgam of Trotskyism, working class protest, and nationalism, with nothing much by way of a program.

From the 1940s, the Labour Party committed itself energetically to the strategy of managing Scottish affairs within the U.K. Discontent was interpreted as exclusively economic, to be assuaged with more public spending and development projects but without any concession on the constitutional front. The strategy received its fullest expression in the diversionary regional policies of the 1960s, presented as a non-zero-sum game in which the development regions in Scotland and elsewhere could benefit from new industry, the boom regions could gain relief from congestion, and the economy as a whole could benefit from the use of idle capacity.[11] At the ideological level, although a residual Home Rule element survived, Labour portrayed Scottish nationalism as archaic, reactionary, and divisive to the working class. Parliamentary sovereignty and political centralization were presented as essential to allowing Labour to legislate its program of reform. At the same time, the old policy of Home Rule within the empire had become redundant as the 1931 Statute of Westminster gave effective independence to the Dominions. Henceforth there was no halfway house between membership in the United Kingdom and independence and, given the relative unimportance of the British Commonwealth, no external support system for an independent Scotland in a dangerous world. In 1958, the Home Rule policy was finally removed from the party platform.

BRITAIN IN EUROPE

In the postwar years, the collapse of the United Kingdom's external support system of empire rapidly became apparent, and governments searched frantically for a replacement in the Commonwealth, in Atlanticism and the illusion of the "special relationship" with the United States, and finally in the

European Community (EC). EC entry, disdained in 1957, was pursued from the early 1960s as an economic panacea. The mechanisms of this were often unclear, although discussion was replete with the sadomasochistic images of the British public (i.e., private) school such as cold showers, shock treatment, and drastic punishment. EC entry was also presented as a project around which centrist forces could unite to preserve the threatened consensus. Community membership could discipline both capital and labor while placing institutional constraints on radical governments. This was most apparent in the 1975 referendum campaign on membership, when political centrists previously opposed to membership rallied in favor, while left-wing erstwhile supporters turned against. (Indeed, in the referendum alliance can be seen the origins of the 1980s Liberal-SDP alliance, although they failed to carry much of the Conservative Party into the new centrist formation.) Membership was opposed by a variety of groups marshaling economic, class, and nationalist arguments. Most economists remained profoundly skeptical of the economic benefits of membership, arguing that Britain's economy would have to be made competitive *before* entry to take advantage of the wider market. The Labour Party left and the trade unions opposed the Community's free market basis, with its ban on protectionism and subsidies.

Three types of nationalists added their voices. Old-style empire loyalists, mainly found in the Conservative Party, continued to defend a world role for Britain while considering the Community adequate for lesser nations. Little Englanders, mainly in the Labour Party, purveyed a different nationalism, focused on the needs of the island state and drawing on myths of British democracy and independence threatened by alien continental influences—Tony Benn is an exponent of this type of view. The Little England tradition, which can be traced to Liberal opposition to empire in the nineteenth century, contained the seeds of England's (and possibly Britain's) missed national revolution, a project for the creation of a developmental national state. In the peripheral nations of the U.K., Little Englandism by definition has limited appeal, and many of their nationalists like to mock the universal pretensions of English culture. Yet EC membership was opposed by local nationalist groups as an example of further centralization, a new obstacle to the recovery of lost sovereignty. In the more remote parts of England, opposition also focused on the issue of peripherality itself and the dangers of development concentrating on the European golden triangle. Specific sectors caused concern: U.K. coal and steel industries were heavily concentrated in the periphery, and Scots saw threats to their fishing and hill farming. While these oppositions are analytically separate, they did have points of contact.

Despite the insistence of the Labour left that their opposition was based on an ideological hostility to market capitalism, they tapped reserves of xenophobia in the working-class consciousness. The inconsistency between their opposition to Scottish nationalism and defense of the British state revealed most clearly that there was a nationalism underlying their attitudes about the Community. The various strands of EC opposition and alternative schemes for national regeneration were brought together in the late 1970s, in Labour's Alternative Economic Strategy, a program of state-sponsored reindustrialization and protectionism.[12] This required a strengthening of the central national state to be achieved through exploiting the potential of parliamentary sovereignty, although the statism of the strategy coexisted uneasily with a form of corporatism in which power would be shared with trade unions and firms. Withdrawal from the European Community would permit national protectionism and widespread state intervention. Within a planned economy and behind protectionist walls, the territorial distribution of economic activity could be ordered by the state. One attempt was made to reconcile the Alternative Economic Strategy with political decentralization, but it was never officially endorsed by the party.[13] In the course of the 1980s, however, with Labour in opposition nationally, a number of municipal councils experimented with local economic development strategies, and the party at large slowly absorbed this experience as it abandoned the Alternative Economic Strategy in the late 1980s.

THE NATIONALIST REVIVAL IN SCOTLAND

From the mid-1960s, there has been a marked revival of nationalism in Scotland, although the causes are difficult to identify. A rise in the diffuse sense of national identity has been linked to the decline of empire and the crisis of the U.K. state. The strengthening of Scottish administrative institutions by governments concerned to consolidate their position in Scotland has in turn led to a focus of debate on Scottish issues and further demands for institutional reform. In the fields of sports and culture, Scottish identity has been reinforced and modernized.[14]

At the same time, the system of territorial management came under increasing strain as British governments failed to deliver on their promises. Having increasingly defined economic issues in spatial terms, the British found that failure was interpreted in the same framework.[15] The weakening of the two-party system created a new opening for territorially based parties, which in the mid-1970s were able to maintain the balance of power in Parliament. By the mid-1970s the system of territorial management was in danger of breaking down altogether, presenting a double crisis for the regime. The threat of separatism posed a danger to its territorial integrity, and the rise of territorial parties threatened the two-party duopoly upon which the constitution hinged.

It is tempting to analyze the rise of nationalism in Scotland in class terms or to see it as a reflection of other types of social movement, but such reductionism is ultimately fruitless. Nationalist voters in the 1970s were a representative cross-section of the population, drawing support from all social classes; in the 1990s they tend to be more working class and similar in profile to Labour voters.[16] Their leaders at one time tended to insist that the party was itself a social movement, based on shared commitment to self-government but encompassing a wide class and ideological spectrum.

Nor should nationalism be seen as an "ethnic" movement based on language, culture, or ascriptive identity. The rise of nationalism in Scotland has accompanied a decline in traditional ethnic-cultural differences between the Highlands and the Lowlands, Irish and Scots, Catholic and Protestants. The status of the three languages, English, Scots, and Gaelic, hardly features in political debate, and it is relatively easy for incomers to assimilate into Scottish society.

It is true that the Nationalists have gained more support in some regions and sectors than others. In the fishing areas of northeast Scotland, they have capitalized on opposition to national and Community policies and built up a large base of support. For a long time, they enjoyed considerable success in Scotland's new towns, products of postwar planning policies to disperse population from the urban centers. New towns tend to have an overrepresentation of skilled blue-collar and clerical workers and an underrepresentation of the top and bottom ends of the social hierarchy. Their early populations were by definition recent arrivals moving out of older neighborhoods. In the 1970s, the Scottish National Party (SNP) also exploited the unpopularity of Labour's national and local administrations to make advances into the low-income public housing estates of Glasgow's periphery, but the SNP's success was short-lived. The SNP has been unable to establish a permanent presence in the cities or exploit urban discontent. Labour's Scottish base has thus remained largely intact.

There are constant tensions within the SNP over the form and direction that the movement should take. On the one side are the traditionalists committed to a simple policy of independence and tending to conservatism on social and economic issues. They emphasize an appeal to all Scots and deplore ideological or class division. Although they would deny that this puts them on the political right, their independent Scotland would be little different from the present one except for the presence of an Edinburgh parliament. On the other side is a left-wing group dreaming of a Socialist Scotland and blaming Scotland's indigenous elites as well as the British connection for the nation's problems. They see a need to prise the urban working class from Labour's grip if the party is to prosper or Scotland to resume its independence. They tend, by and large, to be more moderate on the independence issue and to deride the notion of a united, classless Scottish nation. In the 1980s, they organized in the '79 Group, plunging the party into a period of internal conflict, proscriptions, and resignations. Like all nationalist movements, both right and left in the SNP make liberal use of myth, creating their own imagined nations that are then presented as a mixture of description and aspiration. For the Right, the myth is of a classless, democratic nation, rooted in rural and small-town life, a body of sturdy democratic citizens living in tolerance and good order. For the Left, the myth is of the oppressed nation/class, a naturally Socialist society kept down by its own class structure in collaboration with the British state. Both versions are infused with myths of Scottish democracy going back to the religious conflicts of the seventeenth century, and suffer from severe problems as mobilizing ideologies. In the 1990s, the SNP has settled down as a left-of-center Social Democratic party in the European mode. This makes social democracy a hegemonic ideology in Scottish politics, in stark contrast to the situation in England.

As the nationalists have moved to the center-left, the Labour Party has moved in a nationalist direction. There has always been a nationalist element within the Labour Party and a much smaller one among the Conservative Party. From the late 1960s a combination of electoral concern and rising national consciousness prompted both parties to reconsider their positions, although neither was prepared to consider a radical overhaul of the British constitution itself to accommodate the new territorial pressures. The Conservatives produced a short-lived and decidedly contrived proposal for an elected Scottish Assembly to take the committee stage of Scottish bills, which would then complete their progress at Westminster. They later dropped this and reverted to uncompromising defense of the status quo. Labour, in government from 1974, produced proposals for an elected legislative assembly with its own executive but insisted that this would in no way infringe the unity and sovereignty of Parliament. To reassure those in Scotland who feared for their privileged position at the center, Scotland's overrepresentation in Parliament would continue, as would the presence of the secretary of state in the Cabinet. Economic policymaking would remain the exclusive prerogative of the central government, with the Scottish Assembly confined to social and environmental issues. In the event, Labour could not command a majority in Parliament for its proposals, and a wrecking amendment meant that the small positive majority in the 1979 referendum was insufficient to carry the scheme. The Conservatives, having secured the abstention or opposition of their own supporters with promises to bring in a better devolution scheme of their own, abandoned the idea when they regained office after 1979. In opposition, however, Labour strengthened its belief in devolution.

SCOTLAND AND THE EUROPEAN COMMUNITY

At the same time as Scottish and Welsh nationalism was challenging the territorial constitution of the United Kingdom from below, EC entry was testing it from above. Yet, for many years, little political connection was made between the issues. One reason for this is the unwillingness of the British parties to accept any constitutional modification at all. So both devolution to Scotland and Wales and EC entry were to be achieved by acts of the U.K. Parliament, whose sovereignty would be unabridged. Referendums were conceded in both cases to resolve divisions within the Labour Party and not as a result of a principled decision to take the decisions out of the hands of Parliament. Indeed, in both cases, it was emphasized that the referendums were merely advisory.

Opposition to the Community was deeply felt in the British periphery. To a large extent, this was a function of peripherality itself. In a European free trade area, outlying regions removed from the "golden triangle" are likely to be even more disadvantaged than they already are within the UK. Suspicion of remote government was redoubled in the case of government from Brussels. Specific sectors caused particular concern: With half the U.K. fishing industry, Scotland saw the opening of European waters as a major threat; fishing concerns were a significant factor in several SNP victories in the elections of 1974.

As Labour became increasingly dominant in Scotland in the 1970s, it became increasingly opposed to EC membership. In the vote on the principle of entry, in 1971, Scottish MPs in both major parties divided in more or less the same proportions as their English and Welsh colleagues. By the time of the vote on direct election of the European Parliament, in 1977, there was a marked divergence. Whereas Conservatives were overwhelmingly in favor, Scottish Labour MPs divided 16 to 10 against, in contrast to non-Scottish Labour MPs who divided 122 to 110 in favor. There was no correlation between the attitudes of Labour MPs on devolution and Europe. The SNP opposed EC membership in 1971, ostensibly on the ground that the issue would have to be decided by an independent Scotland. In practice, they attacked the Community as a further removal of power from Scotland. Brussels was presented as an even more remote version of London, equally insensitive to Scottish interests. The SNP did, however, support the principle of direct elections to the European Parliament as a means of enhancing Scottish influence in the Community. Greater Scottish hostility to the EC was reflected in the referendum result of 1975. Although in Scotland as in other parts of the U.K., the majority voted to remain in the Community, the turnout was lower than anywhere except Northern Ireland and the Yes vote just 58 percent, compared to 67 percent in England. Polls in the 1970s and early 1980s showed continuing hostility to the Community in Scotland, with a majority of Labour voters and the vast bulk of SNP voters in favor of withdrawal. They also showed that Scots supporters tended to see membership as benefiting England more than Scotland, whereas opponents considered that Scotland was more severely damaged.[17]

SCOTTISH SELF-GOVERNMENT
AND EUROPEAN INTEGRATION

As early as 1973, some Labour MPs were beginning to make a connection between the revived Scottish constitutional issue and European integration. Indeed, the as yet unclear implications of Community membership led to a cautious reappraisal of Labour's opposition to devolution even before electoral pressure forced its hand in 1974.[18] In 1973, Labour MP Jim Sillars founded the Scottish Labour EC watchdog committee, a group of MPs who would monitor developments in the Community as they affected Scotland. Sillars's position at this time was that Britain should withdraw from the EC and Scotland should have a devolved assembly but that, if Britain remained in the Community, Scotland should have as much independence as would give it independent representation in Brussels. He was moving rapidly in a more nationalist direction and in 1976, after the referendum had confirmed EC membership, quit the Labour Party to form the short-lived Scottish Labour Party (SLP), with a policy of Scottish independence within the EC. The idea had little appeal outside the ranks of Sillars's party, however, and died with the SLP after the general election of 1979. Labour, by the early 1980s committed to a devolved assembly and to withdrawal from the Community without a referendum, declared the question to be irrelevant.

The SNP continued to oppose the EC as strongly as the British connection, as a dilution of the sovereignty to which Scotland was entitled. Indeed, so firmly did the SNP hold their view of Scotland as a historic nation that they refused to join the Bureau of Unrepresented Nations set up by Breton, Welsh, Basque, and Alsatian groups in Brussels to press their case within the Community. In the view of the SNP, these were merely fringe groups with little electoral support seeking representation within the existing Community. They, in contrast, were a mature national movement with mass support ready to assume independent existence. The model that they presented was that of the Scandinavian democracies, all but one of which were outside the EC. They similarly rejected the model of a "Europe of the regions" put forward by some of the peripheral movements on the Continent on the grounds that Scotland is not a region but a nation comparable in status to the existing member states.

Scots failed to see the EC as a solution to the Scottish independence issue because the Community was being presented, particularly in the referendum campaign of 1975, as a prop for the old state order. The pro-EC prospectus called for continuity, consensus, centrist government, and stability, the essentials of the threatened postwar settlement. Because the British economy was failing to provide the material underpinning for this and the state was visibly crumbling in the face of industrial unrest, political extremism, and territorial pressures, a new external support system was called for. Europe would provide this where the empire, Commonwealth, and Atlanticism had successively failed. The competitive stimulus would revive the economy, Community constraints would limit governments, and continuity in policy would be assured. The common purpose showed by the pro-EC side would demonstrate the possibilities for a new consensus politics of the center, with the extremes excluded. The authority of the central governing elite would be restored. With the issues thus defined in terms of the British domestic agenda, radicals tended to gravitate to the no side. The idea that continuing Community membership could be used to subvert the British state itself was confined to a few intellectuals.[19]

INDEPENDENCE IN EUROPE

The option of Scottish independence within the European Community started to be taken seriously only in the late 1980s, as a result of developments in British as well as European politics. After some fifteen years of membership, it was apparent across the political spectrum that pre-Community trading relationships could not be restored and that British membership must be regarded as permanent. The experience of the Thatcher government further modified attitudes on the Left and in the periphery. Its use of the centralized state to put through a radical right-wing program caused many on the Left to revise their opposition to constitutional restraints on government, whereas Margaret Thatcher's strident anti-Europeanism convinced many that the Community could not be all bad.

The experience of the trade unions is particularly important. Excluded from consultation by national government, they found a welcome in Brussels and came to see the proposed social dimension of Jacques Delors's initiative for full economic union in 1992 as a means of recovering rights lost in domestic politics. The Labour Party also abandoned its proposals for withdrawal, although it has yet to formulate a clear vision of the political future of Europe. It is ambivalent about the merits of strengthening the European Parliament, although the fact that the European elections of 1989 provided its first national victory over the Thatcher administration improved the Parliament's image. After 1975, the SNP, too, began to accept the permanence of the Community and the poor prospects for states that remain totally outside it. A crucial role was played by Jim Sillars, former Labour MP and leader of the breakaway SLP. Joining the SNP in the early 1980s, Sillars retained his belief in independence within Europe, and in a November 1988 by-election was able to ride to victory over Labour in the inner city constituency of Govan. By this time, the party as a whole had been converted to the idea of independence within the EC.

This idea is in many ways seductive. As part of the United Kingdom, Scotland can influence Community decisions only through the Scottish lobby, focused on the role of the secretary of state in the Cabinet. As an independent state, it would have its own delegation to the Council of Ministers. If major economic and social decisions are really to be transferred from London to Brussels, then it would be worth sacrificing representation in the former for the latter. Nationalists also point to the European Parliament where Scotland, with a population of five million, has just eight members (six Labour and two SNP), whereas the Republic of Ireland, with a population of three million, has fifteen members.

Independence in Europe also carries great reassurance to Scots fearful of taking a leap in the dark. Like the old policy of Home Rule within the empire, it promises an external support system in a dangerous world and allows nationalists to disclaim the "separatist" label. There is no doubt about the importance of this reassurance factor, although there is evidence that public opinion has moved on since the devolution debates of the 1970s. Throughout the 1980s, there was growing support for some measure of Scottish Home Rule with declining support for the status quo. A poll taken in March 1979 showed only 14 percent favoring independence, 42 percent supporting an assembly with substantial powers, 35 percent wanting no change, and 9 percent unsure. By March 1985, a reversal in the support for independence and the status quo had occurred: Thirty-three percent favored independence, 47 percent were for an assembly with substantial powers, 14 percent favored no change, and 6 percent were unsure. Support for independence appears to have outstripped support for the status quo sometime early during Thatcher's second term. The EC dimension appears to add considerably to the support for Scottish independence. A poll conducted jointly for the *Glasgow Herald* and BBC Scotland found that 61 percent of Scots felt that an independent Scottish government would best represent Scottish interests in the European Community, whereas only 32 percent felt this would be best achieved by the U.K. government. The same poll found that 55 percent thought that Scotland would be better off if it was independent in Europe, 23 percent thought it would be worse off, 11 percent thought neither/no difference, and 11 percent did not know.[20]

The stumbling block for the SNP, however, was that 70 percent thought it either not very likely or not at all likely that Scotland could become an independent member of the EC. Yet in principle the Community cannot exclude European democracies. Neither of the major British parties has indicated that it would resist Scottish independence if that were the expressed view of the Scottish people and, in the event of negotiated independence, it is improbable that other Community members would seek to expel a territory that has been part of the Community since 1973. Indeed, all parties would be likely to insist on Scottish membership in order to minimize the disruption of

secession. Now polls on the constitutional issue regularly include the inde-
pendence-in-Europe option, which gains the support of between a quarter and
a third of the voters. A summary of opinion on the constitutional issue is
given in Figure 8.1.

Figure 8.1
Support for Constitutional Options, Scotland, 1974–1995 (percent)

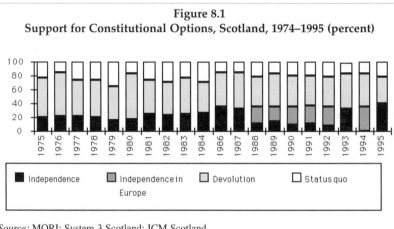

Source: MORI; System 3 Scotland; ICM Scotland.

SCOTTISH NATIONALISM IN THE CONSERVATIVE ERA

The 1980s saw a consolidation of nationalist sentiment in Scotland. Scottish
nationalism was strengthened in the 1980s by the erosion of four essential
sources of support for the union: the British party system; the calculation that
the union serves Scotland's economic interests; the preservation of a Scottish
civil society within the union; and the broad identity of values between
England and Scotland. The rise of third-party voting has ended the two-party
duopoly in the popular vote, although not, given the electoral system, in parliamentary representation. Nor can either of the major parties claim to be truly
British in their appeal. This is part of a postwar trend that has accelerated in
the 1980s. Whereas Labour won parliamentary majorities in five of the six
regions of the United Kingdom in 1945, it was unable to win in more than
four in all subsequent general elections in which it won office.[21] Conservative
parliamentary majorities during the 1950s and in 1970 were dependent upon
the party's predominance in only three of the U.K. regions. The pattern is
clear. Although Labour support is more widely distributed than that of the
Conservatives, both major parties operate from fewer and narrower regional
bases. The 1992 general election further emphasized the regional distinctive-
ness of the two major parties. In Scotland and Wales the governing
Conservatives won just seventeen of 109 seats and under 30 percent of the

popular vote. The two-party system is at its weakest in Scotland, where only 64.7 percent vote Conservative or Labour. The ability of the major parties to continue to play their integrative role is thus placed in question.

The Scottish media gave considerable attention to the "doomsday scenario" before the 1987 general election. In 1992 the same scenario was repeated. This suggested that Scotland would again reject the policies of Conservatism yet have them enforced by an English majority. Labour would be powerless to prevent the implementation of policies that the Scots clearly did not want. It was also suggested both by the SNP and some elements of the Labour Party that the Conservatives lacked a mandate to govern in Scotland.

In the narrow constitutional sense, there is no question of the government's right to rule. The Conservatives won a U.K. parliamentary majority in 1979, 1983, 1987, and 1992 and, by custom and practice, thereby form the government. There is, though, a serious question about political legitimacy, whether a government rejected by a large majority of Scots will be able to govern with the kind of consent that has underlain the British democratic system. In the longer term, there is a fundamental question as to how long a political union survives when the necessary underlying social, economic, and political consensus progressively erodes.

For the Labour opposition, the scenario is equally problematic. As its leaders know, it is unable to sustain the no-mandate argument advanced by some within its ranks as long as it relies on the conventions of parliamentary majorities attained under the present electoral system to legitimate future Labour governments. To play the nationalist card would raise doubts about its ability ever to win a British majority again. Yet without challenging the government's legitimacy, Labour could not effectively respond to nationalist taunts portraying its parliamentary group as the Feeble Fifty.

The SNP, for its part, saw its vote in 1992 increase to 21 percent, but the simple plurality electoral system won it only three seats. The Scottish Liberal Democrats, with half the vote, won three times as many seats. From the other side of the political spectrum, the discrete mechanisms of accommodation by which Scottish interests were managed in the past have been disrupted as some English MPs intervene regularly in Scottish business, complaining about the favorable treatment received by Scotland.

The Erosion of the U.K. Union

The economic advantages of the union have always been a matter of controversy. In the nineteenth century, it opened up imperial markets to Scottish manufacturers, but it is arguable that this left Scotland, like the rest of Britain, excessively dependent on these. National economic policies of protection in the 1930s have been criticized as damaging Scotland's export-based industry.[22] In the 1960s, a lively debate took place on the extent to which the rest of the U.K. subsidized Scotland and on the economic implications of independence.[23] The major British parties campaigned aggressively on the economic benefits of the union to Scotland, in particular the disproportionate share of identifiable public expenditure and the national regional policies aimed at sending industries to the development areas.

In the 1970s, the focus shifted to North Sea oil, with the nationalist slogan "Rich Scots or Poor Britons" inviting Scots to keep the benefits to themselves. The British parties found themselves hoist on their own petard, having made the transfer payments from England to Scotland the centerpiece of their defense of the union. Again, the question is more complicated than might appear at first sight. Oil revenues in themselves do little to improve the condition of life for the majority of Scots without specific economic and social policies to ensure a proper distribution of the benefits. There is a danger, indeed, that an oil-rich Scotland could suffer further contraction of its manufacturing base as its currency appreciated, with increased social division between the employed and the unemployed. In the 1980s, the salience of the oil issue greatly diminished, for reasons that are not entirely clear.

As British government regional policy was run down, Scotland came to depend less on the central state and more on international capital. The recession of the early 1980s was particularly hard on Scottish-owned firms.[24] A growing number of Scots now question the economic benefits of the union. A poll in May 1989 showed 49 percent of Scots believing that the Union works against Scottish economic interests. Only 21 percent believed that economic links with the rest of the U.K. worked for Scottish interests.[25] The 1992 Scottish election survey showed massive support for the proposition that Scotland had fared worse than England due to government policy; even 50 percent of Conservatives shared this view.[26]

Preservation of Scotland's distinct civil society was always seen as part of the union bargain. In the early years, religion was a key element of this, along with education and the local government system. This was possible because of the nature of the British constitution, which combined parliamentary sovereignty with an understanding as to the limited scope of the state. This understanding was broken by the Thatcher government, which took parliamentary sovereignty to mean the unlimited power of government to impose its will in a highly centralist manner. Local governments, trade unions, and universities lost their traditional autonomy. Government agencies were filled with businesspeople or political cadres. In England, this sparked a move for constitutional reform. In Scotland, it added to support for Home Rule.

The final source of support for the Union has been the broad identity of social and political values between Scots and the English. There is evidence of a greater support in Scotland for collectivist values and an interventionist state.[27] Some Conservatives dismiss this, arguing that their electoral failure in Scotland stems from a culture of dependence, the reliance of the Scots on the nanny state, and an unwillingness to fend for themselves. According to this analysis, the mechanisms of administrative devolution and the actions of Scottish ministers in Thatcher's first two terms prevented the harsh medicine from having its effect. Scots' lack of support for the Conservatives is thus due not to an excess but to a lack of Thatcherism. They therefore advocate a more vigorous application of the strategy north of the border. In fact, Scotland has not been exempt from the key elements of the strategy.[28] The British political program has been applied, with the Scottish Office refraining from independent policy initiatives and concentrating on a conventional defense of Scottish interests within the framework of that program. Conservative failure in Scotland must therefore be attributed to a distaste for their policies.

The unpopularity in Scotland of certain government measures is notable. The community charge, or poll tax, has been consistently opposed by over 70 percent of Scot respondents. In December 1988, 37 percent of Scots stated that they supported civil disobedience against the poll tax, with 43 percent disagreeing.[29] This divergence of social and political values between England and Scotland is a more potent threat to the union than the election of eleven SNP members of Parliament in the 1970s. In that case, the threat could be dismissed as a marginal one, with a limited devolution scheme containing the damage and allowing normal two-party politics to resume. It can also be argued that Scottish predominant values are more in line with those of the Jacques Delors/François Mitterrand vision of a social Europe than the Thatcher vision of an unfettered market. So as England has moved farther from Europe, Scotland has moved closer. It can be argued, indeed, that the U.K. does not have a "Scottish problem" but an "English problem" because it is in England that the dominant political party cannot make up its mind to be in Europe or out of it, or what its own national identity is, British or English.

Yet this very divergence of England from the European vision poses serious problems for the policy of Scottish independence in the Community. If the remainder of Britain were to continue under an anti-Community Conservative government (and the prospects for this would increase enormously with a Scottish secession), then Scotland would face the choice of aligning itself with Britain or with Europe. If it chose to join the European Monetary Union (EMU) while Britain stayed out, it would face large exchange rate fluctuations with its main trading partner. If it chose to stay outside EMU, it would remain an economic dependency of Britain, subject to macroeconomic monetary and exchange rate decisions made in London. Its choices in social policy would further be constrained by the need to compete with its main trading partner to the south.

CONCLUSION

The debate within Scottish opposition circles thus moved in the 1980s from opposition to the EC as an integral part of opposition to the British state

(SNP) or transnational capital and the free market (Labour). Rather, the Community is now seen as a mechanism for circumventing a British state itself committed to political centralization and economic liberalism. Opposition to Community membership in Scotland has declined steeply with the shift in position of Labour and the SNP. Danish rejection of the Maastricht Treaty in the first referendum was seen as a rejection of centralization and the dominance of a powerful neighbouring nation. Scots have suffered these inconveniences within the U.K. for long enough to see Europe as a way out. Yet both economic and constitutional futures remain open. Although it is politically committed to Europe, Scotland remains geographically and economically peripheral, vulnerable to the effects of the free internal market. The accession to the EC of Greece, Spain, and Portugal has reduced Scotland's share of development funds, and the Social Charter is unlikely to be the lifesaver that British trade unionists expect.

The situation at the time of writing is extremely confused. An all-party Scottish Convention to discuss a constitutional future for the nation met in the years 1988–1992. Although boycotted by the Conservatives and the SNP, it gained considerable support from Labour, the center parties, smaller groups like the Greens and the Communists, and from trade unions and local government. A convention is an old Scottish device for registering the national will but, in the traditional manner, the last one was a sober, serious affair and not the center of a mass social movement. Nor was it clear what would become of the convention's recommendations when they were complete.

Labour hoped to form a U.K. majority after the 1992 election and legislate for a devolved Scottish assembly within a U.K. that, in turn, would remain part of the European Community. A Parliament in which no party had a majority would have seen the non-Conservative parties cooperating in a program of constitutional reform in which Scotland and Europe would have been central elements. In the event, the Conservatives were returned with an overall majority. Once again, they did extremely poorly in Scotland, with just over 25 percent of the vote. Since this was a marginal improvement on their 1987 score and since the SNP, while gaining votes, failed to capture extra seats, the Conservatives proclaimed a moral victory and indicated that they intended to do nothing at all about the Scottish constitutional issue. A discussion paper, "Scotland and the Union,"[30] offered a few palliatives and some more administrative devolution.

After the 1992 election, the Conservative Party developed a serious division over Europe. On one side are the more liberal, traditional Tories, who tend to support Europe strongly. On the other are the right-wing heirs of Thatcher, wedded to a mixture of economic neoliberalism and social authoritarianism. Seeking to reinforce the British nation-state, they have become increasingly anti-Europe and are opposed to any concession to Scotland. This debate finds little resonance in Scotland and the Europhobic position of the

Tory Right is arguably a new form of English nationalism, directed at threats to the old order from above and below. If this strand should triumph, it will alienate Scotland further from the U.K. political order and bring it more closely into the European mainstream. The Conservative crisis over Europe is more than a mere argument over policy such as has occurred many times in the past. It is a crisis of identity and thus potentially lethal. It is not only the Conservative Party that suffers from divided attitudes on Europe. Labour, in opposition, is able to disguise its own differences only by exploiting the more visible ones in the Conservative Party. A Labour government would also have to reconcile the conflicting demands of consistency in Europe with the multinational character of the United Kingdom.

Figure 8.2
Share of Vote, Scotland, 1955–1992 (percent)

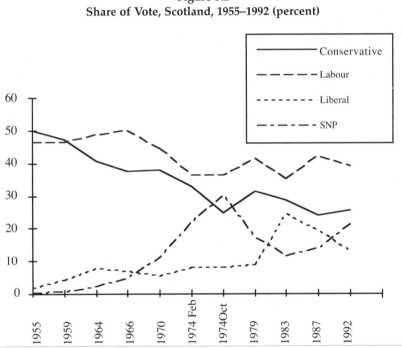

NOTES

1. David Marquand, *The Unprincipled Society* (London: Fontana, 1988).
2. Michael Keating, *State and Regional Nationalism: Territorial Policies and the European State* (Hemel Hempstead, U.K.: Harvester-Wheatsheaf, 1988).
3. Richard Rose, *Understanding the United Kingdom: The Territorial Dimension in Government* (London: Longman 1982), p. 11.

4. Michael Keating and David Bleiman, *Labour and Scottish Nationalism* (London: Macmillan, 1979).

5. Arthur Midwinter, Michael Keating, and James Mitchell, *Politics and Public Policy in Scotland* (London: Macmillan, 1991).

6. Michael Keating, *The Role of the Scottish MP* (Ph.D. diss., CNAA, 1975).

7. Keating and Bleiman, *Labour and Scottish Nationalism*.

8. Ibid.

9. Manuel Castells, *The City and the Grassroots: A Cross-Cultural Theory of Urban Social Movements* (Berkeley: University of California, 1983).

10. Michael Keating, *The City That Refused to Die: Glasgow: The Politics of Urban Regeneration* (Aberdeen, Scotland: Aberdeen University Press, 1988).

11. Regional Studies Association (hereinafter RSA), *Report of an Inquiry into Regional Problems in the United Kingdom* (Norwich: Geo, 1983).

12. Barry Jones and Michael Keating, *Labour and the British State* (Oxford: Clarendon, 1985).

13. John Prescott, *Alternative Regional Strategy* (London: Parliamentary Labour Party Spokesman's Group, 1982).

14. Jack Brand, *The National Movement in Scotland* (London: Routledge and Kegan Paul, 1978).

15. Keating, *State and Regional Nationalism*.

16. On voters in the 1970s, see Brand, *National Movement;* on voters in the 1990s, see Jack Brand, James Mitchell, and Paula Surridge, "Social Constituency and Ideological Profile: Scottish Nationalism in the 1990s," *Political Studies* 42, no. 4 (1994), pp. 616–629.

17. Michael Keating and Nigel Waters, "Scotland in the European Community," in M. Keating and B. Jones, eds., *Regions in the European Community* (Oxford: Clarendon, 1985).

18. *Scotsman,* July 10, 1973.

19. For example, see Tom Nairn, *The Break-l of Britain,* 2nd ed. (London: Verso, 1982).

20. *Glasgow Herald,* April 14, 1989.

21. R. M. Punnett, "Regional Partisanship and the Legitimacy of British Government 1868–1983," *Parliamentary Affairs* 37, no. 2 (1984), pp. 141–159.

22. Christopher Harvie, *No Gods and Precious Few Heroes: Scotland, 1914–1980* (London: Edward Arnold, 1981).

23. G. McCrone, *Scotland's Future* (London: Oxford University Press, 1969).

24. Brian Ashcroft and James Love, *Takeovers, Mergers and the Regional Economy* (Edinburgh: Edinburgh University Press, 1993).

25. *Scotsman,* May 16, 1989.

26. Brand, Mitchell, and Surridge, "Social Constituency."

27. Midwinter, Keating, and Mitchell, *Politics and Public Policy in Scotland*.

28. Ibid.

29. *Scotsman,* December 12, 1988.

30. Secretary of State, Scotland, *Scotland and the Union* (Edinburgh: Her Majesty's Stationery office).

9

The Irish Response to European Integration: Explaining the Persistence of Opposition

John Coakley, Michael Holmes, Nicholas Rees

In 1992, Irish voters approved the Treaty on European Union (Maastricht Treaty) by a clear margin of 69 percent in favor, 31 percent against, in a national referendum. The result reveals some of the ambiguities about Ireland's relationship with European integration. On the one hand, it reinforces the perception of Ireland as a strongly pro-European country, committed to supporting and advancing the process of integration. On the other hand, it shows that despite twenty years of membership and participation in the European Community (EC), there remains a solid core of opposition to integration in the Republic of Ireland.

In this chapter we explore the manner in which Ireland's relationship with an evolving European superstate has unfolded. It concentrates on examining the sources and nature of opposition in the Republic of Ireland to the process of European integration in general and to the European Community in particular and seeks to account for the forms that it has taken. We explain why opposition exists as part of Ireland's response to European integration and demonstrate that even in a pro-European country there are clear obstacles to forging greater unity.

In structuring our analysis, we follow a framework derived from a recent classification of forms of opposition to European integration.[1] Opposition in capitalist societies, it has been suggested, may be classified in terms of two general dimensions: whether it is "integrated" (concerned with specific outcomes) or "unintegrated" (concerned with principles), and whether it is "direct" (explicitly oriented toward a clearly defined target) or "indirect" (oriented toward more diffusely defined goals). We interpret these dimensions as referring respectively to the substance and form of protest behavior. This classification may be considered alongside a more general classification of pressure group activity that brings a theoretical perspective to traditional typologies: Political pressure may be assessed in terms of the range of its objectives (specific, sectoral, global) and the duration of the period over which it is exercised (limited, permanent).[2]

The classification we propose here is based on a marriage of the two discussed above. First, we consider the content of the demands being advanced. Overlap between the substance and range dimensions described above allows us to propose a distinction between "pragmatic" and "principled" demands, the former being specific and perhaps reflecting temporary interests, the latter being explicitly rooted in some fundamental ideological position. Second, we have replaced the two remaining dimensions (form, duration) by one referring to manner of articulation of demands: whether the group is a single issue one or whether it has other primary concerns, becoming mobilized only occasionally on a particular political issue (this corresponds with an old distinction made by Maurice Duverger between "exclusive" and "partial" groups).[3] If we cross-classify these dimensions, we get the matrix presented in Table 9.1. The distinction between the cells in this matrix informs much of the discussion that follows; in particular, although the pragmatic-principled dichotomy represents in reality the poles of a continuum, the distinction between groups whose raison d'être depends on the issue they address and multi-issue groups that tackle such an issue only episodically is rather easier to operationalize. The terminology we have used in describing the cells in this figure (for instance, the distinction between "sectoral" and "promotional" groups) derives from the standard literature on pressure group activity.

Our objective is, then, to examine the nature of opposition to European integration in Ireland with reference to this classification system. In the next section, we examine Irish public mass and elite attitudes regarding European integration in the context of the Irish nationalist tradition. We go on in the following section to look at the development of opposition to the integration process from the period immediately before accession to the present day, focusing especially on the three referendum periods (on the issue of membership in 1972, on the Single European Act [SEA] in 1987, and on the Maastricht Treaty in 1992). In the next section we analyze the patterns of opposition that have emerged among political and other elites. We go on to

Table 9.1   Classification of Groups Opposing and Supporting European Integration

| | Content of Demands | |
Form of Articulation	Pragmatic	Principled
Single-issue	Ad-hoc pressure groups	Organized pro- and anti-EC pressure groups
One issue in multiple-issue groups	"Nonideological" parties; sectoral pressure groups	"Ideological" parties; promotional pressure groups

review the surviving issues of concern in such areas as the economy and the question of neutrality, and activities in a broader framework of opposition. In the concluding section we look at the implications of this continued opposition for the future; we identify the principal areas where opposition to membership or to further extension of the competence of European institutions survives and its implications for Ireland's role in the European Union (EU).

IRISH MASS AND ELITE ATTITUDES TOWARD EUROPEAN INTEGRATION

From one perspective, perhaps what is surprising about Irish attitudes toward European integration is that the country was prepared to consider pooling its national sovereignty in the EC. A striking contrast between Ireland and the other EC member states has been the country's preoccupation with national independence, a consequence of its relatively recent acquisition of statehood and its unusual history as subject rather than ruler in a colonial relationship. The historical bitterness of the relationship between the Irish and the British might have been expected to color attitudes toward incorporation in any larger political community in which the British voice would be capable of drowning out the Irish. Indeed, Irish support for early attempts at European cooperation and integration, such as in the Organization for European Economic Cooperation (OEEC) and the Council of Europe (1949), was limited, and the state's energy was channeled into establishing its national identity and independence. In this context, it is rather surprising that Irish public attitudes toward European integration and more specifically toward the European Community have generally been supportive, while those of the Irish political and economic elite have been even more positive. We may, however, identify four characteristics of the Irish nationalist tradition that help to account for this.

First, public and elites' attitudes have become less nationalist. The wave of nationalist feeling that marked the birth of the state in 1922 and preoccupation with the "unfinished businesses" of the relationship with Britain and partition left little opportunity for experimentation with European ideals. However, forces for change were at work. From the 1940s onward, once Ireland's independence of Britain had been established and Irish unity seemed a long-term rather than an immediately realizable goal, bread-and-butter issues came to play a greater role, particularly at election time. The shift from protectionist to more open economic and trade policies, begun in the late 1950s and culminating in the signing of the Anglo-Irish Free Trade Agreement in 1965, both reflected and encouraged an abandonment of the traditional nationalist objective of aiming for maximum economic self-reliance. The Republic also embarked on a reappraisal of its nationalist stance toward Northern Ireland. Throughout the 1970s and the 1980s, officially sponsored nationalist symbols and rituals were quietly buried, and a new, less nationalist image of the past was cultivated in the schools.

Second, to the extent that nationalist attitudes persist, they are anti-British rather than anti-European. Indeed, Ireland has had certain cultural links with continental Europe consciousness. In the medieval period, these ties were principally in the form of an extensive interchange of scholars and manuscripts. Following the wars of the sixteenth and seventeenth centuries, thousands of members of the Irish gentry sought refuge in continental Europe, typically in the armies of France, Spain, and Austria. Strong cultural contacts remained until the end of the eighteenth century, most notably in the domain of education: Most Irish clergy and many members of the gentry were educated in continental Europe, in such institutions as the Irish colleges at Louvain, Paris, Rome, and Salamanca. Links with these institutions have survived down to the present century, serving as a reminder of the country's reliance on continental European (and especially Catholic) allies in its struggle against its Protestant neighbor.

Third, to the extent that anti-British attitudes persist, these are not incompatible with arguments for a realignment with Europe, in the economic domain at least. Membership in the EC offered the prospect of reducing Ireland's economic dependence on the U.K. In terms of trade links, Ireland had for centuries been dominated by British industry and the British market. In 1800, for instance, over 80 percent of Irish exports went to Great Britain, which also accounted for 79 percent of Irish imports.[4] By 1929, even after the attainment of political independence, trade dependence of the Irish Free State on Great Britain was no less, and by 1960 this dependence remained enormous, Great Britain accounting for 61 percent of Irish exports and 46 percent of Irish imports (a considerable proportion of the remaining trade was with another part of the United Kingdom, Northern Ireland). Although trade with continental Europe was increasing even before accession to the EC, the change in Ireland's trade patterns since 1973 has been dramatic. By 1990, 28 percent of Ireland's exports were to Great Britain, from which it received 38 percent of its imports.[5] While nationalists concerned with overdependence on Great Britain in external trade relationships could find little objectionable in the EC, those worried about poor prices for Irish agricultural exports and about the low level of infrastructural development in the country could point to the prospect of substantial, direct financial assistance from Brussels, a transfer that has been much more obvious than the indirect and frequently negative effects of membership on other sectors of the Irish economy.

Fourth, to the extent that nationalist values of any kind persist, these can be portrayed as being compatible with European integration. The argument has been put, for instance, that acceptance of political links with the EC raised the prospect, ironically, of enhanced political autonomy. Although it was true that sovereignty in certain vital areas would increasingly be shared with Brussels-based institutions, at least Ireland would have a voice in the process of making decisions that would affect it. It was thus not too difficult for members of the Irish political and administrative elite to contemplate the exchange of the reality of continued British domination, especially in the economic and cultural fields, for a looser, multilateral association with the rest of Western Europe. As suggested above, the Irish nationalist tradition was not merely anti-British; with Britain so frequently at loggerheads with the major powers of continental Europe, it could also afford to be pro-European. Most nationalists did not see the EC as a threat, and rejected parallels with the Act of Union of 1800, which brought Ireland into the United Kingdom. The EC was seen as a new and different form of alliance, in which Ireland was now free to choose its partners in a pluralistic Community whose central institutions would allow Ireland a voice out of proportion to its population. This view was articulated clearly by Foreign Minister Michael O'Kennedy in 1977:

> Remember, as a country with only recent independence, we were conscious to a certain extent of the effect which membership would have on our sovereignty, but we also knew that by becoming members of the Community we were being enabled for the first time to influence decisions which would influence us anyway. Therefore, we were contributing to a pooling of sovereignty to enable us to have a more enriched sovereignty.[6]

Irish Public Opinion and European Integration

The evidence provided by public opinion surveys supports the view that Irish attitudes have certainly not been negative toward European integration, although it also suggests that there is a degree of ambivalence underlying Ireland's relationship with the EC. The European Commission's program for monitoring public opinion in member states, of which the *Eurobarometer* surveys are the best-known component, demonstrates this. We may, for example, consider the responses to four of the questions that have been asked regularly in these surveys; they relate to efforts to unify Western Europe, to Ireland's membership in the EC, to the prospect of a dissolution of the Community, and to the benefits gained through membership.[7] The results for the period from 1973 to 1994 are summarized in Figure 9.1.

The similarities between these indicators are striking. Less than a fifth of the samples surveyed expressed negative attitudes toward the EC and the process of European unification in the 1970s. Dissatisfaction levels rose subsequently, however, and appear to have peaked at the beginning of the 1980s. A decisive downward trend in dissatisfaction began in 1983; since then, the proportion expressing negative attitudes toward membership has plummeted from 25 percent in 1983 to 7 percent in 1994, and there has been a corresponding decline in the proportion expressing relief at the prospect of the

Figure 9.1
Negative Attitudes Toward European Integration, Ireland, 1973–1994

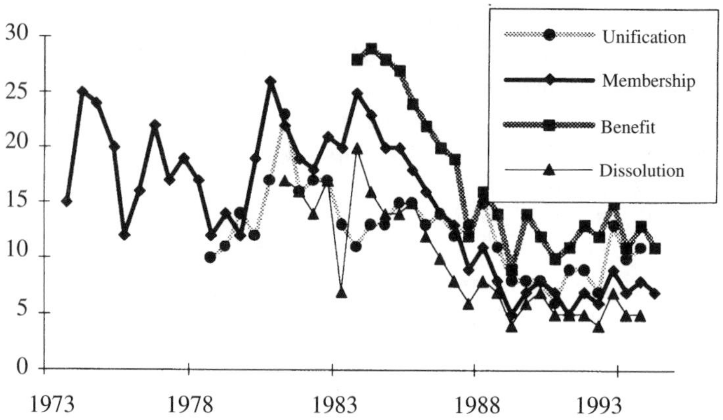

Note: The responses relate to those whose attitudes toward European unification were "against very much" and "against to some extent," who regarded EC membership as "a bad thing," who felt that Ireland "has not benefited" from membership, and who said that they would be "relieved" if the EC dissolved, respectively.
Source: Eurobarometer reports, 1983–1994.

breakup of the EC and in the proportion seeing Ireland's membership as bringing no benefit. Negative attitudes toward European unification for long remained rather more stable, averaging 12 percent in the 1970s, 15 percent in 1980–1984 and 13 percent in 1985–1988, before dipping to 8 percent in 1989–1991 and rising to a little over 10 percent in 1992–1993.

The Irish experience must, of course, be seen in comparative perspective. The relationship between Irish public opinion and that in the other member states since Ireland's accession is summarized in Figure 9.2. This reports answers the question on European unification only and has been simplified by the merger of certain countries and the omission of others. First, the public opinion profiles of the six original member states have been so similar that it is feasible to report them as a group without doing violence to the position in individual countries. Second, since its accession in 1981 the Greek profile has been similar to the Irish, and since their accession in 1986 the Spanish and Portuguese have followed the same pattern as the core states; all three of these countries have therefore been omitted.[8] What is clear from Figure 9.2 is that Irish opposition to the EC has tended to move parallel to that in the six core states, but to be about 4 percent greater until 1989, when it actually dipped below the EC core states' average; since then, it has remained below this average. In this the Irish pattern diverged from the British, where opposition to European unification increased significantly in the late 1980s and, of course, from the Danish pattern, where opposition has exceeded 40 percent.

Figure 9.2
Negative Attitudes Toward European Unification,
Ireland and Other States, 1973–1994

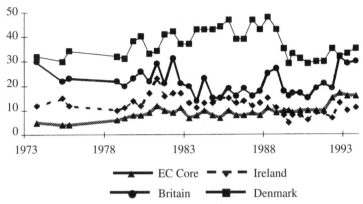

Note: "EC Core" is defined as the original six member states of the EEC. The responses relate to those whose attitudes to European unification were "against very much" and "against to some extent."
Source: Eurobarometer reports, 1983–1994.

The data presented up to now present an oversimplified picture of attitudes toward European integration. We go on in Figure 9.3 to consider in greater detail the profile of Irish attitudes by distinguishing more precisely responses to the question of European unification. Clearly, committed opposition to European unification is entirely overshadowed by committed sup-

Figure 9.3
Attitudes Toward European Unification, Ireland, 1973–1994

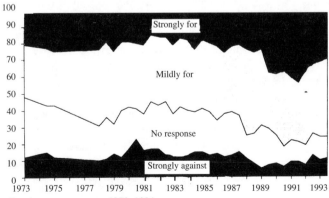

Source: Eurobarometer reports, 1983–1994.

port, and the overall pattern is one of very considerable stability, but with a tendency for the proportion not expressing an opinion to decline and for support to increase. Core opponents of European unification (defined as those "strongly against" it) remain a marginal group, slightly smaller in 1993 (3 percent) than in the first half of the 1970s (5 percent).

While the data reviewed above are neither as penetrating in content nor as extensive over time as we would like (in particular, they do not allow for analysis of the meaning of certain of the attitudes articulated, and they begin only in 1973, thus leaving a gap for the premembership period), certain consistent tendencies emerge. Irish attitudes toward the issues raised by the question of European integration appear to have been assimilated ultimately to those in the core member states. Whatever the indicator, positive perceptions of the EC and of European unity greatly overshadow negative ones, and this imbalance had become more pronounced by the end of the 1980s. The pool of committed opponents of European unification, never very extensive, seems to have dwindled almost to zero.

The Irish Political Elite and European Integration

Given the circumstances described above, the Irish political elite had a relatively free hand in negotiating the country's institutional relationship with continental Europe. The concepts of the common market and of European unity did not evoke negative reactions, and early discussion of a new relationship with Europe took place in a context of elite acquiescence or even indifference. This attitude was evident in the interwar period, when the Fianna Fáil government, fresh in office in 1932 on a radical nationalist program, supported Aristide Briand's proposed system for a European Federal Union.[9] In the aftermath of World War II Ireland continued to move closer to Europe through its participation in the European recovery program. Nevertheless, there was little sustained Irish interest in more wholehearted and adventurous forms of integration. Irish politicians were above all skeptical and cautious when it came to participating in European institutions, many of which seemed distant from Irish concerns.

On a pragmatic economic level the major political parties in Ireland supported cooperation with European institutions but expressed little interest in or enthusiasm for the postwar federal movements that were emerging in Western Europe. Ireland's principal foreign policy concern in the 1940s and 1950s was the partition issue; this had the effect of limiting its scope for cooperation in other European institutions. There was only sporadic interest in European integration among the political elite, and even less interest was shown among the general population.[10] Politically and militarily Ireland continued to apply Eamon de Valera's wartime policy of neutrality by refusing to join military alliances such as the North Atlantic Treaty Organization

(NATO). Nevertheless, the state did join and participate in the Council of Europe and the United Nations (1955), decisions that certainly contributed to an overall widening of the horizons and experience of Irish politicians.

Thus Ireland's application to join the European Economic Community (EEC) in 1961 resulted in little debate in the Republic on the merits of membership. On the whole there was little opposition among the major political parties, Fianna Fáil and Fine Gael, who supported Ireland's membership application but differed over the terms and conditions of entry. The Labour Party was the only significant party to oppose membership in the EEC and to argue for some form of alternative association with the newly formed Community. This lack of controversy reflected a mixture of pragmatism and idealism on the part of the political elite. Once Britain had decided to join the EEC, access to British markets appeared under threat if Ireland did not follow suit, thus placing Ireland in the position of feeling obliged to seek membership. At the same time Irish attitudes toward the EEC were changing, with an increasingly pro-European lobby surfacing among the emerging technocratic class and government officials who supported the country's move to modernize its economy and reduce its dependence on its neighbor through access to a larger European market.

In 1967 Ireland reactivated its application to join the EEC, again responding to Britain's renewed application. The government, in an attempt to bolster support for membership, published its third White Paper on the European Communities in April 1967 outlining the provisions of the treaties and describing the effects of the various instruments.[11] The following July the Taoiseach placed before the Dáil (lower house) a simply worded motion "that Dáil Eireann approves of the decision to reactivate Ireland's application for membership of the European Economic Community." Though in the ensuing debate amendments to the motion were introduced by the opposition parties, Fine Gael and Labour, the government motion was passed without division, suggesting a parliamentary consensus on the matter.

The apparent ease with which the government succeeded in proposing and passing a motion in favor of joining the EEC reflected continued elite support for membership. Nevertheless, in the period between 1967 and Ireland's eventual accession in 1973 there surfaced a number of issues over which opponents and supporters of the EEC were divided. These revolved around the question of whether Irish sovereignty would be impaired, the degree to which Ireland would be able to retain its status as a neutral country, and the effect that membership would have on the economic well-being of the state. These three issues, which were debated during the 1972 referendum, have sporadically reappeared in Irish politics over the intervening years. More recently, the Irish referenda over the SEA and the Maastricht Treaty offered opponents of the EC an opportunity once again to voice opposition to the Community and to its planned expansion.

IRELAND AT THE POLLS: REFERENDA
AND EUROPEAN PARLIAMENT ELECTIONS

Opposition to EC membership was slow to develop, in view of the relatively low level of public and even elite interest in the issue. The first significant public debate on the issue was generated by the fact that Ireland could not sign the Treaty of Accession without amending its constitution.[12] Because a popular referendum is necessary to approve any proposed constitutional change, the referendum on membership in 1972 allowed and indeed forced opponents of membership to prepare a defensible case. By the time the referendum campaign was under way, arguments for and against entry could be placed in four categories of very unequal importance: conservative support for membership, conservative opposition, left-wing support, and left-wing opposition.

In general, groups supporting membership included the two largest parties, Fianna Fáil and Fine Gael, which were both committed to membership. Only one organization of the Left, the tiny Irish Communist Organisation, joined them, arguing that Western European unity followed inevitably from capitalist development and implying that its advent would in the long term hasten the Socialist revolution.[13] Of the state institutions, the Department of Foreign Affairs was the most noticeable supporter, playing an active part in the publicity campaign in support of membership. It prepared a white paper on accession that has been described as "a blunt, honest and incisive description of the reality of foreign policy in Irish circumstances."[14] The Irish Council of the European Movement (ICEM) was the major pressure group involved in advocating and promoting Irish membership and "helped to coordinate a strong 'yes' campaign."[15] Both business and farming organizations supported the membership campaign.

The strongest opposition was to be found on the Left, although there were also less important conservative groups. The Labour Party led the opposition in the referendum, but although official policy was against accession, a number of leading party members were known to favor membership, a fact that weakened the party's campaign. "Official" Sinn Féin and the tiny Communist Party of Ireland also provided left-wing opposition, with two small parties, Aontacht Eireann (made up for the most part of former members of Fianna Fáil) and "Provisional" Sinn Féin comprising the conservative opponents. The most active pressure group in opposing membership was the anti-EC counterpart of the ICEM, the Common Market Study Group, although its presentation of the case might have been better described as nationalist rather than as left-wing.[16]

In terms of the issues raised, "the debate was pitched overwhelmingly at the material level."[17] The arguments in favor of Ireland's membership rested first on its inevitability, in view of Britain's decision to join; second, on the desirable economic consequences that would follow, especially in the agricultural sector, and on the negative effects that Ireland's exclusion from the Community would cause; and, third, but less wholeheartedly, on the capacity it would give Ireland to share in the building of a new Europe.[18] The opposition argued that not only would the country's accession result immediately in restrictions on its sovereignty, but the policy of neutrality in foreign affairs would also be jeopardized in the long term; portions of the industrial sector of the economy and even of the farming community (especially smaller farmers) would suffer; and less drastic alternatives, such as associate membership, were available.[19]

The weak political position of opponents of membership made the outcome of the referendum fairly predictable. In view of what is known of the capacity of political parties to determine the voting behavior of their supporters, it is not surprising that the vote in favor of membership was 83 percent, with 17 percent voting against. Analysis of the 1972 referendum results indeed shows a very high statistical correlation between the yes vote and support for Fianna Fáil and Fine Gael in the 1969 and 1973 general elections, with opposition tending to be concentrated in constituencies where the Labour Party was strong.[20]

Following the decisive referendum result, Ireland settled quickly into membership. Opposition to the EC was clearly weak; only 17 percent had voted no, a figure significantly lower than Denmark's 36 percent and very much lower than the 53 percent who had voted to keep Norway out of the Community. The conservative consensus on the value of membership, together with the overwhelming dominance of conservative forces in Irish society, quickly earned for the Irish a pro-European reputation, especially when set against the much more qualified attitude toward the Community of the other countries that joined in 1973.

Unlike the 1989 campaign, which we will examine later, the European election campaigns of 1979 and 1984 offer only weak evidence regarding the evolution of the fortunes of competing pro- and anti-integration organizations. The relatively high turnout in the 1979 European elections in Ireland (63.6 percent, compared with the Community average of 62.1 percent) has been interpreted as giving evidence of a continued positive attitude toward the Community on the part of the Irish electorate. This view must be qualified. In the first place, the elections coincided with the local government elections, and the participation level was comparable with that in the previous local elections in 1974. The media tended to regard the elections primarily as an internal Irish contest, to a greater extent even than the party leaders.[21] Finally, analysis of the campaign suggests that the parties themselves concentrated on domestic rather than European issues.[22] However, it should be noted that a slight shift had taken place in the positions of the three parties since 1972, in that the Labour Party now belonged to a European political group (the Socialists) that was more committed to integration than the group with which Fianna Fáil was allied (the European Progressive Democrats). Despite differences of emphasis between the three, all now accepted fully the implications of membership of the Community.

Neither the 1979 nor the 1984 elections provided much opportunity for the expression of opposition. In 1979, the only parties contesting the election were Fianna Fáil, Fine Gael, the Labour Party, and Sinn Féin Workers' Party (SFWP, originally "Official" Sinn Féin, later known as the Workers' Party). Only the latter two provided any sort of opposition voice, muted in the case of the Labour Party and minimal in the case of the still very small SFWP. Independent candidates secured only a small proportion of the vote (T. J. Maher gained a farming vote, Neil Blaney a republican one, and Sean Loftus a community one). In 1984, in addition to the larger parties, Sinn Féin, the Democratic Socialist Party, and the Green Party also ran candidates, but again none secured more than 2 percent of the votes in any constituency, and the situation with regard to independent candidates was the same as before.

We must, then, turn to the 1987 referendum on the SEA, the second occasion on which anti-EC sentiment crystallized in an organizational form. The government, at the time a coalition of Fine Gael and the Labour Party, signed the SEA on February 17, 1986. The SEA then had to be ratified by the two houses of parliament and lodged with the Italian government (which held the EC presidency at the time) before it could come into force. The SEA was duly passed by both houses, but before it could be lodged by the government a court case was taken by a private individual to have it declared unconstitutional. The Supreme Court decided on April 9 that the section dealing with foreign policy cooperation was incompatible with the constitution, so a referendum was necessary.[23]

The decision of the Supreme Court was almost completely unexpected—indeed, "the reaction to the decision among the political establishment was one of incredulity"[24] so that neither the supporters nor the opponents of the SEA had made any advance preparations for a referendum. One point of particular interest at this stage was the fact that during the time the Court was considering the case, there had been a general election in Ireland. The Fine Gael–Labour coalition that had signed the SEA and brought it before the Dáil was defeated and replaced by a minority Fianna Fáil government. This raised a question about the attitude the new government would take in relation to the SEA. Although Fianna Fáil had supported Irish membership of the EC, the new Taoiseach, Charles Haughey, had as leader of the opposition expressed fears that the SEA might erode Irish neutrality, and during the Dáil debate on ratification, Fianna Fáil had unsuccessfully moved an amendment seeking to include safeguards for regional aid and neutrality.[25] There was therefore reason to imagine that the Fianna Fáil government might try to append a statement on these issues to the SEA.

However, as it turned out, Fianna Fáil made no such effort, and went ahead with a referendum to seek approval of the original SEA. Thus the same pattern of groups that had campaigned in 1972 began to reemerge. Once more the two main parties, Fianna Fáil and Fine Gael, were on the pro-integration side. They were joined by the newly formed Progressive Democratic Party, largely composed of former members of the two main parties. Of the state institutions, the Department of Foreign Affairs was again anxious to ensure that the SEA was passed, but the Government Information Service was more active. The government later revealed that IEP345,995 had been spent on the information campaign.[26] Of the single issue pressure groups, the ICEM was still the major pro-integration lobby group and led the campaign. Multiple issue pressure groups, such as the farmers' and employers' organizations, whose members were among the major gainers from membership, campaigned strongly for a yes vote.

Opposition came from a range of groups similar to those that emerged in 1972. The Workers' Party (descendants of "Official" Sinn Féin) had sought renegotiation of the SEA in the Dáil, and campaigned against it in the referendum. Sinn Féin (descendants of "Provisional" Sinn Féin, but by this stage best considered a left-wing group) also opposed the SEA. The Labour Party did not adopt an official position, leaving the decision up to individuals, most of whom opposed it. The Irish Sovereignty Movement, which grew out of the Common Market Study Group, could be seen as the heir to the nationalist rather than left-wing opposition to membership. A number of multiple issue pressure groups also played an active part in the campaign. The Irish Campaign for Nuclear Disarmament (ICND), which had lobbied against ratification in the Dáil, was the largest of a number of "peace movement" groups that campaigned on the issue of Irish neutrality. Individual Third World development activists campaigned on a similar platform. Ecology interests, including the small Green Party, raised questions of nuclear power and safety. Finally, conservative Catholic groups, led by Family Solidarity (an organization standing for the defense of traditional values), raised the issue of European secularism and liberalism and the danger that the SEA could "say yes to EEC abortion and divorce laws."[27]

The campaign developed along strategic lines that have been described as follows. "It has been argued that the optimum strategy to win a referendum with an essentially conservative electorate requires the presentation of the opponents' position as a fundamental threat. There is thus an inherent disposition to distort the issues beyond reasonable bounds."[28] The pro-SEA campaign was expressed largely in terms of the economic benefits already enjoyed by Ireland in the Community, implying that a no vote might jeopardize these; as in the Danish referendum, supporters of the SEA claimed that the issue was the country's continued membership in the EC.[29] The anti-SEA campaign, which was organized under two temporary umbrella groups, the

Constitutional Rights Campaign (covering all issues) and Cosainthe Coalition for Peace and Neutrality (peace groups and development activists), presented a maximalist interpretation of the SEA, to the effect that it would lead inexorably to the end of Irish neutrality. This helped to define alternatives such that "voters were unnecessarily allowed to get the impression that they had to choose between the economic benefits of Community membership and foreign policy based more clearly on ethical principles."[30]

Any doubts as to what that choice might be were effectively dispelled when an opinion poll published a week before polling day showed a clear majority in favor of the SEA, and the referendum was carried, 70 percent to 30 percent. Analysis suggests that "party allegiances had a strong bearing on the result, but they did not entirely determine it."[31] The fact that the no vote had grown from 17 percent to 30 percent and the low turnout in comparison with the 1972 referendum led to accusations by both Fianna Fáil and Fine Gael that the other party had not campaigned vigorously enough, although the comment by Fine Gael's Garret FitzGerald that "the two principal parties had moved back from the position they adopted in the 1972 referendum campaign, of openness towards an eventual European confederation or federation" is probably going too far.[32]

But this time, the opposition did not dissipate quite so easily. The 1989 European Parliament (EP) elections provided a not-too-distant focus for continued opposition, and activists from the anti-SEA campaign sought to make use of them. A number of candidates stood on an anti-integration platform, both as individuals and for parties. The two most significant individual candidates that emerged were Raymond Crotty, who polled 5.7 percent of the vote in Dublin, and Joe Noonan, with 3.2 percent of the Munster vote. Crotty, an economist at Dublin University, was the individual who had sought and secured the Supreme Court ruling against the SEA that had led to the referendum. His privately organized campaign was based on concerns for Irish economic sovereignty and development. Noonan, a lawyer from Cork, was the sole candidate of People First–Meitheal, which described itself as "a nonparty organization set up to monitor developments within the EEC."[33] This organization was established in 1989 purely to contest European Parliament elections, and drew its support from a range of peace, ecology, left-wing, and Third World groups.

Both the Crotty and the Noonan campaigns attempted to build on the opposition apparent during the SEA referendum. Arguing against the view that they had no hope in the election, both pointed to the votes cast against the SEA, which would easily have sufficed to elect either candidate, and appealed specifically to those voters to support them. Although neither campaign was successful, they polled well enough to indicate the presence of a specifically anti-EC vote outside the established parties.

The political parties involved in the 1989 campaign were generally the same as in 1984. But there were two significant developments: the success of the Workers' Party in Dublin, where their candidate had the highest personal poll with 15.8 percent of the vote; and the emergence of the Green Party as a political force to be reckoned with. The Workers' Party, more left-wing than Labour, had also been a more consistent opponent of the Community, and the Greens, who espoused the cause of Irish neutrality as well as ecological issues, polled unexpectedly well in both Dublin, with 8.3 percent of the vote, and its hinterland constituency, Leinster, with 6.3 percent. An interesting feature of the Green campaign was the involvement of leading members of the continental Green movements, such as the West German MP Petra Kelly. This built upon the campaign undertaken by European Greens in Ireland during the 1987 SEA referendum.

In the wake of the 1989 EP elections, European issues continued to have a high profile, as the Community negotiated the Treaty on European Union. The Treaty was eventually signed in Maastricht in 1991, but in order for Ireland to be able to ratify it, another constitutional amendment and referendum were required. Initially, the campaign seemed set to follow familiar lines. However, in February and March 1992 a series of events completely changed the tenor of the campaign. The attorney general obtained a High Court injunction to prevent a fourteen-year old child from traveling to England for an abortion, and the subsequent Supreme Court ruling effectively legalized abortion in Ireland in certain circumstances. This brought the issue of abortion to the fore and enmeshed it with the Maastricht referendum. The Irish government had appended a protocol to the treaties when they were signed that had been intended to prevent the Community from imposing changes on Ireland's abortion laws. However, the legal confusion engendered by the Supreme Court's decision was such that both pro- and antiabortion groups feared they would lose out if the referendum were passed and if the protocol were ratified along with the rest of the Treaty.[34]

This issue made the lineup of forces for and against the Maastricht Treaty slightly different from before. On the side for acceptance, the major change was among the political parties. Once again, Fianna Fáil, Fine Gael, and the Progressive Democrats all supported the Treaty, but Fianna Fáil had problems maintaining party cohesion: One member of the Dáil and one senator, both active antiabortion campaigners, were expelled for voting against the party line on Maastricht. However, to counterbalance that loss, the three conservative parties were joined in supporting the treaty by the Labour Party. The leaders of the four parties issued a joint statement in support of a yes vote. The problem for Labour was that the party leadership was unable to carry most party members with it. Once again, state institutions were heavily used to put across the government campaign.[35] Opposition groups complained of a bias against them throughout the campaign, particularly when the government made use of legislation intended for times of national emergency to broadcast an appeal to voters on the semistate television network, without the usual right of equal air time.

Of the single issue pressure groups, the Irish Council of the European Movement featured less prominently in this campaign than previously. Its activities, which included public meetings at which a number of prominent political figures and academics spoke, were organized on a countrywide basis. On the whole, however, its activities took second place to the government's own very active public information campaign. Among the multiple issue pressure groups, despite reforms to the Common Agricultural Policy (CAP) the farming organizations remained thoroughly supportive, as did business interests. More interesting was the decision by the Irish Congress of Trade Unions to support the campaign, mirroring the change in the Labour Party's position. One other multiple issue interest group that came out in favor of a yes vote was the Council for the Status of Women. Women's groups had expressed considerable concern about the possible implications arising from the Supreme Court ruling on abortion, which suggested women did not have an automatic right to travel or to information, and many opposed the Treaty on these grounds. However, the Council, the main umbrella body, opted to support it.

Opposition was again centered on the left. The Green Party was one of the first to declare its opposition to the treaty, and both the Workers' Party and its breakaway faction the Democratic Left also opposed them. These were the only parties with parliamentary seats to oppose Maastricht, but it should be noted that Sinn Féin did so too, and that despite the decision of their leaders, many Labour Party members, including two members of the Dáil, campaigned against Maastricht. Of the single issue pressure groups, the individuals who were most strongly associated with the Irish Sovereignty Movement were involved with the campaign, but the movement itself was not visible. Instead, the individuals concentrated on promoting an overall campaign of all groups under the banner of "Platform for Democracy, Employment and Neutrality." People First–Meitheal resumed its criticisms of the Community and was an active member of the Platform. Among the multiple issue pressure groups, the disarmament, Third World, and ecological groups were active in campaigning for a no vote, as were a number of women's groups. Some trade unions also went against the stance advocated by the Irish Congress of Trade Unions and campaigned with the opposition. These groups sat very uneasily alongside another strand of opposition, that of the conservative Catholic groups, who concentrated exclusively on the abortion issue.

There were two important moments in the course of the campaign.[36] The first was the eruption of the abortion issue, as already described. This threatened the conservative consensus in favor of Maastricht and European integration but also meant that the opposition was virtually running two diametrically opposed campaigns. One emphasized the familiar issues of integration: the absence of the promised economic advantages, the threat to neutrality, and the absence of democratic accountability in the EC. But it also argued on the basis of a perceived threat to women's rights. The other repeated some of the earlier criticisms, but reversed the last one, charging that there was a perceived threat of abortion being foisted upon Ireland.

However, both aspects of the opposition campaign drew inspiration from the second important moment of the campaign, the Danish referendum of June 2, 1992, which rejected the Maastricht Treaty.[37] This made the prospect of voting no less fearsome; if other countries vote no, then why should Ireland not follow suit?

The prospects for a no vote were, however, very slim. The previous referenda had demonstrated the considerable degree of support for integration in Ireland. They had also shown that voters tend to follow the advice of their favored party, so with four parties, including the three largest in the state, formally supporting the campaign, it would have taken a major collapse in party authority for the referendum to be defeated. Furthermore, all of the opinion polls taken prior to the referendum indicated a comfortable majority, a prediction borne out by the eventual 69 percent to 31 percent outcome.

The 1994 European Parliament elections provided further evidence of a continuing challenge to the political establishment on European issues with the election of two Green Party members of the European Parliament (MEPs).[38] However, they also reinforce the view that the challenge remains unfocused and inconsistent. The People First–Meitheal group failed to contest the election, and the Green Party successes seem only to have shuffled around the representation of opposition from left-wing parties to an environmental one.

PATTERNS OF POLITICAL MOBILIZATION

Having looked at the principal instances in which Irish opposition to the EC has been apparent, it is now possible to identify the major groups that have been actively involved in the debates on Europe. From this it is possible to develop a broad picture of Irish responses to the integration process, in accordance with the framework outlined at the outset of this chapter, before going on to look at particular patterns of opposition.

Political Parties

All political parties fall clearly into the multi-issue category in terms of the form of articulation, although the content of their demands is more varied. In dealing with the political parties, it is worth bearing in mind the overwhelming dominance enjoyed by conservative parties in Ireland. The three major right-wing parties of the period of Community membership, Fianna Fáil, Fine Gael, and the Progressive Democrats, have all been consistent supporters of membership, with only occasional fluctuations in enthusiasm. Fianna Fáil is the largest party in the country and draws on a strain of conservative nationalism akin to that of the Gaullists in France, with whom they are allied in the European Parliament. Because of this background, the party has on occasion raised questions concerning certain aspects of Community policy. However, this is usually done from the safety of the opposition benches: Its record in government is pro-EC, as was demonstrated during the SEA and the Maastricht Treaty debates, if somewhat tinged with a materialist outlook.

Fine Gael, the main opposition to Fianna Fáil, is perhaps more enthusiastic about the ideal of European integration. The period of Irish membership has coincided with a move in Fine Gael from pursuing liberal, free market policies toward a policy that encompassed moderate social democratic elements on some issues.[39] Fine Gael has also produced the two Irish politicians perhaps most widely identified as being "good Europeans," Garret FitzGerald and Peter Sutherland. The last of the three conservative parties, the Progressive Democrats, was formed in 1985. Its support for the Community reflects both support for integration and for the current right-wing free market orientation of the Community.

The two conservative parties that opposed membership in 1972 no longer come into consideration here. Aontacht Eireann, a nationalist republican party, has faded away, and "Provisional" Sinn Féin, although still very much opposed to Community membership, is now more accurately seen as a left-wing nationalist party. Thus, the right-wing political parties that support European integration are all major political and governmental actors, without any distinct ideological stances. The content of the demands they put forward may therefore be categorized as pragmatic rather than principled.

This brings us to the left of the political spectrum, which might be expected to espouse a rather more principled, ideologically based set of demands. This is indeed the case, although given the conservative nature of Irish society, that ideological tone has never been markedly radical. It is worth noting that although the left-wing parties derive most of their electoral support from working-class constituencies, the party that wins most working-class votes is Fianna Fáil. The main left-wing party is the Labour Party, whose initial opposition has softened to acceptance of membership as a fact of political life and indeed to formal support for the Maastricht Treaty. The Labour Party is still caught between those who favor further integration, perhaps influenced by their Socialist partners in the European Parliament, and those who are critical of particular policies, such as its free market orientation and the perceived threat to Irish neutrality. The latter probably constitute a majority of the membership as a whole, with the party leadership being closer to the former group.

The Workers' Party, which emerged from its republican origins to become the second major left-wing party, showed signs of undergoing a similar reluctant conversion to support for the Community. Its opposition had been more consistent, but shortly before the 1989 European Parliament elections its annual conference registered a major policy shift, indicating acceptance of the inevitability of Community membership and committing the party to work within the Community framework. The Workers' Party split in 1992, with six of its seven members of parliament leaving to form Democratic Left, but both parties opposed the Maastricht Treaty on similar grounds.[40] A similar stance is evident in the small but emerging Green Party, which finds some common ground with the Left.

Thus, with the adoption of policies of critical acceptance of the Community by the Labour Party, the Democratic Left Party, and the Workers' Party, outright opposition to membership remains the preserve only of the very small Sinn Féin Party and some other minuscule left-wing groups, such as the Communist Party of Ireland. The powerful political right wing in Ireland is overwhelmingly pro-integration.

State Institutions

The attitude of state institutions toward the European integration process is uniformly favorable. To some extent this is simply a reflection of the wishes of their political masters from Fianna Fáil and Fine Gael. But there is also evidence of a socialization process at work. Officials from such departments as agriculture and finance are regularly involved in European-level meetings, and this has helped to build up acceptance of the EC as an established part of Irish affairs. Government departments have also adopted far more overtly political positions in support of the Community than they have on many other issues. This is most true of the Department of Foreign Affairs, which owes its considerable expansion in the 1970s directly to the demands created by accession to the Community, and which has enjoyed greatly enhanced prestige since then.[41] Semistate corporations such as the Industrial Development Authority (IDA) have also benefited from European contacts.

Single-Issue Pressure Groups

By definition, the focus of such groups is on a single issue, based on principled opposition to or support for the EC. Two Irish pressure groups have concentrated specifically on European issues. The ICEM is the pro-integration body. It is a small, full-time organization, supported by the EC, which aims to promote support for European integration in Ireland through organizing and attending conferences, publishing pamphlets, and lobbying politicians. The ICEM would object to being labeled either left-wing or right-wing, regarding itself—and European integration—as "progressive." But given its support for the currently right-wing Community, it might perhaps be treated under a generally right-wing umbrella.

The Irish Sovereignty Movement, which grew out of the Common Market Study Group of the 1972 referendum period, is the ICEM's anti-integration counterpart. Its activities are quite similar to those of the ICEM—attendance at conferences, production of pamphlets, lobbying—but it is a part-time organization run by a handful of activists. Just as the ICEM is hard to pigeonhole, the Irish Sovereignty Movement too does not fit neatly into either right- or left-wing categories. Certainly, many on the Left support it and are involved with it. But again, given its concentration on the EC as an issue of sovereignty and national autonomy, it can be seen as being to the right of the other opposition groups.

A more recently formed pressure group is People First–Meitheal. It might seem rather strange that an organization set up specifically to run a candidate in an election should be classified as a pressure group rather than a political party. But People First–Meitheal explicitly refuses to contest any election other than European Parliament ones, which sets it apart from ordinary political parties. The future of the organization, however, must be open to doubt. With five years between each contest in its chosen electoral arena, it is difficult to see how it will build up any sort of electoral image.

Multiple-Issue Pressure Groups

Analysis of the stances adopted by these groups provides a very basic outline of how Ireland has fared under membership. The powerful farming lobby and the Federated Union of Employers (FUE) have both been consistent supporters of membership, a stance based pragmatically on the benefits that had accrued to the farming community (or at least to the large farmers) and to Ireland's export-oriented industrialists. The trade unions have been less enthusiastic about European integration but have taken no clear-cut position. Some trade unionists were active in opposing membership in the 1972 referendum and similarly some expressed opposition to the SEA, but such comments from individuals have rarely translated into trade union policy. The current position is, hardly surprisingly, close to that of the major left-wing parties—opposition to some policies, particularly any that might threaten neutrality, but support for others, such as the Social Charter. In general, the unions accept membership in the EC, and in 1992 the Irish Congress of Trade Unions came out in favor of acceptance of the Maastricht Treaty.

Certain pressure groups that might otherwise be seen as single-issue groups have also become involved in the debates on European issues. The ecological movement, through such organizations as Greenpeace and

Earthwatch, has expressed fears that membership of the EC might inhibit Ireland's freedom to challenge Britain over nuclear pollution of the Irish Sea and also that it could lead to a lowering of environmental safeguards.

The reappearance of peace movements across Europe in the 1980s was mirrored in Ireland, where the concentration has been on the preservation of Irish neutrality. ICND had been at the forefront of this movement, acting through conferences, publications, and public awareness campaigns, but other smaller groups, including church activists, were also involved. These activists also feature strongly in the Third World development lobby, where the focus has been on the perceived danger that European foreign policy cooperation, through European political cooperation, might force Ireland to support what is seen as U.S. interference in Central America and the rest of the Third World. Opposition to the EC has also been articulated by religious groups of a sharply different orientation, such as the various conservative Catholic groups, led by Family Solidarity, who opposed the SEA on the grounds that it might open the way to European legislation allowing divorce and abortion in Ireland and who emphasized the latter concern in the Maastricht referendum campaign.

Individual Activists

It is worth mentioning briefly the role that individuals have played in referendum campaigns, despite a certain degree of overlap with the categories discussed above. Some noted European activists have been involved in political parties, and certain pressure groups have become closely identified with their leading activists. The manner in which Raymond Crotty brought the court case that led to the SEA referendum is a vivid illustration of the potential of individual action. It also draws attention to the traditional importance of independent candidates in Irish elections, which has carried over into European Parliament elections.

Public Opinion

Analysis of Irish survey data confirms the general similarity of Irish supporters and opponents of European integration to their European counterparts, in terms of their social backgrounds.[42] As in other member states, those in high-income groups, in high-status occupations, and with more advanced levels of education tend to support EC membership most strongly. However, support has also been very strong among farmers, who elsewhere in Europe have been more critical; this may, presumably, be explained in terms of the relatively undeveloped nature of Irish agriculture by European standards. The regional distribution of support is, indeed, peculiar. Support for the EC has consistently been strongest in the western periphery of Connacht-Ulster; next come the provinces of Munster and Leinster, excluding Dublin; finally, in the area of the capital support has been weakest. Although this pattern is in large measure a function of the regional distribution of occupational groups, it is striking that support for the EC tends to be strongest in the poorer agricultural areas. The same kind of relationships that have been observed elsewhere in Europe between attitudes to European integration and certain other attitudes are present also in Ireland. Support for membership is very strongly associated with satisfaction with life in general and with the operation of democracy in particular. As these are likely to be attributes of the political Right, it is not surprising that support is also highest among those placing themselves on the right of the political spectrum and among supporters of the two major parties, which are clearly parties of the center-right. Opposition to the Community survives among supporters of Fianna Fáil and Fine Gael, despite these parties' commitment to membership; but Labour respondents show an increased tendency to support membership despite that party's earlier objections.

ISSUES AND TARGETS IN THE DEBATE

Having identified the principal actors and interests, it is now necessary to try to present a broad picture of Irish responses to European integration. The method used above has been to identify groups as either right- or left-wing and as either pro- or anti-integration, and there is sufficient evidence to suggest that attitudes to the EC in Ireland coincide with a left-right division. But still opinions vary within the opposition camp. Different strands can be identified among these opinions, depending on the issues that each opposition group sees as the most salient, and by looking at the different issues it is also possible to identify the various types of opposition involved, according to the typology put forward by Carl Lankowski, who argues that opposition to European integration derives from ethnic-regionalist, class-based, or postindustrial demands.[43] We may now turn to the principal issues.

The Sovereignty Question

The issue here is that the EC is perceived as a threat to Irish sovereignty, autonomy, and independence, a perception that draws on the Irish nationalist tradition and thus can be interpreted in terms of an ethnic-nationalist or regionalist type of opposition. As has been noted above, Ireland as a newly independent state might be more jealous of its sovereignty, but at the same time it also developed a tradition of cooperation with continental Europe in the process of establishing that independence, so there are limits to this argument. The Irish Sovereignty Movement can be identified as the prime opposition actor in this category.

The Neutrality Question

Bound up with the issue of neutrality is a range of more specific concerns. Opponents of a common EC foreign policy allege that it would lead to curtailment of Irish foreign policy autonomy, the prospect of being drawn into military conflicts, involvement in a military alliance, and the introduction of military conscription. Initially, it might seem that the neutrality issue can be interpreted in the same way as sovereignty—as an expression of Irish nationalism. This certainly needs to be considered, but the groups who are most active on the neutrality issue do not easily fit into this type of nationalist-regionalist opposition. Rather, the opposition of the peace movement and the Third World lobby would seem to fit more smoothly with postindustrial concerns.

The Economic Question

A number of opposition groups refer to the economic problems posed by membership. For some, these include ensuring economic cohesion in the Community, so that Ireland as a peripheral region in a capitalist economy will not be marginalized in the EC. For others, opposition on this issue is a more explicitly anticapitalist phenomenon, based on fears that the EC is developing into an increasingly right-wing entity that will inhibit or preclude Socialist development in member states. Economic opposition from both quarters is based on a critique of the distributional effects of a capitalist system and can be identified as a type of class-based opposition.

The Social Question

The conservative nature of Irish society has given rise to one peculiar form of opposition to the EC, that of the Catholic groups opposed to divorce, abortion, and a generally perceived threat from European liberalism and secularism. The type of opposition this represents is once more that of postindustrialism, although of a very different strain from the neutrality question. It is based on a desire to preserve a traditional lifestyle in the face of the pressures of modernization and industrialization. This conservative opposition emerged at the time of the SEA referendum, after it had been brought onto the national political agenda by referenda on abortion (1983) and divorce (1986). At the time of the Maastricht referendum, the abortion issue again came to the fore. The conservative social response has more to do with internal political debate (albeit occasionally fueled by events arising out of membership) than purely with the Community or integration.

The Targets

Our analysis so far has concentrated on identifying types of opposition to the EC in Ireland. It has not yet dealt with the object of that opposition.

Opposition has been couched in a very wide range of terms and appears to fall into three principal categories: opposition to European integration in general, opposition to the EC more specifically, and opposition to particular concrete policies. For the purposes of the following discussion, we interpret the concept of European integration very loosely, as referring to efforts of any kind to develop a formal institutional linkage between European states.

The first category covers those who are opposed to European integration per se, no matter what form or scope it may take. As such, this style of opposition clearly reflects a desire to preserve national sovereignty and autonomy. The Irish Sovereignty Movement is the most obvious example, and the conservative Catholic opposition might also be placed in this category.

The second category refers to less dogmatic approaches, where integration as defined above is not rejected, but the particular form of integration represented by the EC is. Although it is more difficult to make distinctions clearly here, it might be suggested that the opposition of left-wing groups, in particular the political parties, is of this nature. They do not oppose integration per se—indeed, there is a long tradition of Socialist internationalism—but the capitalist form of integration being pursued by the EC. Of course, this can manifest itself as opposition to the current right-wing economic policies being pursued by the Community rather than to the Community itself. Given the dominance of such economic policies in the affairs of the Community, it seems more reasonable to argue that changing that panoply of policies would be essentially the same as changing the Community in its entirety.

The final category is that of opposition to particular EC policies. This area currently includes Irish opposition to any attempt to build European security or defense cooperation. It is primarily the preserve of the postindustrial groups from the peace movement and the Third World lobby, who can be seen as not necessarily ill-disposed toward the Community itself, beyond these particular policy areas. Of course, the recent rush of development in eastern Europe has hung a question mark over the current military alliances that have been central to perceptions of Irish neutrality,[44] but as yet the response of these groups has not become clear. This reflects the degree to which opposition to the EC has been expressed only sporadically in Ireland.

CONCLUSION

We may now suggest a preliminary conclusion with regard to Irish opposition to the EC. An example of each of the types identified by Lankowski can be seen in Ireland, and there is also an apparent linkage between types of opposition and the object of opposition. The Irish Sovereignty Movement is the main actor that draws its demands from a regionalist-nationalist source, and it is also the most clear-cut example of a group that is opposed to any integration involving a loss of sovereignty. But although the group has survived, its activities are only occasional and sporadic—it has not been able to place the issue of opposition anywhere on the regular political agenda. Class-based opposition stems primarily from the left-wing political parties, supported to some extent by trade unionists, and it is these groups that are most critical of the EC in its current form rather than integration per se or specific policies. Although in many instances this takes the form of opposition to certain economic measures being pursued by the Community, because the Community is still largely an economic entity at present this can be interpreted as a more fundamental challenge to the EC. In this instance, the permanent nature of parties and unions leaves them in a much better position to articulate opposition on a regular basis, and they are much less dependent on the catalytic effect of occasional referenda to generate discussion, making them perhaps the most likely source of long-term opposition to the EC in Ireland. Finally, the range of groups that fall within the postindustrial type of opposition are most likely to oppose only certain EC policies. The peace, ecology, and Third World lobbies, and People First–Meitheal, which draws on all three strands, certainly seem to demonstrate this, although it should be noted that the support within the Green movement for local democracy has led it to view the centralizing tendencies of the Community with some concern. At the same time, there are many aspects of the Community that find favor among these groups—for instance, EC environmental policy[45]—making them a less likely source of continuing opposition, in contrast to what has been suggested in the wider European context by Hueglin (see Chapter 2). The only source of opposition that does not correspond to this perceived link between basis and object of opposition is the conservative Catholic strand. This has been identified here as postindustrial, yet its opposition is directed more toward the dangers of excessive contact with "alien" European ideas. Nevertheless, even here the opposition has been expressed in terms of preventing specific Community policies on divorce and abortion (nonexistent though these may be) from being implemented in Ireland.

What, then, of implications for the future? Since its original accession to the EEC, Ireland's continued support for the Community has rested on pragmatic economic considerations, dictated by the country's peripherality in Europe and poor economic performance in the postwar period rather than on enthusiastic support for European integration. In this respect Irish politicians and the general public by and large have accepted uncritically the necessity of membership in the Community. Whether or not this lack of criticism will last depends on the extent to which Ireland continues to be a net beneficiary of economic assistance from the Community. As one analyst has noted, "Historians may look back at the SEA debate as a watershed in Irish politics. . . . The debate on Europe no longer focuses on whether Ireland should remain a member of the Community. That has been finally and definitively decided

by the SEA referendum. . . . The burden of debate now falls on performance."[46] This implies that future Irish support for European union or further
integration must be seen to be directly beneficial for the state and its people
(debate on the Maastricht Treaty moved some way toward that mark). The
controversy that surrounded the publication of a report by the state advisory
body, the National Economic and Social Council (NESC), *Ireland and the
European Community* (1989), which is highly critical of Ireland's economic
performance in the EC, suggests the very fragile relationship between Ireland
and the EC and the dependence of that relationship on economic considerations rather than political ideals.[47]

On the whole, opposition in Ireland to the Community has been sporadic
and most often directed at particular policies rather than at the underlying
economic rationale of the EC. Interest groups such as farmers' and employers' organizations have been critical of EC policies and of their implementation by the government while maintaining consistent support for the
Community and the idea of integration. Other traditional economic interest
groups have also supported the EC, which is seen as offering a more attractive alternative than the protectionist and inward-looking government policies of the 1950s. Equally, the trade union movement, most usually associated with opposition to the EC, has been slow to develop any critical appraisal
of the Community. This can be explained partly by the divisions in the trade
union movement in the immediate postwar period, resulting in considerable
internal dissension, and until recently the Labour Party's inability to win significant electoral support in Ireland. Furthermore, trade union participation in
the government's economic plans has co-opted trade union criticism of the
government and its handling of the economy. Since the Single European Act,
the labor movement has become increasingly committed to and involved in
pursuing worker's rights through the acceptance of the EC's Social Charter
rather than in offering any direct opposition to the EC.

In the light of these considerations, the sporadic nature of opposition in
Ireland is hardly surprising; it is often concerned with particular EC policies
rather than directly with the EC or with European integration. Nevertheless,
principled opposition has consistently emerged in Ireland in response to
changes in the relationship between Ireland and the Community. Raymond
Crotty's constitutional challenge to the SEA is a vivid and typical example of
the type of latent opposition that remains in Ireland. The Janus-faced character of Irish nationalism should not be underestimated in a state that remem-
bers only too well the long and protracted struggle for independence from
Britain, while peace in Northern Ireland is far from assured. Although the
country remains economically committed to the EC, a number of potentially
divisive issues remain on the political agenda. Among the more obvious are
the question whether Ireland's policy on neutrality can or should be retained
in an increasingly politically active European Union and the degree to which

Ireland should support further European unification. In particular, the 1996 intergovernmental conference may provide a further test of Ireland's commitment to the European Union, with the possibility that a more lively debate may emerge in the country over the nature of Ireland's relationship with the EU, especially in light of the desire of some states to see the Union develop a more *communautaire* approach to the Common Foreign and Security Policy and develop a European-level defense policy. However, the collapse of communism and the complete shift in security perceptions that it engendered has encouraged a reassessment of the value and appropriateness of neutrality as a policy in Ireland.

In the Irish case opposition to an evolving European Union may be more likely to emerge in the future within the EU's own institutions rather than at the state level in the first instance. Ireland's representatives may, as a result of the Community's fourth enlargement, find themselves with more potential allies among the Nordics and Austria. Potential sources of friction may include nonrealization of the economic benefits of the internal market, the risk of being excluded from the third stage of Economic and Monetary Union, increasing political divergence with regard to the Common Foreign and Security Policy, and tension between Irish nationalism and European integration. In particular, the NESC report, which challenges the assumptions of the Cecchini Report on the likely benefits of the internal market, has resulted in an intense debate in Ireland.[48] Again, such debate is indicative of Ireland's economic concerns with regard to the Community and of the fragile relationship between Ireland and the EU. If economic gains are not realized in Ireland then the Community may become the subject of criticism, and opposition to the EU and its policies may increase further.

NOTES

1. Carl Lankowski, "Political Opposition in the EC: The Role of the Community from the Rome Treaty to the Danish Referendum of 1986," *Il politico* 52, no. 2 (1987), pp. 261–293.

2. Daniel-Louis Seiler, *La politique comparée* (Paris: Armand Colin, 1982), pp. 137–140.

3. Maurice Duverger, *Party Politics and Pressure Groups: A Comparative Introduction* (London: Nelson, 1972).

4. Gearoid MacNiocaill and Gearoid ÓTuathaigh, "Ireland and Continental Europe: The Historical Dimension," in P. J. Drudy and Dermot McAleese, eds., *Ireland and the European Community* (Cambridge: Cambridge University Press, 1984), p. 22.

5. John Coakley, "Society and Political Culture," in John Coakley and Michael Gallagher, eds., *Politics in the Republic of Ireland* (Dublin: Folens; Limerick: PSAI Press, 1993), p. 43.

6. Foreign Minister Michael O'Kennedy, quoted in John Cooney, *The EEC in Crisis* (Dublin: Dublin University Press, 1979), p. 139.

7. The wording of the question was as follows: (1) "In general, are you for or against efforts being made to unify Western Europe?" (2) "Generally speaking, do you think that Ireland's membership of the Common Market is a good thing, a bad thing, or neither good nor bad?" (3) "If you were to be told tomorrow that the European Community (Common Market) had been scrapped, would you be very sorry, indifferent, or relieved?" and (4) "Taking everything into consideration, would you say that Ireland has on balance benefited or not from being a member of the European Community (Common Market)?"

8. The significance of the group expressing no opinion on the question relating to European unification should be noted. During the four years 1981–1984 this averaged 13 percent in the six core states but reached levels of 35 percent and 58 percent, respectively, in Spain and Portugal. The three corresponding percentages dropped to 10 percent, 22 percent, and 25 percent averages for the four years 1985–1988, and by 1992 all figures were close to the EC average of 9 percent.

9. Ruth Barrington and John Cooney, *Inside the EEC: An Irish Guide* (Dublin: The O'Brien Press, 1984), pp. 10–13.

10. See Miriam Hederman, *The Road to Europe: Irish Attitudes 1948–61* (Dublin: Institute of Public Administration, 1983).

11. See D. J. Maher, *The Tortuous Path: The Course of Ireland's Entry into the EEC, 1948–73* (Dublin: Institute of Public Administration, 1986).

12. Article 29.4 of the Irish Constitution provided for the executive power of the state in connection with its external relations to be carried out by the government. The amendment took the form of adding a new subsection to that article that would allow the state to join the Community and would deem subsequent legislation consequent on membership to be similarly accepted.

13. The Irish Communist Organisation originated in the late 1960s and was distinguished by the original quality of its political analysis and by its propagation of a "two-nation" interpretation of Irish history that rested on a distinction between the Protestant North and the Catholic South. It had no connection with the (Moscow-oriented) Communist Party of Ireland and later changed its name to the British and Irish Communist Organisation, adopting a more unionist and a more liberal stance. See Irish Communist Organisation, *The European Common Market: A Communist History* (Dublin: Irish Communist Organisation, 1971).

14. J. J. Lee, *Ireland 1912–1982: Politics and Society* (Cambridge: Cambridge University Press, 1989), p. 463.

15. Dermot Keogh, *Ireland and Europe 1919–1989: A Diplomatic and Political History* (Cork and Dublin: Hibernian University Press, 1990), p. 240.

16. Anthony Coughlan, *The Common Market: Why Ireland Should Not Join* (Dublin: Common Market Study Group, 1970).

17. Lee, *Ireland 1912–1982*, p. 464.

18. See Irish Government, *The Accession of Ireland to the European Communities: Laid by the Government Before Each House of the Oireachtas, January 1972* (Dublin: Stationery Office, 1972); Ireland, Department of Foreign Affairs, *Into Europe: Ireland and the EEC* (Dublin: Department of Foreign Affairs, n.d.); Michael Sweetman, *The European Community: Why Ireland Should Join* (Dublin: Irish Council of the European Movement, n.d.).

19. For details of the campaign, see Keogh, *Ireland and Europe*, pp. 236–255.

20. Tom Garvin and Anthony Parker, "Party Loyalty and Irish Voters: The EEC Referendum as a Case Study," *Economic and Social Review* 4, no. 1 (1972), pp. 35–39.

21. Mary J. Kelly, "The Media View of the 1979 European Election Campaign," *Economic and Social Review* 14, no. 2 (1983), pp. 137–152.

22. Desmond S. King, "The Interaction Between Foreign and Domestic Policy in the 1979 European Elections in Ireland," *Irish Studies in International Affairs* 1, no. 3 (1982), pp. 62–81.

23. The Supreme Court decision was not unanimous. Two judges held that Title III did not constitute a breach of the Constitution, as it fell within the scope of the subsequent legislation allowed for by the 1972 amendment. Three judges ruled the opposite, taking a maximalist view of what foreign policy cooperation might entail. The amendment that was thus required again took the form of an addendum to Article 29.4, allowing the state to ratify the SEA.

24. Patrick Keatinge, "Annual Review of Irish Foreign Policy," *Irish Studies in International Affairs* 2, no. 4 (1988), pp. 82.

25. Dáil Debates 370 (December 10, 1986), pp. 2367–2368.

26. Dáil Debates 373 (January 17, 1987), p. 2319.

27. Keatinge, "Annual Review," pp. 83–84; Michael Gallagher, "The Single European Act Referendum," *Irish Political Studies* 3 (1988), pp. 79–80.

28. Keatinge, "Annual Review," p. 84.

29. Gallagher, "Single European Act Referendum," p. 79.

30. John Temple-Lang, "The Irish Court Case Which Delayed the Single European Act: *Crotty v. an Taoiseach and Others*," *Common Market Law Review* 24 (1987), pp. 717; for details of the campaign, see Keogh, *Ireland and Europe*, pp. 267–280.

31. Gallagher, "Single European Act Referendum," p. 81.

32. Garret FitzGerald, "Irish Neutrality," *European Affairs* 2, no. 9 (1987), p. 9.

33. *People First–Meitheal News*, April 14, 1989.

34. The referendum was worded to amend the Constitution so as to allow the government to ratify the treaties.

35. Irish Government, *The Government White Paper on European Union* (Dublin: Stationery Office, 1992).

36. See Michael Holmes, "The Maastricht Treaty Referendum of June 1992," *Irish Political Studies* 8 (1993), pp. 105–110.

37. Thus Conservative Catholics were "inspired," somewhat incongruously, to praise permissive, Protestant Denmark.

38. See Michael Marsh, "The 1994 European Parliament Election in the Republic of Ireland," *Irish Political Studies* 10 (1995), pp. 209–215.

39. Peter Mair, "The Party System," in John Coakley and Michael Gallagher, eds., *Politics in the Republic of Ireland* (Dublin: Folens; Limerick: PSAI Press, 1993), p. 97.

40. See Michael Holmes, "The Establishment of Democratic Left," *Irish Political Studies* 9 (1994), pp. 148–156.

41. Patrick Keatinge, *A Place Among the Nations: Issues of Irish Foreign Policy* (Dublin: Institute of Public Administration, 1978), pp. 210–213.

42. See John Coakley, "The European Dimension in Irish Public Opinion in 1972–82," in David Coombes, ed., *Ireland and the European Communities: Ten Years of Membership* (Dublin: Gill and Macmillan, 1983).

43. Lankowski, "Political Opposition," pp. 272–274.

44. Michael Holmes and Nicholas Rees, "An Ostrich in Quicksand: Ireland's Foreign Policy in a Changing World," in O. Knudsen, ed., *The Inner Fringes of Europe* (Oslo: NUPI Conference Papers, 1990).

45. David Whiteman, "The Progress and Potential of the Green Party in Ireland," *Irish Political Studies* 5 (1990), p. 53.

46. Keogh, *Ireland and Europe*, p. 281.

47. National Economic and Social Council, *Ireland and the European Community* (1989).

48. Ibid.

10

Coming Out of the Cold: Nordic Responses to European Union

Christine Ingebritsen

The five northern European welfare states (Sweden, Denmark, Norway, Iceland, and Finland) are the most resistant to continental plans for European unity.[1] Historically, the Nordic states have resisted the initiatives of France, Germany, Italy, and the Benelux countries to create a political and economic union. Instead, the Nordics followed the lead of Great Britain and preferred less binding forms of cooperation as signatories to the European Free Trade Association (EFTA). Yet as plans for European unity were implemented and the Warsaw Pact and the North Atlantic Treaty Organization (NATO) no longer divided Scandinavia into two separate blocs, the Nordic states increasingly feared being left out in the cold on Europe's northernmost periphery.

In this chapter, I explain the historic ambivalence of the Nordic states toward European integration and why some northern European states have been more willing to cooperate with the European Union (EU) than others. As I argue in the first section, these states have more to lose than other states that have sought a partnership with the EU. From the perspective of northern Europe, there have been sound political and economic motivations for resisting European integration.

Although Northern Europe shares a preference for autonomy from Europe, with British entry into the EU in the 1970s and the revival of European integration in the 1980s, the Nordic states increasingly traded off national sovereignty for supranational cooperation. However, the Nordic states have followed separate paths to Europe. Denmark was the first to join the EU, yet within European institutions the Danes have rejected plans to create a political and economic union. On two separate occasions (1972 and 1994), a majority of Norwegians rejected membership in the European Union. Iceland has no intention of joining the EU in the near future and has followed a Norwegian path of resistance to European integration. Finland, on the other hand, shares a Swedish desire to be in the core of European politics. The Finns and Swedes are even more European than the Danes: As new members, both states accepted all the terms and conditions for political and economic union negotiated at Maastricht when they joined the EU on January 1, 1995. Nordic responses to European integration reveal important differences between these states.

What are the implications of Nordic accession to the EU? As the two Nordic neutrals come out of the cold, Swedish and Finnish entry into the European Union will influence the direction and substance of European integration. However, as the Danish experience in the EU reveals, these states will also be compelled to accept changes in policies that move them farther away from national decisionmaking autonomy and Social Democratic traditions.

RELUCTANT EUROPEANS

Nordic ambivalence toward European integration is an expression of fundamental differences between national priorities and the imperatives of pan-European cooperation. Nordic citizens pay more in taxes, receive higher average wages, and are more likely to be members of trade unions than citizens of EU member states. As Gøsta Esping-Andersen argues, the Scandinavians are unique in their institutionalized commitment to the provision of solidaristic, universal social policies. Despite fundamental changes in the capacities of Nordic welfare states and the limits of social democracy, northern Europeans have a legacy of more solidaristic policies than their continental trading partners.[2]

Traditionally, the Nordic Left viewed the EU with skepticism. As a continental club more concerned with market mechanisms than with social policy, the European Union had little to offer the Nordic states. The Nordics preferred to maintain open trading regimes with the EU yet rejected plans for supranational cooperation and political union. European integration represented a move away from the solidaristic, Social Democratic Scandinavian models of welfare capitalism. For some Nordic states, European integration was an inconceivable alliance with the West.

During the Cold War, the Nordic states were attentive to how the Soviet Union might perceive cooperation with a "capitalist" European bloc of predominately NATO member states. For the two eastern Nordic states, Sweden and Finland, membership in the European Union was deemed incompatible with national security policies. In the 1970s, the Swedish Social Democrats maintained that membership in the European Union would compromise the credibility of Swedish neutrality policy. Although it is now commonly known that Sweden had a secret agreement with NATO during the Cold War, the official policy restricted Swedish participation in European integration for security reasons. The Treaty of Friendship, Cooperation and Mutual Assistance (TFCMA) signed between Finland and the Soviet Union in 1948 restricted Finnish sovereignty in security policy making. Finns were attentive to how their actions would be perceived in Moscow. As a consequence of Cold War politics, the Finns preferred trading agreements to EU membership.

From the perspective of northern Europeans, EU decisionmaking is closer to a Japanese model of corporatism without labor than Peter Katzenstein's

model of "democratic corporatism."[3] The European Trade Union Confederation (ETUC) and the Union of Industrial Employers' Confederations of Europe
(UNICE) have been unable to agree on proposals to establish a common labor
market. Thus, organized labor is comparatively weaker on the European level
than in the domestic political economies of the five Nordic states.

Many Scandinavian citizens express concern over what they perceive as
a "democratic deficit" in Community-wide decisionmaking. As EU institutions become more centralized, decisions are made further and further away
from the people. In the words of Jens-Peter Bonde, the leader of Denmark's
anti-EU movement and a member of the European Parliament: "Every time
you take away decision-making power from elected officials or close deliber-
ations on new laws that before were decided in open parliaments, that makes
it much harder to involve citizens. Lawmaking should be as close to citizens
as possible, and this is something that is highly valued in our tradition of local
democracy."[4] Whereas the southern European states (Greece, Spain, and
Portugal) have viewed European integration as a promising means of consolidating democracy and promoting economic development, the northern
European states have viewed European integration with much greater skepticism.[5] In the controversial domestic debates over European Union, Nordic
publics feared the consequences of aligning with states that have weaker labor
movements and abandoning national policies for European policy regimes.
For many citizens in the affluent north, the European Union is a costly project
that transfers wealth from north to south and weakens welfare state policies,
democratic decisionmaking, and corporatist institutions. Because of the particular challenges associated with European integration, it is thus not surprising that the Nordic states were among the last to join the EU and that they have
been more resistant to proposals to deepen integration.

From the perspective of international relations theory, one might anticipate that small, export-dependent states have few choices than to ally with
larger, more powerful nations. In the words of Robert Keohane, "small states
do not have the luxury of deciding whether or how fast to adjust to external
change. They do not seek adjustment; it is thrust upon them."[6] Northern
Europe, however, has followed three distinct paths to Europe. Danes have
been the most ambivalent, Swedes and Finns have been the most cooperative,
and Norwegians and Icelanders have been the most resistant to European integration. Important differences in the political economies and security policies
of the five Nordic states can account for patterns of accession to the EU.

NORDIC PATHS TO EUROPE

The Nordic states are often viewed as a homogeneous group of small, open
economies, with a tradition of Social Democratic hegemony, universal welfare policies, and corporatist institutions. However, as Lars Mjøset argues, the

nature of each state's leading export sector creates different patterns of policymaking in each of the five Nordic states.[7] Leading export sectors vary *within* the Nordic area from agriculture and small manufacturers in Denmark,
manufacturing and engineering in Sweden and Finland, to fishing in Iceland
and petroleum in Norway. In addition to differences in economic dependence
on international markets, the Nordic states have also had distinct security
policies in relation to the two military blocs.

During the Cold War, northern Europe was divided between east and
west. The three western Nordic states, Norway, Iceland, and Denmark, could
freely join the European Union as members of NATO. The eastern Nordics,
on the other hand, were more constrained because of the Swedish policy of
neutrality and the Finnish policy of semi-alignment with the Soviet Union.
When European integration deepened and the Cold War system unraveled,
some Nordics (Sweden and Finland) were drawn into European cooperation
at a greater speed than others (Norway and Iceland). As a NATO member
state and an agricultural exporter, Denmark was the first of the five Nordics
to join the EU in 1973, yet it did so with reservations.

Denmark's Ambivalent Accession

Agricultural exports were the critical engine behind Denmark's economic
development. The export earnings from agricultural products enabled
Denmark to import raw materials and semifinished goods. Despite the growing importance of manufacturing and services to the economy since the early
1970s, agribusiness has a powerful position in Danish corporatist decisionmaking.[8] For Danish agricultural exporters, Britain was the largest and most
important market. Following World War II, the British and Danish governments negotiated long-term trade agreements that secured a market for
Danish exports and provided the British with agricultural products at below
world market prices.[9]

In 1959, the Danish government joined Britain, Austria, Norway,
Sweden, and Portugal to create EFTA, an antiestablishment institution
designed to enable these states to accept a more limited European partnership
than that specified by the Treaty of Rome. EFTA membership enabled these
states to obtain access to European markets without joining an economic or
political union.

When Britain applied to join the EU in 1961, this created a dilemma for
the Danes. How could they afford to lose their largest agricultural customer
and retain close ties to the other Nordic states? In the 1960s, the Danish government submitted an application to Brussels, conditional upon the EU's
acceptance of Britain's application. President Charles de Gaulle's veto of the
British application on January 14, 1963, subsequently resulted in Denmark
suspending its application.[10]

In 1972, the Danish government resubmitted its application with Britain to join the EU. Economic motivations were the most important determinant of Danish accession, but it was by no means an easy campaign. The bourgeois parties and the Social Democratic Party aligned with agricultural interests in support of European Union membership, while the Socialist People's Party (SF) and other left of center parties actively opposed Danish membership on ideological grounds. The People's Movement Against the European Union (Nei til EU) mobilized a campaign opposing the government's application for membership. The participants included anti-EU parties (the Communist Party, the Left Socialist Party, the Socialist People's Party, and the Justice Party), and economic interest organizations (fisheries) that were threatened by opening their markets to the EU. When the national referendum was held in the fall of 1972, 64 percent of the participants supported EU membership. Denmark joined the EU on January 1, 1973.

According to Danish political economists, the Common Agricultural Policy (CAP) was the primary reason for joining the European Union.[11] Under the terms of Danish accession, the state accepted full participation in the CAP because of economic projections: "In 1971 it was estimated that the value of agricultural exports would be between one thousand and two thousand million kroner higher after entry, whereas the Danish contribution to the financing of the community would only be about five hundred million kroner, so that the new situation from 1973 ceteris paribus would contribute substantially to solving the balance of payments problem."[12] The anti-EU movement did not disappear following Danish accession. Instead, as many as four members of the organization have served in the European Parliament. The goal of the Danish People's Movement Against the EU is resignation from the European Union.

Thus, Denmark entered the EU with ambivalence. Market imperatives prevailed, yet many groups in the society retained a skeptical view of the EU as a supranational organization dominated by larger European countries and powerful corporate interests. Denmark remains a reluctant European, and many of the reasons why Danes were reticent about joining the EU came to the surface again in the 1980s, with the introduction of the Single European Act (SEA).

For the Danes, there were four central concerns with EU plans for improving the decisionmaking capacity of core institutions and unifying the nations of Europe. The transfer of political authority from Copenhagen to Brussels, the loss of veto power under a new system of qualified majority voting, a threat to values embedded in Scandinavian welfare policies (health, environment, safety), and the extension of cooperation to noneconomic areas (foreign policy and defense) were viewed with skepticism.

The Conservative-led government under Prime Minister Schlüter and industry leaders were the first to endorse the internal market program. Social

Democratic Party leader Anker Jørgensen informed Schlüter that the Social Democrats opposed the EU reform program and intended to veto the package. The Radical and Socialist Parties also maintained an anti-SEA position. As a means of resolving the issue, the government scheduled a national referendum.[13] Prior to the vote, the anti-EU organizations mobilized a grassroots campaign against the internal market.[14] The EU opponents tended to be younger, better educated, employees in the public sector, university students, and residents of Copenhagen or provincial areas.[15]

Despite the efforts of the anti-EU social movement, a majority of Danes approved the SEA in 1986: Fifty-six percent voted in favor, and 44 percent voted against. At that time, the public was more pro-integrationist than the politicians. When the Maastricht Treaty was debated the situation was reversed: All the major parties supported the treaty, whereas the public was much more skeptical. As a consequence of the public's yes to the internal market program, the Social Democrats have adopted a more pro-integrationist stance in their platform.[16]

Even though the Danes approved the Single European Act, there were many reservations about the consequences of the internal market program for the Danish welfare state. For example, policy liberalizations required to bring about an internal market have the net effect of reducing public finances. EU proposals to reduce value-added taxes (VAT) decrease revenue collected by public authorities and make it more difficult to sustain social welfare policies. According to estimates made by the Danish government, applying the European Commission's proposals would result in a loss of tax revenue equivalent to forty billion Danish kroner (DKR) or 5.5 percent of the gross domestic product (GDP).[17]

Danish trade unionists have also expressed concern over the effects of integration on the position of labor. The free movement of persons encourages high-skilled workers to move to other EU member states while simultaneously opening up the labor market to all EU citizens. As Paulette Kurzer argues, Social Democratic parties in small, open economies have more difficulty fulfilling promises of full employment as they coordinate policies with the EU and participate in financial market integration.[18]

Denmark's ambivalence toward European integration was visible once again in a national referendum held on political and economic union. On June 2, 1992, Danish voters rejected the Maastricht Treaty by a narrow margin: 50.7 percent voted against Maastricht, and 49.3 percent voted in favor. Only forty-eight thousand accounted for the difference, with 82.9 percent of the electorate participating in the referendum. Danish elites, however, were much stronger supporters of the agreement. One hundred thirty members of the Danish Parliament voted in favor of the Maastricht Treaty and only twenty-five voted against.[19]

Public reticence to forge ahead with plans for political and economic union spread across Europe following the Danish "no" to Maastricht. The French and Irish publics narrowly approved the Treaty, and the British indicated that they would wait until Danish reservations with European union were resolved. The Swedes, Finns, and Norwegians observed the ambivalence of their continental neighbor, and public support for entry into the European Union declined.

In response to the Danish people's "no" to Maastricht, the government drafted a memorandum outlining the Danish reservations with the Treaty. The Danish memorandum was accepted by other EU member states in the December 1992 Edinburgh meeting. Denmark's aspirations for the future development of the EU and reservations with the Maastricht Treaty are outlined in Table 10.1.

On May 18, 1993, the Danish people approved the amended version of the Maastricht Treaty: 56.8 percent of the participants endorsed the agreement,

---

Table 10.1 The Edinburgh Amendments to the Maastricht Treaty

Denmark's Aspirations for the EU:
1. The European Union should become more democratic. Decision-making in EU institutions and in Denmark should be made more accessible to the people.
2. EU guidelines should permit national implementation.
3. A Social Charter should specify minimal standards to protect the rights of workers.
4. A White Book establishing EU guidelines for improving the environment and environmental standards should be adopted.
5. Denmark will determine its own social standards and distributive policies.

Danish Exemptions:
1. Denmark will not participate in the so-called defense policy dimension that includes Western European Union, the creation of a common security policy or defense.
2. Denmark will not participate in the creation of a common currency or economic union embodied in phase three of economic and monetary union. Denmark emphasizes the importance of participation in the EMS. When other EC states move to phase three, Denmark will consider closer cooperation in this area.
3. Denmark will not accept supranational legal cooperation.
4. Denmark will not participate in the creation of union citizenship.

Source: "Danmarks tilrædelse at Edinburgh-Afgørelsen og Maastricht-Traktaten," (Copenhagen: Foreign Ministry, 1993.

---

and 43.2 percent voted no. Public riots broke out following the decision when an anarchist group threw stones at police adjacent to the parliament building.

Thus, Danes remain ambivalent about European integration, even though they have been a member of the European Union for more than two decades.

As in the rest of Scandinavia, the Danish government is more integrationist than the Danish people. Whereas the Danes rejected the Maastricht Treaty, the Swedes and Finns joined the EU on January 1, 1995, subject to all the terms and conditions for the creation of an economic and political union.

Into the Core: The Swedes and Finns Join the EU

In contrast to the Danes, Swedes and Finns are latecomers to the European Union yet they joined with a stronger commitment to European unity than the other Nordic states. Security policy traditionally prevented Sweden and Finland from pursuing a closer partnership with Europe. During the Cold War, neutrality policy provided a certain degree of autonomy from international institutions. However, since the end of the Cold War, both governments demonstrated their willingness to cooperate more closely with the European Union. In post–Cold War Europe, autonomy is no longer so desirable, nor is neutrality a motivation to resist membership in the European Union. In contrast to the other Nordics, Swedes and Finns view European integration as a means of reviving their domestic economies and securing their borders. According to official government policy, nations in Europe cannot act independently but must work cooperatively to solve transnational problems.[20]

The pull of European integration has been particularly strong in Sweden. As a consequence of Sweden's dependence on international, export-oriented companies, the EU's internal market program led to a surge in foreign direct investment. For each year between 1985 and 1988, Swedish industry doubled its investments in Europe.[21] Major companies such as IKEA and Tetra Pak relocated their production facilities outside of Sweden, while others, such as ASEA, merged with other European firms. For Swedish Social Democrats, capital flight had political consequences: Reviving the economy depended on attracting foreign capital. Sweden's largest trade union, Landsorganisationen (LO), adopted a new strategy of cooperation with Europe in order to attract employers to invest in Sweden. In response to European integration, LO and the Central Organization of Salaried Employees (TCO) opened offices in Brussels. The employers' federation and the trade unions initiated detailed internal studies of the consequences of European integration for Sweden's economy. In Sweden, organized capital and organized labor aligned in favor of European integration.

The consequences of European integration for Sweden were the source of intensive study and political debate, which gathered momentum during the summer of 1990. Political controversy focused on how Sweden could maintain its policy of neutrality in the EU, to what extent the Swedish model would change, and the implications of EU membership for the health of Sweden's economy. Industrial leaders, trade union officials, Swedish academics, and Social Democratic leaders actively debated the pros and cons of European integration in the press. Public opinion solidly favored membership, and the Conservative Party, led by Carl Bildt, endorsed EU membership.

The Swedish Social Democratic leader Ingvar Carlsson announced the intention of the government to pursue a closer agreement with the EU during the fall of 1990. By July 1991, Sweden had submitted its application to Brussels. For Sweden, the European Economic Area (EEA) Agreement was not enough: Only through EU membership could Swedes be guaranteed a voice in the development of European institutions. As Swedish political scientist Bo Rothstein argues, European integration requires an active industrial policy at the regional level. Improving Sweden's competitive position in European markets necessitates a combined effort of business and public sector cooperation, according to Rothstein.[22] In the accession debates, the Swedes were optimistic about the capacity to influence the direction and substance of European integration. By joining the EU, it was argued, Sweden would have the possibility of influencing European political developments. As an example of Swedish Euro-optimism, the 1991 election campaign featured a red rose superimposed on the EU flag: "a Social Democratic European Union." In Sweden, all of the major political parties (the Social Democratic Party, the Conservative Party, the Liberal Party) endorsed closer ties to the European Union.[23] However, societal interests grew more skeptical, particularly following Denmark's rejection of the Maastricht Treaty.

In a startling reversal of foreign policy, the Finns followed the Swedish path to Brussels. During the Cold War, Finland was extremely cautious in its relations with its neighbor, and membership in the European Union was never seriously considered. Yet in 1987, an important change occurred in Finnish foreign policy. The prime minister and the foreign office announced that Finland's policy of neutrality no longer prevented the state from participation in European institutions.[24] As in Sweden, the desire for a continental security guarantee was accompanied by political pressure from multinational corporations who sought new markets in the EU. Between 1985 and 1990, Finnish foreign investment increased sixfold, from 2.18 to 12.47 billion Finnish markka (FIM).[25]

As in Sweden, national security considerations figured prominently in the EU debate. The political instability of neighboring Russia and the signing of a new treaty ending the Finnish-Soviet Cold War security arrangement in January 1992 made European integration more attractive. The Finnish government adopted a position similar to that of the Swedish government with respect to reconciling neutrality policy and the obligations of the Maastricht Treaty. In an official policy statement made in October 1992, the Finnish government outlined the compatibility of neutrality policy and European Union membership: "The Maastricht Treaty will not make the European Union a military alliance, nor will it replace the present defence arrangements of EC members. The core of Finland's traditional neutrality, military non-alignment and a credible independent defence, is in harmony with the obligations of the Maastricht Treaty, and as a defensive arrangement will retain its significance for Finnish security."[26] Finland, to a much greater extent than the other Nordic states, suffered the economic consequences of Soviet disintegration. The levels of unemployment soared to 20 percent, as the Finns lost the stability of the eastern market. Finland's economic crisis necessitated a dramatic reversal in policy, and European integration was widely viewed as the appropriate solution. Public support for entry into the EU was stronger in Finland than anywhere else in northern Europe.

As a consequence of support for entry among the Finns, the Finnish referendum on European Union membership was held earlier than the others, with the intent of achieving a domino effect: More skeptical Swedes and Norwegians would (it was argued) be swayed by Finnish accession. Two of the Nordic publics embraced European integration, but the Norwegians again resisted.

In the October 16, 1994, national referendum on EU membership, 57 percent of Finns approved the treaty. Some weeks later, the Swedes narrowly approved the treaty, by a margin of 52 percent to 47 percent (with 1 percent of the participants submitting blank protest ballots). Since the Swedes joined Europe, public opinion polls suggest that the promise of integration has yet to be realized, with a majority of citizens against EU membership.[27] However, opposition to the European Union was not as well organized or as deeply rooted as in neighboring Norway.

Thus, Finns and Swedes sought an even closer partnership with the European Union than the Danes. As a consequence of Swedish and Finnish adherence to the Maastricht Treaty, Danes may be compelled to reconsider the Edinburgh reservations. However, another referendum must be held in order to bring the Danes into the European political and economic union. Despite Euro-optimism among the Nordic neutral states, the two western NATO member states (Norway and Iceland) held many more objections to the European project.

Norwegian and Icelandic Resistance

In contrast to the other Nordic states, Norway and Iceland feared the economic and political consequences of joining a partnership of more powerful European states. As NATO members, Norway and Iceland had fewer political motivations to align with Europe than Sweden or Finland. As a petroleum-dependent state with a more sheltered economy, the Norwegians were not as convinced about the economic advantages of EU membership. After all, Norwegians have been in a "union" (with other Scandinavian states), and they prefer to remain as independent as possible from foreign influence. In Iceland and Norway, the EEA agreement was viewed as a satisfactory way to maintain access to markets without compromising sovereignty over natural resources or national policies.

On November 28, 1994, a majority of Norwegians (52 percent) rejected membership in the European Union. For Norwegian Prime Minister Gro Harlem Brundtland, the referendum outcome was a major disappointment. For the second time in twenty-three years, the anti-EU organization, "Nei til EU," effectively mobilized a nationwide campaign against European integration. The leader of Norway's anti-EU Center Party, Anne Enger Lahnstein, was an important voice in the "no" movement. Lahnstein appealed to the sentiment of those who feared that European integration represents a threat to the Norwegian way of life, particularly those residing in the rural areas of Norway. Just as in 1972, the EU referendum was a triumph of the periphery over the center.[28] Farmers and fishermen actively opposed EU membership, and their concerns were central to the emotional appeals raised by the anti-EU organization and the Norwegian Center Party. Fifty-seven percent of women in Norway voted against membership, because of fears that participation in the European Union threatens many of the achievements of the postwar women's movement.

Norwegians were not as convinced as the Swedes or Finns that European integration would resolve economic problems at home. As the single most important energy exporter to the EU, Norway found itself in a unique position in the integration debate. The state's petroleum is sold on long-term contracts with individual member states, and integration does not alter this relationship. Thus, Norway's primary export industry is already integrated in Europe, and the revenues from the sector sustain a high standard of living. According to Norwegian energy analysts, offshore resources will last well into the next century. As Norway proclaimed a budget surplus in 1995, and was the only country in the Organization for Economic Cooperation and Development (OECD) to do so, the Norwegians felt even more assured that they did not need the European Union.

In Iceland, the economy is dependent on the export of fish and fish products. European Union membership would require Iceland to abide by the Common Fisheries Agreement and open its waters to EU fishermen. In the words of Icelandic Minister of Foreign Affairs and External Trade Jon Baldvin Hannibalsson, "The main obstacle to membership in the EU has been the common fisheries policy. Looking at articles 38 to 47 of the Rome Treaty, it is apparent that the founding fathers of the community were not as concerned about fisheries as they were about agriculture. The fisheries policy of the Union, as it now stands, is unacceptable to Iceland."[29]

As a consequence of domestic political resistance to European integration, Norway and Iceland will remain outside the Union for the foreseeable future. The European Economic Area agreement is about as much European cooperation as these states are willing to accept. However, Norwegians and

Icelanders will be watching with interest as their Nordic neighbors become increasingly entangled in the web of European policy cooperation.

The Danish experience with European integration offers some interesting lessons for the other Nordic states. As an EU member, Denmark has less autonomy to pursue independent economic policies, yet there are new political opportunities for Danes to exercise their influence in European Union institutions. What can the other Nordics learn from twenty years of Danish experience in the EU?

THE NORDICS IN THE EU

From a Danish perspective, European integration is changing the capacity of national governments to exercise political authority in three important ways. The first change relates to the "institutional intertwining"[30] inherent in the EU policymaking process. Multilateral cooperation between EU member states has an unintended side effect: There is a substantial degree of autonomy left to Danish authorities to interpret and implement Community directives. For example, the EU's internal market reform program requires member states to adopt 170 separate measures to free the movement of goods, services, persons, and capital. While the Danish government must comply with these EU measures, it still retains the power to implement EU requirements as it sees fit. Because of Danish administrative efficiency, the state has one of the best records of implementing EU directives.[31] By August 1992, Denmark led the way in adapting national laws to EU policies in comparison to the record of other EU member states.[32]

The second, albeit related change in post-1985 Europe is the willingness of national governments to empower European-wide institutions. This is visible in the transition to a system of qualified majority voting, the expanded jurisdiction of the European Court of Justice, and the ambitions to create a common political and economic union designating that powers traditionally in the realm of national authorities be coordinated at the EU level. By cooperating closely with the EU, the Danes have less autonomy over core policies once considered to be the responsibility of national governments.

Denmark has accepted more constraints on economic policymaking than its Nordic neighbors as an early participant in the European Monetary System (EMS).[33] Following an EU Council meeting held in Copenhagen in April 1978, the Danish government agreed to participate in the EMS. Denmark, Germany, the Netherlands, Belgium, and Luxembourg had participated in the snake since 1972.[34] The EMS system imposed more discipline on its participants than the snake and created a new currency unit (ECU). Rules adopted under the EMS included restrictions on deviation from a commonly agreed upon exchange rate (fluctuation band of 2.25 percent, with temporary variation of 6 percent); a flexible, commonly agreed upon central exchange rate; access to short-term credit from the central banks of participating states; and the creation of a ECU. The system was designed to enable broad participation: Countries could enjoy credit and ECU benefits as EMS members without fully adjusting their currencies within the commonly agreed upon parameters. By imposing discipline on governments, the EMS was intended to discourage expansionary fiscal policies and hence reduce inflation. Fixed exchange rates were also viewed as necessary for the full economic benefits of a common market to be realized and as an important stage in the process of creating a monetary union.

Denmark's capacity to independently devalue its currency has been restricted by participation in the EMS. In 1982, the Danish and Belgium governments appealed to EU member states to devalue their currencies. Denmark's request for a 7 percent devaluation was denied by the EU, largely because of Germany's opposition.[35] In 1987, Denmark again succumbed to the preferences of larger states by reluctantly adjusting its exchange rate to the value of the franc.[36] Although independent devaluations are possible, Finn Ostrup points out that the political costs associated with "going your own way" have substantially increased under the EMS system.

Thus, Danish leaders have traded off domestic autonomy over currency policy in return for more stable exchange rates and lower inflation and interest rates. In the long run, participation in the EMS is expected to reduce interest rates and stimulate economic growth. However, as the 1992/93 exchange rate mechanism (ERM) crisis demonstrated, small states such as Denmark, Sweden, Norway, and Finland are subject to the destabilizing effects of short-term European currency adjustments.[37]

Finally, as EU institutions become more powerful entities, there is a new playing field for political bargaining. Denmark's most important organized interests (agriculture, industry, and labor unions) actively participate in organizations at the EU level. For example, the Danish Agricultural Council is a member of the Committee of Professional Agricultural Organizations (COPA) of the European Union and has "obtained considerable influence. COPA is in general considered to be the most effective and professional interest organization at the EU level."[38] The Industrirådet, Danish Federation of Employers, and trade union LO established offices in Brussels following the implementation of the Single European Act. Two Danish firms, A. P. Møller (shipping) and Carlsberg Brewers, participate in the European Business Roundtable, a private organization of forty-one European companies.

In EU institutions, Danish Social Democrats advocate "green norms." Under the Danish presidency of Eureka (1987–1988), a green organization called Euroenviron was established with a secretariat in Copenhagen. Euroenviron promotes environmental research and development on problems of industrial, urban, and agricultural wastes; air and noise pollution; water quality; pesticides and herbicides; and other resource management issues.[39] Danish activism in the EU also enabled the state to preserve national standards for health, safety, and the environment, a particular concern of the labor unions. The EU allows these standards to be maintained as long as they do not constitute technical barriers to trade.[40]

Another example of Danish Euro-corporatism is of vital interest to the public: access to summer homes. Many Danes are concerned about the possibility of foreigners (particularly Germans) acquiring coastal properties. Denmark was granted permission from the EU to allow restrictions on the acquisition of property by foreigners.[41] These restrictions will be viewed with promise by Finns and Swedes, who retreat regularly to mountain or seaside cabins.

Thus, in critical policy areas that threaten the welfare state, Denmark pursues an EU strategy: to transfer Social Democratic values and policies to EU member states. Denmark's transnational response to European integration mediates the state's growing dependence on a unified Germany. According to Nikolaj Petersen, "the looser the future European structure, the more freedom of maneuver for Germany. Therefore, France and other European countries, including Denmark, have become more integrationist lately."[42]

CONCLUSION: A NORDIC EUROPE, OR MORE EUROPEAN NORDICS?

With the deepening of European integration and the transformation of the East-West security system, the Nordic states are coming out of the cold and pursuing closer cooperation with the European core. As I have argued in this chapter, the Nordic states have followed separate paths to European Union. The Danes joined earlier than the other Nordics (in 1973), yet they retain a healthy skepticism toward supranational cooperation. The people's rejection of the Maastricht Treaty, the presence of anti-EU representatives in the European Parliament, and the government's willingness to cooperate with EU policy regimes (such as the EMS) are examples of Denmark's ambivalent accession. Sweden and Finland are latecomers to the European Union, yet they have readily accepted supranationalism. Swedes and Finns are cooperative partners in the EU, unlikely to rock the boat as the Danes have done. Norway and Iceland, on the other hand, have been the most resistant to European integration and preferred a looser form of cooperation with the EU as signatories of the EEA. Despite the noble efforts of Social Democratic Prime Minister Gro Harlem Brundtland to convince Norwegians to join the EU, the public rejected membership for the second time on November 28, 1994. Although it is possible that Norway and Iceland will eventually follow their Nordic neighbors into the EU, these states will have more in common with the British than with the pro-integrationist Nordic neutrals, Finland and Sweden.

To what extent will the entry of two more Nordic states influence the course of European integration? Will these states be compelled to abandon national solutions, or will European institutions become a little more Nordic? As a consequence of accession, Sweden and Finland are signing on to a collaborative project that runs counter to the traditions and policies of Nordic social democracy. With the Swedish and Finnish economies experiencing the worst crisis since the Great Depression, European integration appears more attractive in the 1990s. As committed multilateralists, the new entrants will pursue an agenda within the EU that includes the widening of European Union membership to the east, and the pursuit of Social Democratic norms at the European level.

As a consequence of accession, the two Nordic neutrals have introduced new political issues in European institutions. For the first time, the geographic boundaries of the EU extend as far north as the Arctic Circle and as far east as the Russian border. Swedish and Finnish entry into the EU has broadened the scope of the political debate to include environmental, trade, and security questions unique to the Scandinavian-Baltic region. For example, Swedish and Finnish foreign policy makers are strong advocates of Baltic accession to the EU and have taken the lead in bringing regional security concerns to the attention of EU member states.[43] Thus, widening the EU to include Scandinavia's "near abroad" (Latvia, Lithuania, and Estonia) is a central mission of the two eastern Nordic states.

Nor has Scandinavia passively adapted to the forces of European integration. As Maria Green Cowles has shown in her research on the establishment of the European Business Roundtable, Sweden has exported its corporatist institutions to the EU.[44] It was the Volvo CEO Pehr Gyllenhammar who advocated the creation of an employer's federation at the European level. Although business cooperation exceeds the achievements of organized labor, this cooperation is beneficial to northern European unions. Nordic governments retain their nationally determined wage agreements and are not bound by an EU-level labor accord. For a group of countries that share stronger traditions of labor solidarity, this is viewed favorably by trade unionists in northern Europe.

From the perspective of European Union member states, Sweden and Finland are desirable new partners. Through Nordic accession, the EU gains two new, enthusiastic members and large contributors to EU funds. In contrast to the Danes, Swedes and Finns are committed Europeans. If Norway and Iceland decide to join in the future, the EU should brace themselves for trouble: These states will align with those political forces in Europe that seek to slow the pace and depth of European integration.

Denmark's experience in the EU suggests that the state has been more and more willing to accept infringements on national sovereignty, from participation in the EMS to implementing the internal market program and accepting a version of the Maastricht Treaty. Yet Danes hold strong reservations about the neoliberal, antidemocratic, and non-Scandinavian norms of European integration. Now that Sweden and Finland have also traded off national sovereignty for new political opportunities in the EU, they too bring with them Social Democratic norms of egalitarianism, environmentalism, and social justice. The Nordic voice will be stronger within the EU because of the accession of Sweden and Finland, an important development on the eve of the intergovernmental conference in 1996.

Ironically, even though the Nordic model is in crisis at home, the desire to export the Social Democratic way to the European Union is an agenda shared by all three Nordic EU member states. The attitude that they can influence the EU from within is perhaps optimistic, yet nonetheless these states will have an effect on the substance and direction of European integration by forging coalitions *within* the EU. States such as Austria, the Netherlands, and Germany share many of the domestic political priorities of the Nordic states. However, the trade-off for northern Europeans is high, now that the Danish, Swedish, and Finnish states are compelled, to a much greater extent than in the past, to conform to the norms, rules, and decisionmaking procedures of European Union policy regimes.

NOTES

The author wishes to thank Alan Cafruny, Carl Lankowski, James Caporaso, and an anonymous reviewer for their comments on an earlier version of this manuscript. The Norwegian Marshall Fund provided travel support to Scandinavia during the EU referenda in 1994.

1. Throughout the chapter, I refer to the European Economic Community (EEC) or the European Community (EC) as the European Union (EU).

2. Gøsta Esping-Andersen, *Politics Against Markets* (Princeton: Princeton University Press, 1985); Jonas Pontusson, *The Limits of Social Democracy* (Ithaca: Cornell University Press, 1992).

3. In Peter J. Katzenstein's *Small States in World Markets: Industrial Policy in Europe*, (Ithaca, N.Y.: Cornell University Press, 1985), p. 42, the three defining characteristics of "democratic corporatism" are an ideology of social partnership; a centralized and concentrated system of interest group intermediation; and voluntary, informal bargaining.

4. Interview with Jens-Peter Bonde, Copenhagen, UPI, May 17, 1993.

5. See Peter J. Katzenstein, *Tamed Power: Germany in Europe* (forthcoming).

6. Robert Keohane, *After Hegemony: Cooperation and Discord in the World Political Economy* (Princeton: Princeton University Press, 1984), p. 179.

7. Lars Mjøset, "Nordic Economic Policies in the 1970s and 1980s," *International Organization* 41, no. 3 (summer 1987), pp. 403-456.

8. Danish agricultural interests are represented by the Danish Agricultural Council. The council encompasses virtually every aspect of agricultural production: exports, fur producers, the Federation of Agricultural Societies, and the small landholders organization. The Agricultural Council is regularly consulted on all decisions pertaining to the sector.

9. Bengt Nilson, "Butter, Bacon and Coal: Anglo-Danish Commercial Relations, 1947-51" *Scandinavian Journal of History* 13 (1988), pp. 257-277.

10. Charles de Gaulle's reservations with British entry are outlined in David Lewis, *The Road to Europe* (New York: Peter Lang, 1993), pp. 41-45.

11. Lise Lyck, ed., *Denmark and EC Membership Evaluated* (London: Pinter, 1992), p. 109.

12. Hans Christian Johansen, *The Danish Economy in the Twentieth Century* (London: Croom Helm, 1987), p. 164.

13. The Danish Constitution (Section 20) specifies how power is to be transferred to supranational authorities. According to the constitution, a five-sixths vote by members of the Danish Parliament is required to approve the transfer of authority. If this is not attained, the vote must then reside with the people, and the outcome is binding on the government.

14. For an excellent analysis of the Danish referendum on the SEA, see Torben Worre, "Denmark at the Crossroads: The Danish Referendum of 28 February 1986 on the EC Reform Package," *Journal of Common Market Studies*, 26, no.4 (June 1988), pp. 361-388.

15. Lyck, *Denmark and EC Membership Evaluated*, p. 70.

16. Interview with international advisor to the Social Democratic Party, Copenhagen, 1991.

17. Per Vejrup Hansen, "Fiscal/Taxation Policy," in Lyck, *Denmark and EC Membership Evaluated*, p. 155.

18. Paulette Kurzer, *Business and Banking* (Ithaca, N.Y.: Cornell University Press, 1993).

19. Gunnar Selgård, "Uventet nei til EF-unionen," *Aftenposten*, June 3, 1992, p. 4.

20. See Regeringens Proposition, "Sveriges medlemskap i Europeiska unionen," 1994/95:19, p. 28; and Lauri Karvonen and Bengt Sundelius, "Fran nej till ja: Sverige, Finland och den europeiska integrationen," report presented to Europaprogrammet, Norway, March 9-10, 1994.

21. Ulf Olsson, "Sweden and Europe in the Twentieth Century: Economics and Politics," *Scandinavian Journal of History*, 18, no.1 (1993), p. 33.

22. Bo Rothstein, "Sverige kan missa industriorder," *Dagens Nyheter*, November 12, 1994, A4.

23. There were some leading Social Democrats who were opposed to Swedish membership in the EU. However, the opposition from within the party was not as divisive as in Norway.

24. For an excellent analysis of changes in Finland's EU policy, see Raimo Väyrynen, "Finland and the European Community: Changing Elite Bargains," *Cooperation and Conflict* 28, no.1 (1993), pp. 31-46.

25. Väyrynen, "Finland and the European Community," p. 35.

26. Finnish Ministry of Foreign Affairs, "Finnish Foreign Policy and EC Membership," *Finnish Features*, October 1992, p. 2.

27. According to 1995 public opinion data, if the Swedes were asked to reconsider, a majority would vote against entry into the EU.

28. Interview with Henry Valen, November 30, 1994.

29. Jan Baldvin Hannibalsson, "Iceland and the Enlargement of the European Union" (paper presented at the Conference of the French-Icelandic Chamber of Commerce, Paris, October 21, 1994), p. 4.

30. Alberta Sbragia, *Euro-Politics* (Washington, D.C.: Brookings Institution, 1992), p. 5.

31. Lise Lyck, *Denmark and EC Membership Evaluated*, p. 79.

32. *The New York Times*, November 16, 1992, p. C1.

33. For a comparative analysis of adapting to the EMS, see Wayne Sandholtz, "Choosing Union: Monetary Politics and Maastricht," *International Organization* 47, no. 1 (winter 1993), pp. 1-39.

34. The "snake" refers to a floating currency exchange rate system with a band of allowable fluctuation of 2.25 percent and was implemented in April 1972 by the original six signatories of the Treaty of Rome, the United Kingdom, Ireland, Denmark, and Norway. See Timothy Devinney and William Hightower, *European Markets After 1992* (Lexington: D. C. Heath, 1991), pp. 133-137.

35. Finn Ostrup, *The Development of the European Monetary System* (Copenhagen: DJOF Publishing, 1992), pp. 46-47.

36. Ibid., p. 49.

37. See also Christine Ingebritsen, "Pulling in Different Directions: The Europeanization of Scandinavian Political Economies," in Peter J. Katzenstein, *Tamed Power: Germany in Europe* (forthcoming).

38. Lise Lyck, *Denmark and EC Membership Evaluated*, p. 57.

39. "Tomorrow's Technology," *Denmark Review*, April 1990, p. 22.

40. Lise Lyck, *Denmark and EC Membership Evaluated*, p. 141.

41. See Article 6(4) of the Fourth Directive on capital liberalization and Article 2(3) in the Directives on the right of residence for pensioners and the group of rights in EC Law, Danish Government, *White Paper on Denmark and the Maastricht Treaty* (Copenhagen, 1992), p. 152.

42. Nikolaj Petersen, "Denmark's Foreign Relations in the 1990s," in Martin Heisler, *The Nordic Region: Changing Perspectives in International Relations*, (Thousand Oaks, Calif.: Sage, 1990), pp. 98–99. See also Jens Henrik Haahr, who traces the changes in Danish EC policy from the perspective of divisions within the Social Democratic Party in "European Integration and the Left in Britain and Denmark," *Journal of Common Market Studies* (March 1992), pp. 77–100.

43. See, for example, "Sweden and the Security of the Baltic States," remarks by Minister of Foreign Affairs Lena Hjelm-Wallen at the Brookings Institution, Washington, D.C., June 30, 1995.

44. Maria Green Cowles, "The European Round Table of Industrialists," in Justin Greenwood, ed. *European Casebook on Business Alliances* (UK: Prentice Hall, 1995), pp. 225-236.

About the Authors

Alan W. Cafruny is Henry Bristol Professor of International Affairs and chair, Department of Government at Hamilton College; and External Professor, European University Institute, Florence, Italy.

John Coakley is lecturer in politics at University College Dublin, and secretary general of the International Political Science Association. His publications include *The Social Origins of Nationalist Movements* (contributing editor); *The Territorial Management of Ethnic Conflict* (contributing editor); and *Politics in the Republic of Ireland* (contributing coeditor).

Michael Holmes is lecturer in European studies at University College Cork, and visiting lecturer at the Centre for Peace Studies, Dublin. He has published numerous works on Irish foreign policy, Ireland in the European Union, and political parties in the European Union.

Liesbet Hooghe is assistant professor of political science at the University of Toronto and Jean Monnet Fellow (1996–1997) at the European University Institute. She is the author of *Separatisme* (Leuven, 1989); *A Leap in the Dark: Nationalist Conflict Management in Belgium*; and editor of the forthcoming *Cohesion Policy and European Integration: Building Multi-Level Governance*.

Thomas O. Hueglin is professor of political science at Wilfrid Laurier University in Canada. He received his Ph.D. from St. Gall University, Switzerland, and a postdoctoral degree from Konstanz University, Germany. His research areas include political theory and comparative federalism. His most recent book is *Community—Subsidiarity—Federalism: The Political Theory of Althusius*.

Christine Ingebritsen received her doctorate in political science from Cornell University in 1993. She has published several articles on Scandinavia and European integration, and is currently completing a book manuscript, *The Nordic States and European Unity: From Economic Interdependence to Political Integration*. She is assistant professor in the Department of Scandinavian Studies and an adjunct professor in the Department of Political Science at the University of Washington, Seattle.

Michael Keating is professor of political science at the University of Western Ontario, and has taught in universities in Britain, the United States, France, and Belgium. He has published widely on urban and regional politics and minority nationalism. His most recent book is *Nations Against the State: The New Politics of Nationalism in Quebec, Catalonia, and Scotland*, published in English, Spanish, and French.

Carl Lankowski is research director at the American Institute for Contemporary German Studies, the Johns Hopkins University, Washington, D.C.

Gary Marks is professor of political science at the University of North Carolina, Chapel Hill, and director of the UNC Center for European Studies. His most recent book is *Governance in the European Union* (with Fritz Scharpf, Philippe Schmitter, and Wolfgang Streeck). He is currently studying issues of multilevel governance in the European Union, and is coediting a book on the political economy of advanced capitalist societies.

Nicholas Rees is Jean Monnet Professor of European Institutions and International Relations and director of the Centre for European Studies at the University of Limerick. He has recently published a conference volume on Ireland and the 1996 Intergovernmental Conference (Limerick: Centre for European Studies). He also recently coauthored *The Poor Relation: Irish Foreign Policy and the Third World*.

Michael Shackleton is principal administrator in the European Parliament, where he has most recently been Head of the Secretariat of the Committee of Inquiry into the Community Transit System. He has also published widely on European Union affairs and is a visiting professor at the College of Europe in Bruges, Belgium.

Shalini Venturelli is assistant professor of international communication policy and law in the School of International Service at the American University. She is also chair of the Communication and Human Rights Committee of the International Association for Mass Communication Research. She specializes in constitutional reform and communication policy within the European Union, with particular emphasis on the rights of information and expression.

Pia Christina Wood is associate professor of political science at Old Dominion University. She received her doctorate in political science from the University of Geneva. She has written numerous articles on the European Union and French foreign policy, and is currently completing a book manuscript, *France and the Arab-Israeli Conflict: From DeGaulle to Mitterrand*.

Index

About the Book

Although the European Union as an entity now enjoys support from across most of the political spectrum, this has by no means resulted in the acceptance of a single vision of the EU. The apparent successes engendered by the Single European Act and the Maastricht Treaty have led instead to both a broadening and a reformulation of opposition. The nations of Western Europe have thus forged an ambiguous unity.

The authors of this volume focus on the connections between processes of European integration and the articulation of alternative programs and policies. Part 1 considers the key unresolved dilemmas of the emerging economic and political union. Part 2 offers case studies of political and social movements throughout the EU, examining states that traditionally have voiced the greatest doubts about the Union, as well as those in which support has been strong.